THE HEART OF **RECOVERY**

Real People.
Real Lives.
Real Success Stories.

DOUG BOPST

FOREWORD BY AMY DRESNER

TABLE OF CONTENTS

FOREWORD

Before I met Doug, "fitness" was one of the few "f-words" I did not use. Fitness was for other people: sane, disciplined ones. It was not for someone who lived in her head, earned money with her brain, and sat on her ass all day. It was not for me who can't dance, always felt like her body was an ill-fitting clunky space suit or used her body solely as a vehicle to escape reality and my feelings (hello drugs!).

Fitness people annoyed me with their perky "you can do it" attitude, their ab pics, and their water bottles. I envied their ability to look themselves in the mirror as they did endless squats. I hated them for their confidence to wear tight fitting yoga pants and clean expensive sneakers. I loathed them for their perfect posture and early morning runs.

I've always been thin ("skinny desert Jew" is how I describe myself) so weight loss was never a problem. However, after a brutal heartbreak I took up smoking and another 10 pounds slipped off leaving me looking not so much "modelesque" or "heroin chic" but more like I was out on a day pass from an eating disorder unit. A year went by and I couldn't put the weight back on. I got tired of people asking me if I was okay. I was sick of Thai masseuses telling me "you need eat more!"

Then my mother broke her hip and became wheelchair bound. She had been very inactive. My father, the same age, was delivering food to the elderly when he was the elderly. One obvious difference? Fitness. My dad worked out and walked and swam. My mom did none of that. It scared me enough to take some action. Also, vanity was a part of it. In your late 40's, being skinny doesn't cut it anymore. Gravity was doing its thing and elements were . . . um . . . dropping.

Through a mutual friend I met Doug and he agreed to help me out. He provided a list of foods to buy and trained me via Skype 3 times a week. Slowly my living room became littered with dumbbells and medicine balls and resistance bands. Soon I was texting him and saying "Can we train today? I really need it!" I was becoming the person I'd hated.

After eight months of me moaning and complaining, I look healthy again. I have strength. I have confidence. My mood is better.

Before Doug, I'd heard of the importance of exercise in sobriety but I'd never really experienced it. Besides having some muscles and curves, I've proven to myself that I can change. I've developed discipline (which I can apply to other parts of my life.) I don't buy into my "I don't feel like it" anymore.

Sobriety, recovery, can be so heady. Talk, talk, talk. Sometimes we forget that we can change our moods through our body: exercise, massage, meditation, yoga, breathwork.

So when Doug asked me to write him a foreword for his book of interviews about the multitude ways we can recover, I said yes. What choice did I have? What other trainer was gonna let me swear at him like a sailor? Plus, my ass didn't look like an expensive 24-year-old stripper yet so we still had some work to do.

Thank you, Doug. And for the rest of you, enjoy the book. There are many gems within.

– Amy Dresner, author of *My Fair Junkie: A Memoir of Getting Dirty and Staying Clean*

FROM THE AUTHOR

There is a common "beat" that everyone in recovery shares: being able to "feel" again with our hearts. We can all see, hear, touch, smell, and taste with our other organs, but we can only feel with our hearts. Lasting recovery is all about the heart. It is about getting beyond the negative energy blockages of our past addictions and behaviors. These negative energy blockages include anger, fear, resentment, and anxiety. We should all strive to replace these negative vibes with openness, appreciation, and love for ourselves and others, all while living joyfully in the present.

My book, *The Heart of Recovery*, shares heartfelt stories of people who entered recovery to start living well again. The people interviewed for this book are experiencing life with a full heart to the best of their ability. Ultimately, "The Heart of Recovery" is about people committing to live and not to die; to love and not to hate; to shine light and not live in darkness. The world is a better place with these beautiful hearts, whose stories you will read and hopefully be inspired by. They have all come forward courageously for a greater purpose. I am a blessed and better man for connecting with them.

Let's face it: a person can rarely go anywhere without running into somebody who has not been affected by our country's current drug epidemic. We are unsure of where it will go, what will happen, and what can be done to solve it or even improve it.

I am confident that this book will be an important tool in aiding to solve this crisis, and to offer immediate support to those seeking to overcome drug and/or alcohol addiction.

As a person who has been in recovery for over a decade, I entered it in what's considered a "non-traditional" way. I got into recovery while incarcerated with the help of my cellmate. While in jail, he encouraged me to start exercising and taking responsibility for myself. His support of me was unconditional. I wanted to repay him in whatever way I could, so now I am committed to being of service to others that are struggling. I still have that workout regime he wrote out for me, in pencil, framed on my wall. I never want to forget where I came from.

When I was released from jail, I did not enter a traditional 12-Step or recovery program. Despite that, I have remained in recovery for over a decade. It wasn't that I had anything against them. Many of my friends are members of 12-Step programs or other traditional recovery communities. Those options were not offered to me so I organically started filling my life with healthy habits, friends, and spiritual practices. I also began to take responsibility for the choices and decisions that I had made. And to be honest, I was really terrified of going back to jail or prison. I highly respect 12-Step programs or any other program that helps others find sobriety. And I must thank my grandparents who took me in after my incarceration under some strict ground rules. They were my saving grace and supported me to get back on my feet.

Exercise was an important tool to help change my life. I can honestly say I wouldn't be where I am today if my cellmate had not forced me to start working out during my incarceration. I didn't do pushups, sit-ups, and run and then suddenly not want to get high anymore. It was much more complicated than that.

Exercise forced me to be uncomfortable and challenged me to believe in myself to do the things I never thought I could accomplish. When I entered jail, I couldn't run a mile or do a single pushup . . . even from my knees. As I stayed the course and kept to a routine I saw progress. Realizing I could change, I was motivated to quit smoking cigarettes. All of these hurdles and successes built self-confidence. Fitness gave me purpose and meaning in life-something that is crucial in maintaining recovery. Fitness also taught commitment and how to stick to a routine, which is the main reason I could finally hold a job after I got out of jail.

Commitment is everything in recovery. I have learned there is so much power in commitment, dedication, and believing in yourself. Many addicts think they can never get sober. Especially after years of using and relapse, they have lost all hope that their lives can get better. This hopelessness becomes a roadblock in their motivation to change. Exercising, for me and many others, was and is a stepping stone to accomplishment. It has the ability to teach you that anything worthwhile takes time and . . . yes, commitment.

Please don't misunderstand: fitness isn't the only thing I did. There were other moving parts. I developed a strong support group of friends, some in recovery, others who were simply focused on personal growth and living a healthy life. Whenever I am struggling, acting out, or have an important decision to make, I always call a friend or someone in my inner circle. It's sort of like having multiple "sponsors." Community has been inspirational for me, helping me realize that I am not alone, and I can also be there to help others.

Spirituality, for me, came in time. It wasn't until about 5 years ago that I really started to believe in God. I always thought God didn't exist. I thought, "I am a drug addict, in jail, and suicidal." So, if God is supposed to be all about love, how does this make sense?

As I looked back and saw the things that I was fortunate to accomplish, I began to believe that God was with me the whole time. I couldn't have done all of this by myself. The more I began to believe, the more I began to be at peace with my past. I wasn't proud of many of the decisions I made, but God had a plan. I realized I was kept alive for a reason, to help others become better versions of themselves.

The further I got into my recovery, the more I realized that a lot of the things I was doing were similar to the work of other recovery programs. I knew that I had a problem with drugs. I believed in God. I surrounded myself with like-minded people and I was a man of service.

I was dismayed when I saw that many people would get discouraged if they did not fit into or connect with a specific program, and return to a life of addiction as a result. I also observed that many ex-addicts got easily upset or bored in recovery. They were sober, but not happy. In time, they would relapse because their recovery was not providing them with the necessary psychological and emotional change.

Drugs and/or alcohol numbs a person, and gives them a false sense of happiness and a distorted view of reality. While a great first step is eliminating drugs and alcohol from your life, filling the void left behind with healthy things is a must in order to thrive in recovery. Of course, we all get stressed, anxious, depressed, and upset from time to time. That's perfectly normal. It's life. However, we will either manage these feelings in a healthy or an unhealthy way.

As I did more research into what successful, sober people were doing to flourish in recovery, I found that no matter what program they were working, they all shared many similarities. Staying away from whatever drug they had a history of abusing was crucial. These people were also aware of the things that needed to be done to maintain their recovery and knew when their recovery was not up to par.

This book showcases the many effective tips and strategies of several inspirational, sober individuals, individuals from all walks of life. Many of the people I interviewed do not follow traditional 12-step recovery approach. Methods used range from 12-Step programs to Christianity, harm reduction to fitness, and many others. This book features 50 different personal interviews that I pray will provide hope for people struggling with addiction and encourage enthusiasm for those already in recovery.

I asked each individual the same five questions in order to display 50 different journeys. I chose the five questions that I believe to be the crucial staples of recovery. I also chose a question that allowed the interviewees to open up about a tell-tale moment in their lives that confirmed for themselves that they needed to embrace recovery. These stories vary from the sad to the hilarious to the mundane, accurately reflecting life, addiction, and recovery.

FOR WHOM THIS BOOK IS WRITTEN

This book was written for a variety of people. It is for anyone who is currently struggling with addiction and looking to change their lives and achieve recovery. It is also for anyone who is newly sober, in recovery, or merely seeking to acquire more information and strategies on what can be done to achieve and maintain sobriety using the method(s) that best works for any given individual. Maybe you are that person who has been in recovery for a long period of time, but feels a bit stale and needs additional motivation to achieve long term sobriety. If that is the case, then this book is for you.

You could also be that person who has been contemplating getting sober and is curious if there is hope. Trust me, there is hope. The stories contained in this book, and the strategies and tactics that can be employed will be relatable to most people in same shape or fashion. This book is also for family members who know someone struggling with addiction, or have been affected by the challenges and difficulties of loved ones with addiction.

Lastly, perhaps you are that young person, or a parent of a young person that is considering dabbling in drugs, or alcohol, and wondering where it could lead. Then this book is definitely a must-read for you so that you can learn from other people about what can happen from doing drugs.

INTERVIEW QUESTIONS

The answers to the questions asked of each person interviewed for this book regarding how they take care of their bodies (physically), the quality of their inner circle of friends and associates, and their view on spirituality reveal how important these aspects of their lives are in determining their success of ongoing recovery.

When I, and many other people like me have battled drug addiction, we were managing stress, trauma, anxiety, depression, and other insecurities in an unhealthy way. In my case, it was abusing and selling drugs. I wanted to give readers of this book hope that they can recover, but it is going to take some work.

People suffering from addiction will have to change their mindset, and be willing to engage in activities that will help us deal with life's battles in a healthy way. Not using drugs is just the start, and a great one for sure. Just because we are not using drugs at any given time does not mean that life will be become easy instantaneously. It just simply means we will not be using drugs to medicate, mask reality, and deal with life's problems.

Drugs provide some people with the false sense that we are happy, secure, and successful. Once we can identify other ways to get those same feelings, we can start to win the game. This is why it is extremely important to surround yourself with the right people, nourish yourself physically, and stay positive and grateful when life hits us with both the good and the bad. Many people believe that drug addiction is a disease, while others believe it is a behavior.

Regardless of your belief, do not let drug addiction define you. Managing drug addiction requires change in a person's daily life. Let it inspire you to learn lessons, find what works, and be your best, authentic self.

Keep in mind that the manner in which the interviews were conducted varied from in person, phone, Zoom/Skype and email.

COMMON JOURNEYS

Presented below are some common features of the journeys experienced by people with drug addiction and their subsequent recoveries:

1. Their relationships changed for the better once they got into recovery.

2. They all recognize the importance of fitness.

3. They all have their own unique view on spirituality.

4. Many believe that it is a "one-size-fits-all" approach to be spiritual. That could not be further from the truth. People should use spirituality in whatever way is the best fit for your recovery.

5. Many people share a sense of awareness. They know what they need to do (or not do) on a daily basis in recovery, and to abstain from the drugs they were abusing.

6. Everyone is challenged with some form of adversity in their life that has made them who they are today. We ALL go through challenging times, whether you struggle with addiction or not. Life has its ups and downs, and we have to manage these challenges in a healthy manner.

7. Most people owned their choices about their circumstances in life and caused them to seek recovery.

This book has a plethora of information aimed to help anyone struggling with addiction. Here is how to get the most out of it:

1. Keep on open mind:
   There is no "one-size-fits-all" approach to treating addiction. The reason that I interviewed such a diverse group of people was to inform the audience that there are many different paths to recovery. A person should choose what works best for that particular individual. In this book, you will find things that you can and cannot relate to, and that's to be expected and is acceptable. You will read about things that individuals do that are very unique and may be new to you. This book will show you that no matter what gender, race, profession, or religion you are affiliated with, there will be things that will inspire you to become involved with, and to stay in recovery in whatever way works best for you.

2. Keep a pen and paper handy:
   You will see a behind-the-scenes look at what some of the most inspiring sober individuals are doing on a daily basis to thrive in recovery. You will want to take notes on some things that they are doing that could positively impact your own road to recovery. These lessons could be implemented into your own life. Notice the common themes and realize that you or a loved one is not alone. The struggle is real, but there is hope.

3. Peruse the book at your leisure:
   The reason that an index exists at the front of the book is so the reader is able to selectively read through the book, and choose which stories and sections you want to read. Please do not feel obligated to read this book front to back (it is not designed that way). Instead, perhaps pick a story or two each day to read and go from there.

4. Do your best to implement some of these tactics and tips that are given by the individuals in the book:
   While some recovery tactics may at first appear to be farfetched or unrealistic, consider the potential for a positive outcome. There are enough tips and tricks across the board from all walks of life that it will be easy to relate with much of what is in this book. The tips in this book are sure to help you not only get and stay sober, but to also build a solid foundation to allow you to become healthy, happy, and rejuvenated for the remainder of your life.

5. Do not compare yourself to others in the book:
   As much as I believe that this book will be relatable for the reader in many ways, this does not mean that you need to compare your journey with the people that I interviewed for this book. Focus on your journey, while keeping an open mind to learning on how to improve your recovery using this book.

ANDREW ZIMMERN

"I think there's a natural progression for people who stay clean for a long time to start to take care of their diet better, to start to do some sort of exercise, and all that other good stuff. And that's become a really big part of my recovery."
– Andrew Zimmern

Bio: Andrew Zimmern is a four-time James Beard award-winning TV personality, chef, writer, teacher, and social justice advocate. As the creator, executive producer, and host of Travel Channel's Bizarre *Foods* franchise, *Andrew Zimmern's Driven by Food, The Zimmern List,* and Food Network's *Big Food Truck Tip,* he has explored cultures in more than 170 countries, promoting impactful ways to think about, create, and live with food. He has written four books, appears monthly in Delta *Sky* Magazine, is a contributor at *Food & Wine* Magazine, and an entrepreneur-in-residence at Babson College. Andrew is the founder and CEO of both Intuitive Content, a full-service television and digital production company, and Passport Hospitality, a restaurant and food service development company. He is devoted to his charitable endeavors and sits on the board of directors for Services for the UnderServed and Taste of the NFL. His life's work is about demonstrating and promoting cultural acceptance, tolerance, and understanding through food. More at www.andrewzimmern.com.

Occupation: Chef, Author, Teacher, Television Gastronaut

Drug of choice: I was a New York City garbage head, so when I started using at age 13, it started with booze and weed and within a year, cocaine, hallucinogenics, pills, and by the time I graduated high school, I had already started using heroin and from there on out it was always a cocktail of everything. Two years before current sobriety I went exclusively to booze, and then it was a quick free fall to a hard bottom.

Length of sobriety: 27 years

DB: What do you do on a daily basis to maintain your sobriety, and what is the most challenging part about it?

AZ: Oh Gosh. It's a big question. Well, I regularly attend 12-Step meetings, I have a sponsor, I work the steps out of the book, I do service work, in my 12-Step programs, and I have a pretty rigid daily discipline. And I start my day doing prayer and meditation, and sometimes that's just for a couple minutes, sometimes longer, and I end my day with a pretty rigorous thank you. But . . . probably the biggest thing that I do regularly is I'm pretty rigorous about the suggestions in the big book of AA, at the bottom of page 84. I think people sometimes confuse the recommendations around Step 11, regarding prayer and meditation to be something that's done at the end of the night. And I follow the script on the bottom of page 84. So, when I'm angry, resentful, jealous, and afraid, I do the instructions there. And it was a real life-changer for me, because 22, 23 years ago, when I first started, well some old-timer in Vermont put me over the hood of a car and explained to me that I didn't know jack-shit about what I was talking about with Step 11, and pointed out to me what's at the bottom there. In many places, it talks in the book about being in service to other alcoholics, and at the bottom of page 84, it says we need to do something for others. It does not specify other alcoholics. And it expanded my service life immensely.

There [are] challenges every day. That's what that Step is for. I'm not worried about drinking 10 minutes from now, I'm worried about being an asshole 10 minutes from now.

DB: How have you reconnected with your body since being in recovery, and what are some things you include in your daily life to increase your health and vitality?

AZ: Oh God. Well, not putting chemicals into your system, I think there's a natural progression for people who stay clean for a long time to start to take care of their diet better, to start to do some sort of exercise, and all that other good stuff. And that's become a really big part of my recovery. And there is no substitute for care for yourself. It's either complete or it's not complete. That doesn't mean I'm perfect, but it does mean that I'm very, very much someone who tries to pursue health and wellness in every part of my life.

I've found a couple of sports that I love that I play as many times a week as I can, that has become my yoga . . .disc golf being the big one. Tennis being the other one. And I'm pretty rigorous about them.

DB: How have your relationships changed (types of people, length/meaning of relationships, etc.) from when you were actively using to being in recovery?

AZ: Well, at the end of my drinking and drugging career, I don't think I had any relationships. I mean, I had no relationship with myself, as far as relationships with other people, I was a user of people and a taker of things. And if you're a user of people and a taker of things, it doesn't take very long for everyone to toss you out the door.

I had a very long using career with a lot of very low moments, and I very, very low-bottomed. I eventually became homeless and tried to kill myself in a hotel room, in early January of, mid-January of '92. And . . . my parents thought I was dead, my friends couldn't have cared less, I'd burned every bridge, so I didn't have relationships. The nice thing about putting the cork in the bottle is that 99% of your problems go away. You stop getting DUIs, you stop going to detox, you start waking up on time, you start being responsible, and it just happens.

And then you spend the rest of your life working on that other 1% of the problems that become your main focus. And relationships with other people is something that people who are low-bottom alcoholics really, really struggle with. When we are using, all those people out there, they're not people, they're just shadows. And when we clean up, we realize that the world is actually, the most important thing in the world are the people who are in it. And what I found myself most ill-suited to do was to have relationships with people.

I naturally want to handle things on my own. Make my own decisions. I'm hard-wired to take care of myself. I'm a survivor. So, all those things sort of fly in the face of doing things like talking to your spouse or partner and saying, "Hey, I'm think about calling Bill today." "Hey, I'm thinking about taking a walk with the dog." Just do them. And I think, going back to when I was a teenager, girlfriends, friends, I would hear this all the time, "Having a relationship with you is like having a relationship with myself. We're sitting in the living room and you just get up and go walk the dog."

And so I had to learn to take my inner monologue and make it my external monologue. And all these years later, I'm still working on that. I'm a lot better at it. I've made a lot of progress at it, but it's something that I still . . . relational work with people is still the biggest focus of my recovery. And the people who have, I'm closest to, I was lucky, I had several of my best, best, best, best friends sober up around the time I did. And my best friend moved here and got sober about a year after I did.

DB: Who are the top three to five people you surround yourself with and why are they influential in your recovery?

AZ: I'm lucky that I have my sponsor, I have my childhood best friend, I have my wife, I have my son, I have some colleagues here at work that I've shared my life with for the last 20 years. So I'm super, super lucky that I have those types of relationships. And there's a very tight-knit group of people who I love very dearly who are around me, and then I have my loose-knit group of people who I love very dearly, and love me, which are people that I share meetings with, do service work with, sponsees, things like that . . . that round out what is, for me now, a very full and robust life.

DB: What is your spiritual life like and what do you do on a daily basis to integrate it into your life, and why do you think spirituality is important for growth and sustainability in recovery?

AZ: Well I don't think spirituality is important for growth and sustainability in recovery. I think it's the only way to do it. If your higher power is yourself, or if it's your chemicals, and mine was a combination of both, recovery is impossible. The minute I made the move internally to change my wiring and accept the fact that there was something out there bigger than me, my life changed. And that is the focus of the start to my day, every day. Which is, using that time in prayer and meditation to kind of align myself with the universe and remind myself that I'm not in charge of it.

And it is the dominant—I talk to my higher power, sometimes minute by minute, sometimes once an hour, I have a running conversation in my head, with the God of my understanding. I mean, all day long. I make jokes in my head to that higher power. It's constantly reminding me, yes, it's a cliché, but it's also true, my higher power shows up in other people that challenge me, push me, keep me nimble, in terms of my spiritual attitude. And if you look at all the spiritual axioms, and different kinds of spiritual beliefs and you can pick any one that you like. One of my favorites, you can act your way into right thinking, but you can't think your way into right acting. So there's something that is in my internal monologue constantly throughout the day. And people come up to me, and I'm put in situations that challenge that all the time. And I have to remember that my recovery is about doing, not about thinking and stewing. So it's a constant, constant, constant reminder.

DB: What was one situation you found yourself in that confirmed in your mind that you must seek treatment and recovery and why?

AZ: Well, the end for me, I had, I was homeless. I was squatting a building on Sullivan Street in lower Manhattan. I would steal a bottle of Comet cleanser every day from the bodega and sprinkle it around the dirty pile of clothes that I would pass out on every night. And I did that so the rats and roaches wouldn't crawl all over me when I passed out. And after 11 months of living like that, never showering, we pirated electricity from the building next door, I crashed this building with a bottle gang that I bumped into the night at the local beer and shot bar after I got evicted from my last official domicile in New York.

And I realized that this was no kind of life. So rather than do what any rational human being would do, which is, "Oh my God, look where my drugs and alcohol has brought me, I can't live like this, I need to ask for help," my decision making was, let's steal some jewelry from my Godmother, hock it, get a nest egg, get a room in a flophouse hotel in New York, pull the phone out of the wall, and order a couple cases of vodka up to the room and try to drink myself to death.

And I did that because I thought there were winners and losers in life, and I clearly was a loser. There was no point in going on. And three, four, five days later, I still wasn't dead. And I came to one morning, and the ace bandage of tension that had been around my chest throughout my whole life, wasn't there. It was gone. And I had no explanation for it. Zero. And I literally, it was like, I don't know if you've ever seen that move, *The Rock*, with Sean Connery?

But there's that moment where there's that giant sliding thing and that furnace, and they have to time their jump and kinda scoop through this thing. I saw this opening, this crack, that if I didn't sort of superhero dive through this crack, I was going to die. And then I realized, "Oh my God, I came here to die," and now it was, "I don't want to," and I had this overwhelming urge to do what I had never done in my life, which was reach out to a friend and ask for help. And the moment that I did that, it set me on the course to get, it took me four more days to get to a treatment center and get help, but that simple divine moment, because I didn't do anything for it, I experienced a divinely inspired moment that gave me an opportunity to reach out and connect to another human being. And that was the moment for me that set me on the course to change my life.

AUSTIN F. COOPER

"Through fitness and nutrition I have been able to connect with my body . . ."
– Austin Cooper

Bio: My name is Austin Cooper and I have been in recovery since April 10, 2013. I am the creator of Sober Evolution which is an inspirational, online space for those who are in recovery and for those who are looking to begin their recovery.

Occupation: Life Building Coach

Drug of choice: Alcohol/cocaine/pills/marijuana

Length of sobriety: 5 years

DB: What do you do on a daily basis to maintain your sobriety, and what is the most challenging part about it?

AFC: I make sure to eat healthy as well as exercise daily. I also focus on building new life skills and on accomplishing my goals. It's hard for me to say that any of this is challenging as I have learned to enjoy pushing myself towards bettering my life.

DB: How have you reconnected with your body since being in recovery, and what are some things you include in your daily life to increase your health and vitality?

AFC: Through fitness and nutrition I have been able to connect with my body by literally feeling the changes in my mood, energy, and sleep from eating a healthy meal and exercising. I recently started Intermittent Fasting which has greatly improved my energy and focus throughout the day. It has also given me more structure to my life and helps me regulate my metabolic rate. I get my heart pumping for about 10 minutes each morning after I wake up, I pack my diet full of nutrients and I use certain breathing exercises to help me keep a healthy pace throughout each day.

DB: How have your relationships changed (types of people, length/meaning of relationships, etc.) from when you were actively using to being in recovery?

AFC: Since realizing how detrimental relationships could be towards my life, I have taken the importance of which kinds of relationships to have more seriously. I have eliminated those who speak ill of others, those who are constantly negative and those who bring my mood down from my life. As hard as that was to do, I had to understand that the most important person in my life had to be me. Today, I surround myself with those who encourage me, support me, challenge me in positive ways, people whom I can learn from, like-minded people and those who are continuously positive.

DB: Who are the top three to five people you surround yourself with and why are they influential in your recovery?

AFC: My girlfriend, Lara Frazier has been the most influential person in my life ever since knowing her. She is constantly encouraging me with everything that I do, she inspires me in all aspects of life and she is the most positive person I know.

My father Gary. He is the hardest working person I have ever known. His work ethic is something I look up to and think about often. He has been such a huge support in my recovery and has provided for my family going above and beyond for each one of us.

My mother Kelly. She raised me to be open minded. Her positive outlooks on life have always been inspiring to me. She is someone who always tries new things and has encouraged me with each new thing I put my mind to.

My sister Bailey. She is someone that's always been there for me. She also has an extremely hard work ethic and has been following her dreams for longer than I have. Her love really was such a driving force for me deciding to move forward with treatment and I honestly don't believe that I would be here without her.

DB: What is your spiritual life like and what do you do on a daily basis to integrate it into your life, and why do you think spirituality is important for growth and sustainability in recovery?

AFC: I believe deeply into the ways of the universe. I believe that there are incredible forces in which we can't exactly see. To put this simply, I am typically able to pick up on someone else's mood as soon as they walk in the room. I became very open to this as soon as I started getting healthy. I also am very in tuned with the power of intention. These things give me peace and help me regroup when I need to. Sciences show that these things are very real whether someone is conscious of them or not. I do believe that one will have the upper hand in recovery if they have some thought or entity to think or pray about to make them feel better and drive up their endorphin levels.

DB: What was one situation you found yourself in that confirmed in your mind that you must seek treatment and recovery and why?

AFC: When my sister was going through a rough relationship, I remember out of the blue, I was sober when she called asking for help. I was able to get up out of the dead of night, pick her up, and take her home safely. After that, each time I would drink or use, I would become fearful because I knew that I was too messed up to drive anywhere if my sister needed me. The problem was, I would try cutting down, but I would end up right back to being plastered out of my mind like before. I was unable to manage my drinking no matter how hard I tried on my own. After years of going around the black hole of addiction, I was offered an opportunity to go to treatment and I took it without thinking too hard about it. I went to treatment for 22 days and have been in recovery ever since.

ANTONIA CRANE

"My relationship with my body has changed over the years and as a daily runner, I appreciate my strength and endurance."
– Antonia Crane

Bio: Antonia Crane is the author of the memoir *Spent* (Barnacle Books, Rare Bird Books). She is a writing instructor, stripper, and performer in Los Angeles. She has written for *The New York Times, The Believer, The Toast, Playboy, Cosmopolitan,* Salon.com, *The Rumpus, Electric Literature, DAME, The Establishment, The Los Angeles Review, Quartz: The Atlantic Media,* Medium.com, *Buzzfeed, Lenny Letter*, and many other publications. Her screenplay *The Lusty* (co-written by transparent director, writer Silas Howard), based on the true story of the exotic dancer's labor union, is a recipient of the San Francisco Film Society/Kenneth Rainin Foundation Grant in screenwriting. She has appeared on CNN's *This is Life With Lisa Ling* and has been interviewed on *WTF with Marc Maron* and with Michael Smerconish on https://www.siriusxm.com/potus where he compared dancers to Uber drivers. She is currently making cool shit by and for the sex worker community in Los Angeles.

Occupation: Writer, Stripper, Professor

Drug of choice: Meth

Length of sobriety: 23 years

DB: What do you do on a daily basis to maintain your sobriety, and what is the most challenging part about it?

AC: Most days, I read a daily reflection and pray for humility and to be of service. I also run every day three to five miles up a mountain near my house: this is my moving meditation. These small things help me to remain grounded and calm no matter what calamity life presents. The biggest challenge is to put my sobriety and recovery first no matter what is going on in life.

DB: How have you reconnected with your body since being in recovery, and what are some things you include in your daily life to increase your health and vitality?

AC: At first it was hell. Since I used the drugs to get me out of my feelings and make me thin, I struggled with "unspecified eating disorders" (my therapist's phrase) before, during, and after getting clean and sober. When I quit, I put on 35 pounds in three months. As a sex worker (stripper) that was hard. My relationship with my body has changed over the years and as a daily runner, I appreciate my strength and endurance. I drink water and take vitamins. I try to avoid trigger foods like sugar and flour but I don't approach my diet with an iron fist or an incredible amount of restriction. I get to start my day over if I want to with a shower and meditation. I have started my day over three times before. I just try to eat clean and make thoughtful decisions. I don't do it perfectly and I don't have to. Getting enough sleep is important and as I age, this is a huge challenge so my self-care routine around sleep has become pretty elaborate: tea, melatonin, reading material.

DB: How have your relationships changed (types of people, length/meaning of relationships, etc.) from when you were actively using to being in recovery?

AC: This is a three-hour conversation! I don't hang with my dealer or any hard drug users anymore and I build friendships that are bases on respect and trust that flows in both directions.

I go through long periods of abstinence in romantic engagements. I'm in SLAA (Sex and Love Addicts Anonymous), which is all about self-love and self-value. SLAA teaches me how to detach in a healthy way, how to date in an emotionally sober way, and how to see red flags and not paint them white. In SLAA I've learned to enjoy my own company and connect with my spirituality. In sex work, I set boundaries more readily and ask for things I need. I don't keep people in my life who are heart-breakingly flaky, unavailable, mean, or inconsiderate.

DB: Who are the top three to five people you surround yourself with and why are they influential in your recovery?

AC: I did a double take at "people" because that excludes my cat, Squeaker, who I surround myself with as much as possible. I hang out with other writers who are also in recovery—mostly women. They teach me how to stay accountable and how to communicate effectively. I constantly send e-mails to several women for input as to how to be compassionate and direct to people in my life, both professionally and personally. Artist women who have become successful are my heroes because they've figured out how to be both creative and abundant. I learn how to stay connected to people and show up and participate in and celebrate other's lives. Other people, fellowship, and women are a huge asset to my life and my recovery.

DB: What is your spiritual life like and what do you do on a daily basis to integrate it into your life, and why do you think spirituality is important for growth and sustainability in recovery?

AC: I'm constantly keeping an eye out for God. That means tabling my desires and wants and leaving room for God to come in and direct my thinking and my day. My day is miserable if I am only thinking about how to get what I want and need. Also, it makes other people responsible for my happiness—which is a recipe for resentment. So, I have to be willing to pause and ask for help and direction all day long. Sometimes I'm bad at this, like in traffic or if someone yells at me or I get hate mail or something hurts my feelings. Even if I'm convinced something is personal, it's not. People are just doing their best and you never know what people are going through. Spiritually, I want to lead with compassion and trust.

DB: What was one situation you found yourself in that confirmed in your mind that you must seek treatment and recovery and why?

AC: Oh, this is easy. I rode in an ambulance and was held on a 72-hour hold at Davies Medical Center. I had opened my wrist and required stitches and a social worker. I'd been going to AA off and on, on the spin cycle of quitting speed and picking it up again. That was a pivotal moment for me and I knew I could not do this alone. I needed help. It was life or death. That simple. That hard. That brutal.

ADAM SUD

"I don't look at my recovery as an abstinence-based recovery program. It was more of an acceptance of positive behaviors that would outweigh the destructive behaviors that were ruining my life."
– Adam Sud

Bio: At age 30, Adam Sud weighed over 320 pounds, was severely addicted to drugs and fast food, and was afflicted with Type 2 diabetes, high blood pressure, high cholesterol, anxiety disorder, sleep disorder, and suicidal depression. His downward spiral culminated with an overdose as a result of a suicide attempt while he was alone in his filthy, hoarder-like apartment. He checked into rehab and with the help of his parents and a plant-based diet, he began a journey that led to a remarkable recovery—not only to reverse his chronic diseases and lose 170 pounds but live a happy and healthy life of purpose. He is helping others discover how to find the joy in owning their health, their wellbeing, and to develop self-love, including his twin brother, who he helped reverse his Type 2 diabetes, high blood pressure, and lose 90 pounds with a plant-based diet. Adam is now a diabetes and food addiction coach for Mastering Diabetes (masteringdiabetes.org). A program that focuses on reversing insulin resistance to master Type 1, Type 1.5, pre-diabetes, and Type 2 diabetes using low fat, whole food, plant-based nutrition. He is an international speaker for the plant-based movement. Adam has also worked in recovery centers using plant-based nutrition as a tool for strengthening recovery and relapse prevention. He firmly believes that the simplest change on your fork can make the most profound change of your life. Instagram: @plantbasedaddict Facebook: Plant-Based Addict

Occupation: Diabetes and Food Addiction Coach

Drug of choice: Adderall

Length of sobriety: 6 years

DB: What do you do to stay sober on a daily basis and what's the most challenging part about it, if anything?

AS: Well, so staying sober, it's not something that I do. Really, it's become something that I am. Right? So, I found a way to fall in love with the process of the things that made me feel good about who I was, that created self-care and self-love on a daily basis. In the beginning, you know, that was adopting a plant-based diet, moving my body, going for runs, being a part of a community of people that were all trying to achieve the same thing, which is to create a new lifestyle in which my destructive lifestyle habits no longer existed. I don't look at my recovery as an abstinence-based recovery program. It was more of an acceptance of positive behaviors that would outweigh the destructive behaviors that were ruining my life.

So, for me, it's getting up every day and doing a gratitude affirmation and living a plant-based lifestyle, eating a plant-based diet that is in itself an act of self-care and an act of self-love, because it allows me to create a healthier version of myself today than I was the day before. And early on in my recovery, that was for me an affirmation of sobriety. That was me saying to myself that today, I'm choosing to do whatever it takes to create a lifestyle that allows me to be a happier, healthier person at the end of the day than I was the day before. So, I really don't think it's any one thing. It's more about the way in which I approach my everything that I do in life as an acceptance rather than an abstinence.

DB: How have you reconnected with your body since being into recovery and what are some things you do on a daily basis to increase your health and vitality?

AS: So, when I checked into rehab, I was 350 pounds. I didn't know it at the time, but I had Type 2 diabetes. I had high blood pressure. I had high cholesterol. I knew I had erectile dysfunction and I had just survived a suicide attempt and everything about my day before I attempted suicide and before I checked into rehab was about avoiding any way of connecting with my body, because I hated it so much that I didn't want to be aware of it. I didn't want to be aware of how removed from the ability to live my lifestyle had created for me as a physical person.

You know, there's a saying that says that when you're sick and when you're obese, people pay attention to you and they ignore you at the exact same time. I knew that in my body, I felt handicapped from life and as a result of adopting a plant-based diet and as a result of moving my body through running. Running, for me, has become an act of mindfulness meditation. Through those fundamental changes, I have been able to learn to accept my body for what it is and lose the weight, reverse my chronic diseases, reverse my diabetes, my high blood pressure, my cholesterol, my erectile dysfunction, get off of all my medications, including my antidepressants and mood stabilizers, sleeping medications, anxiety medications.

I have finally, not because of my physical appearance, but I love the body that I have and see it as a true gift, because before, I would view that I needed to, you know, try and exercise my problems away or diet my problems away, but now, I see movement and food as a celebration of what my body is, and it is this incredible gift. I think of life as a person in recovery as everything is about acceptance and gratitude and appreciation. Right? So, I accept that I'm grateful for the opportunity that the universe has put the incredibly healing, powerful foods in my environment. I have access to them, and so I take them in and I use them to create a body that allows me to show the universe how grateful I am for it by moving my body in incredible ways. Like going for a long run, that's an act of gratitude to the universe by me saying "Thank you for giving me what I need to create this life. Here's how I celebrate it through movement."

DB: How have your relationships changed since being in recovery? Who would you say are the top three to five people you surround yourself with and why are they influential in your recovery?

AS: Well, so here's the way I look at it, man. I was really talented at what I did as an addict. Right? I mean, I was never so productive as in the days when I needed my drugs and when I needed to find a way to afford them, whether it was scamming or stealing or dealing or whatever it was, and it was hard work. Right? It's hard work to morally bankrupt yourself on a daily basis. It's hard work to physically bankrupt your health on a daily basis, and it is really hard work to ruin every single relationship that I had, including the ones with my family and my friends, the point to where it to where I had no one around me, not because they didn't want to be there for me, but because I had made sure that nobody was going to be around me, because I couldn't stand to have people be near me, because all it did was show me how far from my life I had fallen.

Whereas now, my life is about understanding the incredible opportunity that it is to feel connected to other people. To move through the world where my connection with other people doesn't just have to be about me in order for me to get something from it. When I was an addict, every interaction I had with somebody was a confrontation or a scam. It was how can I be angry at you because just being with you makes me see myself for what I really am, and so I'm going to make you feel bad for it, or how can I use you in order to get what I need to get my drugs or whatever it is. It was all me, me, me, me, me, and that's how I thought life was supposed to be. But now, I can be with people and just be with them and offer myself and gain so much from the experience that it is really change everything about the way that I move through the world.

You know, I felt I needed to be right all the time in order to disprove everybody's so-called beliefs about me that I don't even know were true, it's just based on my insecurities. But when I stopped feeling like I had to be right all the time, I was able to learn how to live a lifestyle that is unlike anything I've ever experienced in my life and it allows me to connect to people in ways I've never been able to.

DB: Thoughts on top people?

AS: Well, my family, so my mom and my dad. I treated them really, really poorly when I was an addict. I used them on a regular basis and when I wasn't trying to scam them out of something, I was blaming them or shaming them for everything that was wrong in my life. Even in spite of the horrible ways I treated them, they never gave up on me, even when I completely given up on myself, and I am not only alive today but happy, healthy, and sober because they never gave up on me. Because of that, I will always want to have them in my life and to keep me humble, to keep me, you know, on track. They're not only my parents now, they're my best friends. They're mentors for me. But as a gift to myself, I can authentically be with them for the first time since my addiction started back when I was in high school and that's an incredible thing . . . to authentically be their son is a gift to myself.

Not only that, my twin brother and my little sister, of course. My twin brother is literally my identical other half, and my sister, you know, she wasn't talking to me for a while when I was an addict, and rightfully so, but when I got my one year sober, she flew out from Austin in order to go to my meeting to see me get my chip, and she is a very special person.

It's really my family, it is. When it comes down to it, the people that matter most to you, no matter how horribly you treated them, they will be there for you, because addiction is a behavior. It's not who you are as a person, and people that truly love you will know that. They will be there for you when you decide that the behavior that you're doing is destructive and you can no longer continue to do it. That's what it's about. You know? When I realized that my parents and my brother and sister weren't talking about who I was as a person but the behaviors that were ruining the life that I was living, I was able to authentically sort of break open and allow myself the opportunity to try something new. It's those people that keep me humble and keep me on track.

DB: What's your spiritual life like and how do you integrate it into your day and why do you think spirituality is important for growth and sustainability in recovery?

AS: Yeah, so I'm not a religious person. I was raised Jewish, but I'm not a religious person. I'm proud of my Jewish heritage, but my spirituality is the power in connection. To be connected to the living world around me, to the environment around me, to the non-human animals that I share this incredible planet with, to recognize that there's nothing special about me. There's nothing that separates me from any other human, from any other non-human, and the fact that I could look into the eyes of a non-human animal and see myself in themselves, and the fact that they can look into my eyes and see themselves in me is part of what makes this experience of life on this planet so incredibly beautiful and unique and wonderful.

I think of it as, I don't need something, I don't need the fantastic to exist for fantastic things to happen for me every single day, and that is my spirituality. Connecting to the experience of the world going on around me, and know that I'm not separate from it, and because of that, I'm not special, but it is special to witness that happening. In order to continue to do that, I have to continue with my daily practice of caring for the environment and other non-human animals through my choices on my plate, moving my body, and being committed to my recovery in a way that allows me as a person to be physically capable to connect to the universe and this planet the way that I want to, and spiritually and emotionally and physically connect to it.

DB: What was one moment that confirmed in your mind that you needed to seek recovery and/or treatment and why?

AS: Well, I had known, obviously had known for years, that I had a serious issue; but I was never able to say it out loud. It's funny, I think that I was afraid of allowing my ears to actually hear me say I was an addict and I need help. While I could say it in my head, I would never say it out loud out of fear of hearing the sound of my own voice saying I was an addict. And that fear led me down a really dark hole until, you know, it was on August 21, 2012, I attempted suicide by overdose. I was living in a hoarder's apartment, I was a hoarder of junk, a stimulant addict, a fast food addict, and you know, I remember having this thought that, you know, nothing's ever going to get any better and I need to spare myself and everyone else around me the misery that I'm causing.

It was weird, it wasn't like a lot of precontemplation. It was sort of like, this is going to happen right now. And I passed out, I popped a bunch of pills and I passed out on the floor and I woke up I don't know how much longer later, but I was in a puddle of my own vomit. I was in a pile of fast food garbage and I had a very surreal moment where I realized that if I didn't radically change my life that my family was going to have to spend the rest of their lives trying to figure out why I needed to eat and drug myself to death. And you know, for whatever reason, I didn't die. I was going to give myself the opportunity to see if I could make that, you know, make sure that that never happened, and maybe find out that I actually do see something valuable in myself and that there may actually be a reason for me to want to stay alive. That was a reason enough for me to pick up the phone and call my parents and for the first time say to anybody that I needed help. I don't know if I was honestly sincere about wanting to stay sober

100% from that day, but I know that that was the moment where I decided that I needed to ask for help.

CARRIE WHITE

"I blame no one and hold myself responsible for my recovery which brings PEACE."
- Carrie White

Bio: Carrie White has more than left her mark as the First Lady of Hairdressing. During a career that spans 45 years, that bridges the iconic look of Elvis Presley and to the ever-changing style of Sandra Bullock, from the movie *Shampoo* to QVC, from Beverly Hills to India, from roller-skating in spandex as she coiffed the likes of Nancy Reagan and Betsey Bloomingdale to trimming and caring for her 10 grandchildren, Carrie White continues to share her unmatched skills with a scissor, her bottomless passion for life, and her incredible and indelible stories.

Carrie White picked up her survival skill very early in life, as she mixed drinks for her alcoholic mother and endured her step-father's sexual abuse—a skill she honed through her years on the streets of Pacoima and the glamour of Hollywood High, where she discovered beauty school and a career opportunity, unaware of the universe that a pair of scissors could open up for her.

Through it all—the glamour, such as being named Playboy centerfold—the honor of being in the company of legends such as James Galanos, Jimi Hendrix, and Jennifer Jones; the tragedies, such as the loss of her dear friend Sharon Tate; the drug and alcohol fueled destruction of self and loved ones, Carrie White never lost her pure and innocent love for life.

And it is this passion that has brought her back to where she belongs: the top of her profession. Carrie White has reclaimed the respect and earned the forgiveness of family, friends, and clients old and new. Her namesake salon thrives across the street from the Peninsula Hotel, a dream life that continues a long way from where she began . . . and only a few blocks away from Burton Way, where she was born.

Occupation: Hairdresser / Published Author / Published Poet / Recovery Speaker

Drug of choice: Alcohol, cocaine, heroin

Length of sobriety: 34 years

DB: What do you do on a daily basis to maintain your sobriety, and what is the most challenging part about it?

CW: I talk to newcomers or people I sponsor about sobriety on a daily basis. This insures my gratitude and commitment to my sobriety reminding me where I came from and the value of my life and wisdom I have today.

DB: How have you reconnected with your body since being in recovery, and what are some things you include in your daily life to increase your health and vitality?

CW: First of all I eat better . . . fresh, organic, and I don't smoke let alone consume drugs and alcohol. I joined the gym to quit smoking in 1987. Aerobics. I got a trainer twice a week at Golds Gym for 20 years after that. I also got very involved with Kundalini yoga. Today I go to the gym six days a week for 40 minutes and do Pilates once a week. At home, I have a rowing machine and weights.

DB: How have your relationships changed (types of people, length/meaning of relationships, etc.) from when you were actively using to being in recovery?

CW: Oooo please—what a question! My drinks and drugs made all my decisions before I got sober. Who I was with, what I could get, who wouldn't complain about my using and who used like me—until they complained was my way of "people in my life" selection. Everyone was basically an extra in my movie.

DB: Who are the top three to five people you surround yourself with and why are they influential in your recovery?

CW: This April I lost my sponsor of 34 years, a guiding loving woman I saw once a week minimum . . . for all this time. I did her hair and we talked.

And three days later my best friend since we were teenagers, Aloma Ichinose, died. She needed and discovered sobriety before me . . . she 12 stepped me literally for 12 years, and finally after six hospitals, introduced me to my sponsor and her recovery home: Peggy Albrecht of the Peggy Albrecht Friendly House.

Since this . . . I took on a new sponsor and a new sponsee to deepen roots for my protection and program. I have a sober boyfriend. We live together.

My five children and 10 grandchildren are a constant in my life and my trusting sober assistant of 27 years. Their daily presence keeping me in view keeps me on track and insures my concern to be a good example of sobriety.

DB: What is your spiritual life like and what do you do on a daily basis to integrate it into your life, and why do you think spirituality is important for growth and sustainability in recovery?

CW: My life has no separation with my spiritual life. Today . . . every morning and night and through the day . . . I say thank you to the universe and my higher power by recognizing the beauty in my world, and by my actions. I smile and practice kindness and courtesy even when I'm not in the mood and it reminds me to get in this mood.

I go to meetings—three a week. To keep myself teachable, be of service, and connect with gratitude. I keep a clean home, I have a garden I tend that keeps me with the beauty of nature . . . I trust my destiny by my participation. I stay enthusiastic to life by love, music, dance, film, theater, art, museums, and travel. Without my recovery none of this will exist . . . my spirit is "This Love of Life" and my amends are by staying sober. This I know like a tattoo on my heart.

DB: What was one situation you found yourself in that confirmed in your mind that you must seek treatment and recovery and why?

CW: More like why ONE MILLION THINGS CONFIRM MY ALCOHOLISM . . . from being arrested for being drink at age 10 to losing everything I worked for all my life by age of 39. My heart and soul knew to change from my desperate life of fear for my final loss: my life. Knowing others have recovered from using like me—gave me hope.

I blame no one and hold myself responsible for my recovery which brings PEACE, by being honest with myself and others, and staying current with all 12 Steps . . . which include, improvement one day at a time, being of service, giving back, recognizing the needs of others, in this way . . . I continue with the insurance to say thank you, stay grateful and mean it.

COLICCHIE

"I'm here to be the voice for every friend I ever lost."
– Colicchie

Bio: "Colicchie" (aka Chas Smith) is most known for using his rap music to inspire others to beat addiction. His song *Drug Addiction* has gotten over 15 million views on YouTube and has been instrumental in helping others.

Occupation: Rapper/Recovery Advocate

Drug of choice: Heroin

Length of sobriety: 3 years

DB: What do you do to stay sober on a daily basis and what's the most challenging part about it?

C: I mean it really comes down to like six things and I'll elaborate, but it really is about calling my sponsor, going to meetings, doing Step work, sharing with others, prayer, and helping others.

You know I wish I did every single one of them things perfect on a daily basis, but you know, I don't. My prayer has always been really, really strong. My meeting attendance has always been good. Even if I'm traveling, even if I'm too busy with my daughter or whatever, I'll always make time for meetings.

And helping others is something that has really filled my spirit. Honestly, over the last 10 years, since I first got clean for the first time, it's always been something to take me out of myself in a good way, because I've only gotten to where I am by other people helping me and by basically predecessors showing me the way that this works.

It really comes down to that and the 12-Step Fellowship that I'm involved in and everything that it represents is really what I try to do on a daily basis for the most part.

Challenging? I would say complications between me and my child's mother, but it's really nothing when I have faith and it's really nothing when I have people to love and care about me and they just want to do me good and succeed.

You know there's nothing in my life that I keep a secret. For the most part, 99.9% of it, I rap about, but that very, very small percent I talk with a lot of people. I have a lot of really good friends, like recent new friends, but also friends that I've had for many years, especially in my city, that also go to the same 12-Step Fellowship as me.

I have struggled in the past obviously from depression, anxiety, you name it, and this is even with years clean. There was times when I had years clean where I would just be suffocated in depression for no apparent reason, like I'd be living right, but I'd still would like subconsciously filled with guilt and shame. I would talk about it and it would leave, but it would come back. It was really just something that I had to deal with and just get through, but I'm proud to say that ever since my daughter was born 14 months ago I really haven't been depressed. I really haven't had like that gut-wrenching like depression that has paralyzed me, so for that I'm grateful.

DB: Now how have you reconnected with your body since being in recovery and what are some things you do on a daily

basis to increase your health and vitality?

C: I mean in moments, I have ate right. I really wish that I always ate right, but I don't. Once again, this is also intervals, you know, since I started recovery many years ago. I believe in working out obviously, running, lifting, and stuff like that. When I do stuff that feeds my body in a positive way, it makes my mind feel good.

I don't want to say that's the only reason I do it, but it is a big part of it, because this really is a mental, physical, and spiritual sickness that I suffer from, so I really have to take care of all three of them. I can't neglect one part and then just worry about the other. I have to really focus on all three of them. So, for me to lift and to try to eat right is difficult at times, but it's something that I try to pursue.

DB: How have your relationships changed from addiction and now being in recovery, and who are the top three to five people you surround yourself with and why are they influential in your life and recovery?

C: Well obviously when I used I really didn't have any relationships. Obviously, I had those people that I got high with. People that I got high with 10 years ago, right . . . when I was really introduced to addiction and all that, out of like the 10 of us, they're all either dead or in prison. The only one that's clean and living right is my sister.

I really didn't trust nobody. Nobody trusted me. I burned every single bridge, including my closest family members. I couldn't hold a job, never had money. I was disrespectful in any way, shape, or form. I really was a terrorist, and I talk about that all the time. I was a taker. If you were in my life, I looked at you as how I'm going to be able to benefit from you being in my life. How am I going to get money off you? How am I going to gain from even being around you?

Today my life is nothing like that. I have people in my life that I try to just give to. People trust me. I'm accountable. I'm responsible. I have a career. I make money. I have a vehicle. I have a place. Like the transformation that has happened from when I was using to, you know, where I am today really is almost like I lived two different lives.

But I don't ever get it twisted, like I can never return there, because I've had multiple years clean a couple times and have gone back out. I mean really that quick, you know. But the first time I would use, it would literally bring me to my knees, because I know the life that I can live but I chose to go back out.

But honesty my life today, you know, it really is incredible and it's by all the things I mentioned earlier in this interview, like it's by doing them things and, you know, staying like spiritually maintained on a daily basis, like those are the things that build my character and those are the things that like keep me motivated and dedicated to want to constantly push myself to just do better and better, because I realize that this really is not about me anymore.

This is really about my daughter, my family, and everybody else that I surround myself with, because when I help one person it really does indirectly help so many others. I believe in benevolence and I believe in just helping others and just giving selfless service, because like I said, that's really the only way to attack addiction, because I know that I can't do this alone. I really need like an entire army with me to battle something that is so much more powerful than me.

DB: As far as the top people?

C: I'd probably say my friend Rich, my sister Lisa, my friend Matt, my friend Jimbo, and my friend Andrew. I mean there's so many, but those are the top five that came to my head. I want to say these because they're all positive, they're all clean, except for my friends Jimbo and Andrew had years clean at one time, but they're just coming back. But they're just still so positive, you know.

My other friends have like five to 10 to 15 years clean. I surround myself with [those] type of people, because a lot of times I don't believe the good things about myself. I don't want to say I need validation or I need reassurance, but sometimes my thinking can be crazy. Those are the type of people that pull me back into reality and let me know exactly the person I am, because it's important for me. It's important for me to know that I'm growing, therefore I want to continue doing this.

But they are, they're all just special, amazing people that really have helped me in so many different ways and have made a positive impact on my life in one way or another, whether it was just hanging out with them and laughing and just making fun of each other, or us talking about recovery in certain steps and how they've gotten through it.

Those spiritual principles that I practice and I carry, I was taught by somebody else . . . how to do that, how to live that, how to lead by example, and how to basically just, you know, completely change my entire life and my thinking and my behaviors. I mean everything that comes along with recovery, because addiction really does go much deeper than the drugs I used.

The drugs were honestly just the tip of the iceberg. It really comes down to my ideas, attitudes, and behaviors. If I'm surrounding myself around good people I can keep my mind on that would be my focus, like just constantly change for the better.

DB: What's your spiritual life like? And what do you do on a daily basis for spirituality and why do you think it's important for sustainability and growth and recovery?

C: Once again, this is something that has definitely fluctuated over the years. And when I say fluctuated, I mean I've always had a good relationship with God and I've always been very spiritual, but there's just been moments in my recovery where prayer was maybe artificial or I was doing the act just to do the act.

But, then there was times, you know, where I used to spend literally hours on my knees at night praying and feeling the prayers and bawling my eyes while praying. I believe spirituality is important because of Step work. It really can't be done for myself, you know, without it.

But I would always say blessed, fortunate, lucky, whatever you want to say, like why I'm still alive. It took a long time for me to accept that I made it. Just for today, you know, like I'm still alive and some of my friends are dead. Like I'm still here because I serve a purpose. I really do believe that we all do serve a purpose.

We're all being used for good. Like when God calls my number, it's time to go, but my spirituality has been the one thing that like has conditioned me to be a better person, because if I'm not connected with God and I'm not connected with like a higher power, then, like that's really where I get strength from and that's like really where I draw all my power from.

It's always been super imperative for me to have a relationship with God, because a lot of times too, I wouldn't want to talk to people, or share in meetings. But, I always had the strength to pray. I always felt comfort from it. I always felt solace from it. I always felt relieved about just spilling my issues out or spilling whatever is going on in my head, to just talk about it and to just completely put it out there.

My relationship with God is something that's very personal, and it really is very personal for each one of us. But it is something that I would say that is absolutely vital in order for myself to recover on a daily basis.

DB: What was the one situation that confirmed for you in

your mind you must seek treatment and recovery, and why?

C: I'll use just my last time as an example. At this time, I had about 13 months clean. I was dealing with the end of a relationship where I really thought that this girl was the one. It didn't work out that way and I suffered and tortured myself for two weeks, sharing about it in meetings. It really was like a feeling that I never felt before. To this day it's kind of even hard to identify in detail, you know, to verbalize how I felt.

But, I basically hit a point where I thought that drugs would be the solution even for a moment, and I found out that it wasn't very quickly, and after a five-day run of shooting a substantial amount of heroin, you know, like I said, I had been in recovery and I just didn't want to live that way.

It really did get to a point for myself where I just broke down and I prayed and I basically just stopped. I never in a million years have ever been able to do anything like that. Now, it was very, very hard for me in the beginning. I was tremendously obsessed. I wasn't sleeping. I mean this is even after just five days of using. Like I wasn't sleeping. All I wanted to do was use.

I still was going to work at that time. I had a physical job. I was working construction. But, I just pushed forward. The only reason I was able to do that is because I believe in recovery so much, and I already had such an amazing foundation.

Although I did slip and I fell short, I was still so connected to so many good people, and that's really what got me through like the first 30 days. You know, the six things that I told you in the beginning. I just increased it and I just went hard, to be honest. Because I was obviously missing something.

I'm not saying that as an excuse, but I slipped and I quickly caught myself and I got back on track. But, you know, so many spiritual bottoms I hit at times, I know that I needed to make that phone call to go to rehab, or just because I felt like I was never able to do it on my own.

It really just hit that point of being spiritually bankrupt. It wasn't like I was facing cases, or it wasn't even like oh, my mom's going to kick me out, or it wasn't even like man, I'm broke. I wish I had money, let me get clean. It always came down to the feelings for me.

I suffered with so much self-hatred and so much guilt and so much shame, remorse, regret for everything that I was doing, that I would hit these points where I just knew that I needed to change or I was going to die, and if I wasn't going to die from the drugs then I was going to kill myself, because that's how low I felt. That's how I viewed myself. I literally viewed myself as scum, as dirt. I felt like something that nobody wanted to be around.

So, for me it was really all that feeling of me just being completely spiritually broken and spiritually bankrupt.

LAURA MCKOWEN

"All of my relationships have changed for the better in that the ones that are still there are so much more real and strong and honest"
– Laura McKowen

Bio: Laura is a writer, yoga teacher, speaker, and recovery advocate. She writes an internationally recognized, award-winning blog at LauraMcKowen.com and was the co-host of HOME podcast. Laura earned her MBA from Babson College and worked in advertising and marketing for 15 years, where she led international teams and managed stupidly large marketing budgets for Fortune 50 companies. In 2016, she made the leap to entrepreneurship and now writes, teaches yoga-based workshops, and retreats all over the U.S., and consults on marketing, personal branding, and online business strategy.

Laura lives with her daughter on the north shore of Boston and is currently writing her first book, a memoir.

Occupation: Writer, Yoga Teacher, Recovery Advocate

Drug of choice: Alcohol

Length of sobriety: 4 years

DB: What do you do to stay sober on a daily basis and what's the most challenging part about it?

LM: The actual staying sober is not difficult anymore because I do so many things. I don't try. I don't have to think about not drinking or using drugs anymore, but that's because I've built up a whole different life. I would say the thing that has helped me the most or has helped me and sort of keep me level is that I do physical activity. This has been a consistent thing throughout my sobriety. I think it's just so important. I actually went to Orangetheory this morning for the first time in a long time. It's weird, the past three or four months I've been really not doing much physically, which is very strange for me. I started to really feel like shit, like depressed and I think my body needed to not be pushed after being pushed for so long. But then there's this slippery slope. I think my brain is just not getting the endorphins anymore and it makes a massive difference.

Today I feel alive again, you know? I still do participate in meetings here and there. I have a sponsor. I do a lot of personal development work. I mean, because of the work that I do for a career now I'm constantly in that. I think that that once you have a certain level of awareness of what impacts your mental health and how your psychology works and all that, it almost becomes impossible to imagine going backwards. I continue to deal with the underlying root causes, which is what ultimately I think keeps us all sober or allows us to be healthy in sobriety.

DB: How would you say you've reconnected with your body since being in recovery, and what are some things you do on a daily basis to increase your health and vitality?

LM: Reconnecting with the body is one of the first things I teach people. I mean, I never really stopped running. I did stop doing yoga because it was just too painful for me to be with myself on a mat. But yoga was a huge part of getting sober again because it's the mind/body thing, right? Learning to breathe and realizing that our heads get so sick and we identify so much with what our minds are doing . . . that connecting with your body allows you to have another voice or a way out. I did all the things. I ran, mostly did yoga, just tried to be outside a ton. I was also really tired when I first got sober so I also had to learn to not push myself too hard in that way. I think some people come in and they have no connection to their body and they haven't been physical for a long time but that wasn't the case for me. It honestly just felt like I wasn't doing it anymore to overcome a hangover. I was doing it because it actually felt good.

I'm really trying to eat a lot better. For me, that means not just eating sugar all the time. I could be wrong, but I don't know that there are many women who don't know how to eat well anymore. I went through eating disorders. I know more about nutrition and the body than is probably necessary. It's as if I knew how to eat well. I just didn't know how to have a healthy relationship with food. Long-winded way of saying that is that's what I'm working on right now.

DB: How have your relationships transformed from when you were struggling with addiction to now being in recovery and who are the top three to five people you surround yourself with and why are they influential in your recovery?

LM: All of my relationships have changed for the better in that the ones that are still there are so much more real and strong and honest. I don't have a lot of the same relationships that I used to have, meaning a lot of people fell off. Both for my side and theirs. I think it's a natural fallout. I have fewer friends, there are fewer relationships but they're better. It's definitely a quality over quantity type of situation.

I have a daughter. I don't put that in the same bucket as the other relationships because she's my daughter. She's also my greatest teacher. I honestly have a very small group of two or three core friends: one or two from the days that I was drinking and a couple from the world of sobriety. My ex-husband is a big part of my life too because we have a child together. They're all relationships that I had to do a lot of work on. Over time I had to learn how to be honest with people to show up as I actually am and to allow them to do the same. I mean, I think relationships are the hardest and most rewarding part of sobriety and I think it's one of those things where it takes a long time to learn how to be in a relationship of any kind: friendship, romantic relationship, parent–daughter, whatever. Because I started drinking very young, I was extremely immature emotionally and I don't think that just goes for people who have been addicted to things. I think that's most people.

DB: What's your spiritual life like and why do you think spirituality is important for recovery and what do you do on a daily basis to integrate it into your life?

LM: I've always had a sort of relationship with a god. That wasn't new for me in sobriety, but the relationship that I have with . . . and I just say God because that's what makes sense to me . . . but other people say something else. The relationship continues to deepen and change and shift. Really, the biggest catalyst for that was sobriety: when I couldn't get sober and had to rely on something else. In terms of recovery, my relationship with God is about: reminding myself that I don't have control. I think that's an issue that really confuses a lot of people. It's not that I'm powerless over everything, but I am powerless over a lot. I'm powerless, I don't have control of the world, and I don't have control of other people and I don't have control over reality or the truth of what is.

That is the basis of my spirituality: it's a continual letting go and a trust. The other side of that is a faith and a trust that there is a God that is interested in my growth. Things don't always work out in the way that I want or hope or that feel good, but there is an underlying reason why. I haven't gone to church since I was a kid. The religious thing, I would not consider myself religious. I like a lot of different religions: Buddhism makes a lot of sense to me, Christianity makes lot of sense to me, the list goes on.

I don't have any problem with church at all, but I think the

God thing trips a lot of people up in getting sober. AA is the fundamental program that we have in the U.S. It's basically associated 100% with getting sober. Then in the 12 Steps, there's a lot about God, or there's a couple pieces about God. I think it trips a lot of people up. But I've never had a problem with that. I don't know, even from being a kid, I've just always had this idea or this knowing of this presence of something else. It has never tripped me up. It's actually been quite the opposite.

DB: What was one situation you found yourself in that confirmed in your mind you must seek either treatment or recovery and why?

LM: Oh dear God, there were so many. I mean, I didn't have a single rock bottom incident. I was skidding along the bottom for a very long time. The big one for me is I put my daughter in danger one time specifically. There were many times but this was very acute and that started me on this path because I realized. I knew how bad or dark it was, but I didn't know that I could go to that place where I could lose track of her or whatever. That just put a big pin in my denial at that point. I started going to meetings then and just sort of started on it. There are lines that we draw: "Well, if it gets that bad or if it gets like that, or if it gets like that, or if I do that, or if I do that. . ." I thought, there's a line that I would never cross and that was putting my daughter in danger, that I would never supplant my mama instinct, you know, and I did. That definitely caused me to go, yeah, okay so I can't control my drinking or using.

JASON WAHLER

"Through working out and boxing specifically, I am able to complete my physical, mental, and spiritual attunement as well as achieving the natural high from the workout itself."
– Jason Wahler

Bio: Jason Wahler is a host, actor, and TV personality, and philanthropist who appeared on hit shows like MTV'S *Laguna Beach, The Hills,* and *Celebrity Rap Superstar*. After years of publicly battling with addiction, he appeared on Dr. Drew's *Celebrity Rehab*. Since getting sober, Jason has dedicated his life to raising awareness towards addiction and hopes to one day change the public's negative perception of this deadly disease. Through his hard work and dedication, the E! Network produced a *True Hollywood Story* featuring Jason's remarkable transformation. Moreover, in 2017, he received the esteemed Faces & Voice's "Voice of Recovery Award" in Washington, D.C. Today, as founder of Widespread Recovery and Director of Marketing for Tres Vistas Recovery, Jason's goal is to set the standard in aftercare. His direct involvement with the recovery community has changed his life and allows him to be a resource for thousands of individuals who need help but don't know where to turn. Steadfast, Jason works closely with media outlets, celebrities, young adults, schools, law enforcement, churches, and athletes to promote addiction education and prevention through the sharing of his own experiences and stories of hope. He leverages his personal story along with his seat in the public eye to inspire his fellows struggling with addiction. Jason's exposure within recovery communities nationwide has been primed by partnering with key advocates including renowned Dr. Daniel Headrick, a distinguished fellow of the American Society of Addiction Medicine; "Dr. Drew" Pinskey; and, Tim Storey, acclaimed author, speaker, and life coach. Jason also serves on the boards of the Los Angeles Mission and the Brent Shapiro Foundation. "Looking back over the course of the past 10 years I never thought I would be where I am at today. If you told me I would find my passion and motivation working with and for other alcoholics and addicts, I would have thought you were delusional. Today, I can't imagine doing anything else." (Jason Wahler)

Occupation: Host, Actor, TV Personality, and Entrepreneur

Drug of choice: Alcohol, cocaine, and Adderall

Length of sobriety: 110 days (at time of interview)

DB: What caused you to go back out?

JW: What caused me to go back out ultimately was complacency. I inundated myself with work and because of this lack of balance, I became overwhelmed without the proper structure and foundation to keep me on track.

DB: What do you do to stay sober on a daily basis and what's the most challenging part about it?

JW: My daily routine has become a culmination of years of experience witnessing what works and what doesn't. Although every individual will have suggestions and advice, the beauty of humanity is our individuality. With that in mind, healthy habits and routines are all about creating patterns that work for you personally but I would like to share my routine as I believe there may be someone out there it can apply to and help.

One key to my morning routine is consistency. Consistency allows me to hold myself accountable for any shortcomings or procrastinations. By getting into a repeated routine, it's easy to determine where the wheels fell of the cart. By creating consistency and structure at the start of the day, it makes carrying that consistency and structure throughout the day much easier as well.

The beginning of my day starts promptly at 6:00 a.m. This is the first pillar of consistency of my day and it's very important for me to be up at 6:00 sharp so that I have time to perform my morning rituals without the added stress of being late. So many individuals love their "snooze" button; however, the mindfulness of the effect of that button is what gets me to rise and shine. Once I'm up, I like to collect my thoughts in a period of meditation. This gives me a sense of sanctuary to truly get my ducks lined up so that I can knock them down efficiently. It also helps me connect with myself and establish goals for the day. Without goals, a person is just "there" but not really doing anything.

Once I've collected my thoughts and established my goals, I like to further reinforce my connection on a fellowship level by spending quality family time. Although I only spend about 30 minutes with my loving wife and our most recent addition, our beautiful baby girl, Delilah, I would like everyone to remember that life is about love, memories, and the legacy you leave behind.

Moving on from the spiritual side of my morning and transiting to the physical side, I find myself at the gym. Through working out and boxing specifically, I am able to complete my physical, mental, and spiritual attunement as well as achieving the natural high from the workout itself. This is my "first cup of coffee" so to speak as it gets my blood flowing and ready for the day ahead. After I'm done with my workout, I'm on a mission to find my real cup of coffee and a healthy breakfast to refuel, replenish, and reinforce my wellbeing.

Next on the agenda is a much-needed shower mainly so I'm not gross as I'm going about my day because let's be honest, nobody wants a smelly Jason Wahler. The shower with the running water is also another period of meditation for me to reflect on the progress of my morning thus far. This usually gets me pretty pumped to continue on to the next part of my morning day.

Where most people usually cringe getting ready for work, I love it. I relate this to a professional athlete in the sense that I'm in the locker room ready to make my plate appearance and smash one out of the park. My passion is helping people and getting dressed for work establishes a great sense of self-worth because not only am I going to help people, but getting dressed and making sure everything is primped and proper reinforces my self-esteem. Feel good, look good, do good.

Lastly, I am out the door, coffee in hand, on my way to do my day's duties. Although I set goals initially from the onset, I have periodic routine self-evaluations because I strongly believe that if you're standing still, you can't move forward; therefore, I like to make sure I'm moving in the right direction. While my routine works wonders for me and how I go about my day, I believe that this can apply to many people, especially the ones constantly trying to create more time in the day.

DB: How would you say you've reconnected with your body since being in recovery, and what are some things you do on a daily basis to increase your health and vitality?

JW: Since recovery, I was able to hit the reset button on my own wellness. By making the time to focus and work on myself, I restarted eating healthier, working out more frequently, starting yoga, performing daily meditations, and most importantly, reinforcing these positive activities with stronger boundaries. These boundaries have allowed me more time to spend with friends, family, and nature, which help me create memories. These memories are life's treasures and my key to happiness.

DB: How have your relationships transformed from when you were struggling with addiction to now being in recovery and who are the top three to five people you surround yourself with and why are they influential in your recovery?

JW: To say my relationships changed between active addiction and active recovery is an understatement. I was able to see the differences between the negative and positive relationships and, thanks to having a clearer mind, I was able to remove a lot of those negative relationships. You're a product of your environment so it's imperative to surround yourself with individuals who not only care about you but will elevate you.

Dr. Drew Pinsky: He is and has been a mentor to me, someone I can lean on for support or insight. He's been with me along this journey and has seen me at my best and my worst.

Rick Wahler Sr.: My dad has been my confidant and a big part of my support system. He has given me unconditional love, support, and guidance. Where many other parents might give up on their child, my dad has stuck with me through thick and thin, always trying to make me better.

Ashley Wahler: My wife, my best friend, my partner. She keeps me accountable by calling me out when she sees something out of the norm. She has also been with me through some of the hardest years but fortunately, things have been swinging up and we've been creating great memories.

Alex Meschi: One of my childhood best friends and now a business partner, he has been helping me with managing my business and some personal affairs. Business is much easier when you work with someone who is not only loyal, but will also give you constructive criticism versus just rolling over and accepting everything.

Tim Storey: I have made it a goal of mine to reestablish my faith and in doing so, I have connected with Mr. Storey. He is not just a beacon of faith for me but also he is a great motivator and speaker. I love hearing him talk as I feel invigorated to accomplish my goals but he's also a dear friend and colleague.

DB: What's your spiritual life like and why do you think spirituality is important for recovery and what do you do on a daily basis to integrate it into your life?

JW: I grew up Christian and have continued my pursuit of faith in God. Every day, I start my mornings with prayer and meditation along with reading scriptures. I feel that it is important to believe in something bigger than one's self and having that direct connection gives me support and hope no matter the circumstance.

DB: What was one situation you found yourself in that confirmed in your mind you must seek either treatment or recovery and why?

JW: I don't think I could say there was "one" specific instance, but I knew I had to arrest my disease. Unfortunately, I was unable to do so on my own as I did try multiple times with the help of my sponsor at the time. After continuing to fail on my own, I finally surrendered and reached out for proper help.

MELISSA HARTWIG

"I am a firm believer that we hold our emotions and feelings in our muscle tissues."
– Melissa Hartwig

Bio: Melissa Hartwig is a Certified Sports Nutritionist who specializes in helping people change their relationship with food and create life-long, healthy habits. She is the co-creator of the original Whole30 program, and a five-time *New York Times* bestselling author. She has been featured by *Dr. Oz, Good Morning America,* the *New York Times,* the *Wall Street Journal, Forbes,* and *CNBC*, and ranked #19 on "Greatest Top 100 Most Influential People in Health and Fitness in 2018." Melissa has presented more than 150 health and nutrition seminars worldwide and is a prominent keynote speaker on social media and branding, health trends, and entrepreneurship. She lives in Salt Lake City, UT.

Occupation: Co-Founder/CEO Whole30

Drug of choice: Everything

Length of sobriety: 18 years (clean)

DB: What do you do on a daily basis to maintain your sobriety, and what is the most challenging part about it?

MH: I consider myself to be "clean," not sober, as I do occasionally drink alcohol. (I am clean from all of the drugs I was abusing.) I recognize this is not typical for an addict, but after a year of being clean and sober, my therapist and I agreed that in my context, it was acceptable for me to continue drinking alcohol. I've since taken long periods of time off from drinking (up to a year straight), but have never had any of the same issues with or draw to alcohol as I did with drugs.

At this point, being clean is not particularly challenging, although I will always remain vigilant in my recovery practices. In the beginning, however, it was immensely challenging. It was tough learning how to cope with current life stressors and past trauma without the use of some sort of numbing agent.

It was also very challenging to learn to sit in my feelings and process the things I had been running from, particularly the sexual abuse that led me to use in the first place. However, I didn't do it by myself. I was in therapy with the same counselor for the better part of a dozen years to work through these issues and make sure my recovery remained intact.

From Day 1 in my recovery, I began to surround myself with people, things, habits, and practices to support the fact that I am a healthy person with healthy habits. My friends are into healthy eating and movement. I read books, go to the gym every day, meditate daily, hike regularly, prioritize sleep, and have a solid morning and evening routine, along with maintaining a healthy, balanced diet that works for my goals and context.

I am constantly surrounded by my new identity. I have nothing in my life anymore that reminds me of the time when I was using—which has been such an important factor in my recovery. I changed everything about my life when I got clean, and I never once thought that was too drastic of an action to take.

DB: How have you reconnected with your body since being in recovery, and what are some things you include in your daily

life to increase your health and vitality?

MH: Yoga, in the beginning, was a huge part of reconnecting with my body. It still is, along with exercise, hiking, and self-care practices like massage and meditation.

I am a firm believer that we hold our emotions and feelings in our muscle tissues. When I began getting massage and doing yoga regularly, it helped me release some of the toxic energy I was holding in my body—the stuff I was, at the same time, processing psychologically and emotionally in therapy. It may sound crazy, but I've experience drug flashbacks in yoga, recovered buried memories, and ended up crying on my mat on many occasions. It's been very therapeutic, combining a physical practice with my talk therapy and meditation.

The foundation of my current lifestyle is my diet. I find that for many, food is the foundation for an overall self-confidence and sense of power. When you're going through a stressful time, it can feel impossible to take good care of yourself—you feel so reactive and helpless. I find that if you can just do one thing—maintain your healthy diet and not give into "well everything's a mess anyway, might as well eat like crap"—you'll be able to maintain a better sense of self-confidence, remain more calm in the face of stress, and more easily maintain other self-care practices. As my first book title suggests, it really does start with food.

DB: How have your relationships changed since being in recovery? And, from when you were actively in recovery, Who would you say are the top three to five people you surround yourself with and why are they influential in your recovery?

MH: I didn't have any close friends when I was using. I couldn't, I was so out of touch with my emotions, I was so disconnected. I couldn't even connect with myself. To keep my secret (how serious the drug use was), I had to distance myself from my loving family and hide from friends. The only people I could spend time with were those who were just as messed up as I was, and I felt very alone.

Today, thanks to my recovery, therapy, and a decade of personal growth efforts, I have so many meaningful relationships with the people in my life. I've restored relations with my family, have created a wonderful circle of friends (both male and female), and am able to open myself up far more authentically and vulnerably to create strong, intimate connections.

First and foremost, my sister. She has seen every version of Melissa and has loved me and supported me through all of it. It is something so comforting to have someone in your life who has seen all of your s*** and loves you anyway. She's my strongest touchstone, and to this day the only person I trust 100% with the biggest and smallest of life decisions.

I also have an awesome group of girlfriends; something I never really had growing up. (I was always too insecure to bond closely with other girls.) We are able to have deep conversations outside of health and wellness—talks about God and relationships and self-worth and entrepreneur life . . . these kinds of connections feed me now, the way drugs never could.

Finally, I have a deeply personal connection to God, in a way I never did before my recovery. We talk every day, and I've received so much guidance and direction from the universe through my meditation practice. I take great comfort in my faith today.

DB: What is your spiritual life like and what do you do on a daily basis to integrate it into your life, and why do you think spirituality is important for growth and sustainability in recovery?

MH: I think connecting with something bigger than yourself is so important, whether you call it "god" or "energy" or "the universe" (I tend to use all three interchangeably). My relationship with

God has really evolved over the years. I connect with the universe every day in my morning meditation and I call the mountains my "church," because when I'm out in nature hiking, I feel like I can connect in the purest sense. It keeps me grounded and calms the chatter in my head in such a powerful way.

DB: What was one situation you found yourself in that confirmed in your mind that you must seek treatment and recovery and why?

MH: My family tells the story of my sister's 21st birthday dinner. My parents were there, along with my sister and her boyfriend. I don't remember much about the dinner, to be honest. It was a Mexican restaurant and I showed up late, and apparently high. My family told me later my behavior was most unpleasant. I was loud, telling rambling stories about keying someone's car because they parked too close to me . . . I don't remember the specifics, but they all said I was out of control and incredibly argumentative. At the time, I don't even think I realized anything was wrong. But a few weeks later, the wheels totally fell off my bus, and I ended up agreeing to go into treatment.

CRAIG SHOEMAKER

"Virtually the only drink I consume is water and when I drink it, I envision it giving my internal organs and system exactly what it needs."
– Craig Shoemaker

Bio: Craig Shoemaker's extensive accomplishments, spanning more than three decades, are beyond impressive. He has performed for major television and cable networks, writes for the hit sitcom *Fuller House*, a radio guest on countless stations, hosted his own syndicated radio and podcast shows, on stage stand up, performances on Broadway, has written two children's books, invented ON Hold advertising and hosted motivational presentations and speeches; all with audiences ranging from 50 to over 70,000 people. These efforts have earned him accolades including, but not limited to: Comedian of the Year by American Comedy Awards; Number One comedy routine of all time by XM Radio, iTunes #1 comedy album; *The Last Stand Up*, voted in the Top 20 on Comedy Central; two Emmy awards; an induction into the Association of Transformational Leaders; and the Communicator Award Crystal prize. And, let's not forget to mention, the honor of performing for four United States Presidents.

Occupation: Stand Up Comedian/Keynote Speaker/TV and Film Producer

Drug of choice: Alcohol, cocaine, mushrooms, pot, acid

Length of sobriety: 30 years

DB: What do you do on a daily basis to maintain your sobriety, and what is the most challenging part about it?

CS: Meditate, call my sponsor, go to meetings. Most difficult thing is to try to do those things while supporting a wife, ex-wife and four children. It is sometimes difficult to balance all that, along with a torrid work schedule, and remain present.

DB: How have you reconnected with your body since being in recovery, and what are some things you include in your daily life to increase your health and vitality?

CS: I am in tune much more with mind, body, and spirit; the results of which are predicated upon spiritual practice. Virtually the only drink I consume is water and when I drink it, I envision it giving my internal organs and system exactly what it needs. I also drink three shots a day of a liquid nutritional that contains seven natural, organic botanicals. Haven't missed a day in eight years and it is fantastic.

DB: How have your relationships changed (types of people, length/meaning of relationships, etc.) from when you were actively using to being in recovery?

CS: One thing that remains, but less so, is my penchant for jumping in on relationships without full vetting. I tend to see red flags and paint them green. However, with time and gained wisdom, my connections with people are now more true and authentic.

DB: Who are the top three to five people you surround yourself with and why are they influential in your recovery?

CS: I could list my wife as all three because she is, quite simply, the best human being I have ever met. But to answer the question, obviously Mika is number one, and after that there are quite a few people I find myself resonating and vibrating with, since we all share similar basic values. One friend I cherish like a brother is my old pal Dave Cerami. It's amazing to me that I have known him since we were 11 years old, partying with him through middle school and high school, yet we both have evolved into a divine connectivity. I also jive with my sponsor Jerry, we laugh together and share a positive spirit about life.

DB: What is your spiritual life like and what do you do on a daily basis to integrate it into your life, and why do you think spirituality is important for growth and sustainability in recovery?

CS: Seven out of the twelve Steps deal with higher power, so I believe it to be the most important aspect of recovery. One thing I do often is to take a pause to allow an ethereal force to take over, rather than my ego or fear-based thoughts. Spiritus is a Latin word meaning "breath." I simply breathe deeply when feeling anxiety, friction, or anger. A calm comes over me, usually manifesting in a much better outcome than if I let my darker self be revealed. I also laugh a lot and several years ago formed a nonprofit organization called Laughter Heals. Laughter really is the best medicine. Open wide and say "HAHA!"

DB: What was one situation you found yourself in that confirmed in your mind that you must seek treatment and recovery and why?

CS: During a trip to Negril, Jamaica, I overloaded on Red Stripe beer, cocaine, ganja, ganja cake, and hallucinogenic mushroom tea. I was at a small, outdoor Rasta concert and passed out while standing up. My head smashed on the cement and bounced like a bowling ball, as there was nothing to break the fall. I believe I died that day and hovered over my body in a white light. It wasn't my last day drinking and using but certainly lead to more awareness of the problem.

COURTNEY FRIEL

"There's no more flaking or forgetting birthdays, calling out sick and coming up with an excuse to miss plans because I'm really hungover."
– Courtney Friel

Bio: Courtney is a news anchor and reporter at KTLA in Los Angeles. She previously worked as a correspondent for Fox News Channel in New York City. You may have also seen Courtney hosting the "World Poker Tour" and reporting on E! News, Extra, Court TV, and America's Most Wanted. She has two children, a son Cash and a daughter Cameron.

Occupation: TV News Anchor/Reporter

Drug of choice: Alcohol, cocaine, pills

Length of sobriety: 9 years

DB: What do you do on a daily basis to maintain your sobriety, and what is the most challenging part about it?

CF: I'm a huge fan of meditating. I do 20–40 minutes almost daily. It keeps me calm, present, and worry free. The challenge is finding the time for it. I sneak away from the kids or do it in the greenroom closet at work in between newscasts. It also helps me put a barrier between the horrible stories I am covering out in the field that suck my empath energy and make me sad/stressed.

DB: How have you reconnected with your body since being in recovery, and what are some things you include in your daily life to increase your health and vitality?

CF: I treated my body so poorly while I was using, and not just with the chemicals I was putting into it. I was incredibly shallow and had no intuition. Through sobriety I have explored natural ways of healing and connecting with my body, mind and soul, and become a deeper, open-minded person. I will try anything: acro-yoga, sound baths, crystal healers, float labs, spiritual colonics!

DB: How have your relationships changed (types of people, length/meaning of relationships, etc.) from when you were actively using to being in recovery?

CF: I am now accountable in sobriety. I show up for people in my life and the important events. There's no more flaking or forgetting birthdays, calling out sick and coming up with an excuse to miss plans because I'm really hungover. My interactions are real, intimate, and mean more. I can be present and listen to people, process the information better, then remember it all too. When I drank, I was the definition of "loose lips sink ships." Now, I am a trustworthy person that people confide in.

DB: Who are the top three to five people you surround yourself with and why are they influential in your recovery?

CF: My kids are the number one priority for me. I got pregnant with them in the earlier years of my recovery and they help me stay sober every day. I am proud that they were "baked" healthy, and they've never seen me under the influence.

Trainer Bob is my constant. I've known him since 2003 and we work out two to three times a week. I always feel better after seeing him, plus he doubles as my therapist! Work keeps me extremely busy too, and I am lucky to have co-workers, who are also my friends, that support my recovery.

DB: What is your spiritual life like and what do you do on a daily basis to integrate it into your life, and why do you think spirituality is important for growth and sustainability in recovery?

CF: My parents dragged me to Presbyterian church every Sunday until I was 18, so that is where my core spiritual values come from, and I'm constantly praying and giving gratitude all day long. Now in recovery, I bounce back and forth between Rick Warren's SaddleBack Church, and the more meditation driven "Self-Realization Center." Whether it's Buddhism tones in yoga and meditation, a 12-Step program, or church . . . the underlying message is all the same. There is something bigger out there (God, Universe, Higher Power) than you, and you must have compassion and be accountable with your actions.

DB: What was one situation you found yourself in that confirmed in your mind that you must seek treatment and recovery and why?

CF: I had several defining moments where I knew my partying days would be probably be ending soon, but the trigger was finally pulled when I woke up to seven of my friends surrounding my bed in an impromptu intervention. I was angry at first, but then I listened to what they each had to say, and ultimately decided moments later that going to rehab would be the best decision I would ever make. It came down to me realizing I deserved more for my life, that I had more to offer this world, and that I'd had a 15-year party career, but it was time to hang up my "drunken antics" hat.

DOUG'S TWO CENTS ON ROCK BOTTOM

For many, getting into recovery starts with a decision. The decision is that you want your life to be better tomorrow than it is today. Some of us had an intervention or an overdose and decided to get treatment. Others had to go to jail before they made that decision. Maybe you lost a loved one or lost your job and that's what did it for you.

On the other hand, there are those that didn't have one of these dramatic "make or break moments." They just knew that the path they were on was not working for them and that they needed to change things. The point is the path to recovery is different for everyone. Don't compare your journey to someone else's. This is something we constantly have to remind ourselves of.

As you see from these stories, they are all different. Some have similarities certainly, but none of them are exactly the same. I urge you to focus on what works for you. The term "rock bottom" gets tossed around a lot these days. Some love the term, others don't. No matter how you feel about it, we can all agree that we have to reach a point in our lives when we make that decision. Even after that decision, recovery requires that we make the right choices day in and day out.

Aristotle wrote "nature abhors a vacuum." This applies to recovery as well. What this means to me is that you need to replace the drugs and alcohol with healthier things; such as exercise, positive community, and some sort of spirituality practice. New habits must take the place of the old ones. If what you are doing is working, then great, continue. But if not, it might be time to switch some things up. Being aware of when things aren't going well is equally important.

I know for me, I must exercise, eat smart, hang out with good people, help others, and remain purpose-driven for my recovery to remain strong. When things feel "off," it's normally because I am slacking in one of those areas. It's easy as a personal trainer and entrepreneur to become overwhelmed or burnt out. At that point, I get extremely anxious, stressed, and agitated. I have had to learn over the years to put myself first sometimes and to not take myself too seriously. When I was on probation for five years, I was always having to watch every single move I made. Unfortunately, that feeling of having to consistently "watch my back," has stuck with me a bit. Part of my work in recovery is to let loose and not be so much of a "worry wart." Letting loose for me simply means not working all the time, not sweating the small stuff, and actually making time for fun.

MISHKA SHUBALY

"Less than a year after quitting drinking,
I ran my first ultra-marathon."
– Mishka Shubaly

Bio: Mishka Shubaly is a best-selling author and a cult singer-songwriter. He teaches a summer writing workshop at Yale and in 2017, he achieved his highest honor when he became a clue on *Jeopardy!*

Occupation: Writer/Musician

Drug of choice: Alcohol

Length of sobriety: 9 years in 2018

DB: What do you do on a daily basis to maintain your sobriety, and what is the most challenging part about it?

MS: I try to take care of the machine that houses my mind: my body. I try to sleep eight to nine hours every night, no naps, moderate to strenuous exercise nearly every day, no refined foods (especially sugar), no caffeine after 2 p.m., get up early and go to bed early, eat a plant-based whole-food diet. It's frustrating to me that we still often default to binaries that don't serve us, like "mind versus body" and "natural versus unnatural." If you try to get sober and stay sober by only treating your mind or only treating your body, you're making a difficult task that much harder. Similarly, the way many people see "natural" as good and "unnatural" as bad is foolish to dangerous. Poison ivy is natural, toilet paper is unnatural: which of these are you going to choose when you go to the bathroom? Alcohol is a naturally occurring substance. You could make organic vegan cocaine or heroin and it would still ruin your life if not kill you. Americans tend to overmedicate, but antidepressants and other psychotropic medications have saved thousands of lives, maybe hundreds of thousands. Getting on antidepressants was a huge help to me in early sobriety. Conversely, Xanax is a poison for me. Use your brain when it comes to your recovery. Do not trust anecdotes or hearsay or hunches. Talk to a licensed psychiatrist.

And once I've cared for my body . . . yeah, I have to push back hard against my mind. I'm a pessimist, I'm a fatalist, I'm a nihilist. It's like I got the song backwards, I accentuate the negative and eliminate the positive. My life is incredibly rich—I drank and drugged like an animal for years, came out of it with no lasting damage to my physical health, became an ultra-runner and turned my misspent youth into a successful writing career. My writing has won me praise from friends and strangers, helped me build friendships with some of my childhood heroes, and given me a career. Still, each morning when I wake up, I'm like "Christ . . . this again?" I try to stay positive. I've never succeeded, but I haven't stopped trying, so I haven't failed. But staying positive is infinitely easier when I'm running and eating right and getting enough sleep.

DB: How have you reconnected with your body since being in recovery, and what are some things you include in your daily life to increase your health and vitality?

MS: I was fairly athletic as a kid, always playing sports at school, riding my bike, etc. When I started drinking heavily when I was 15, I abandoned all of that. Once I got over my acute physical withdrawal, I started exercising as a means of killing time, trying to care about my life again, and tiring myself out enough that I could sleep. I'd never been a runner, even when I was a kid, but at 32, I discovered that I could run. Learning how to run, how to care for and take pride in my body and my accomplishments, that was absolutely transformative. My father ran marathons and I despaired that I would ever match his accomplishments. Less than a year after quitting drinking, I ran my first ultra-marathon. Then I ran two sub-four-hour marathons in a week, two marathons in a weekend, two marathons in a day, etc. Yes, I beat myself up in the process and eventually had to learn how to run in a healthy manner. I don't crank out incredibly long distances anymore, but it's my hope that I'll be able to run into my 60s. Yoga has been incredible for rehabilitating my body, and boxing and kickboxing have been incredibly therapeutic for my mind.

DB: How have your relationships changed since being in recovery? Who would you say are the top three to five people you surround yourself with and why are they influential in your recovery?

MS: I'm still pretty close with most of the folks I was friends with when I was drinking. I like to think I'm a better friend now, if marginally less entertaining. I'm not friends with a lot of practicing alcoholics, but then I wasn't even when I was drinking. Most of my friends still drink or use drugs casually, though I have gained a lot of sober friends in the last nine years and friends who just aren't big drinkers. I understand my experience to be atypical in that, though. Even nine years sober, I have a hard time just socializing. When I was drinking, I was happy to meet a friend at a bar and spend the next 10 hours there. Now, we always have to be doing something: running, training, building a guitar, working on a project, something. Overall, I think my relationships have improved—my relationships with my family and with myself have improved astronomically—but it's important to point out that all my relationships are still flawed. I still get annoyed, I still get my feelings hurt, I still make people angry, I still get my heart broken. Sobriety is a cure for alcoholism, not a cure for the human condition.

As a touring musician, I don't really have the luxury of surrounding myself with anyone . . . or maybe it's a luxury that I don't have to surround myself with anyone? Either way, I keep in close touch with my family, a couple of old rock 'n roll buddies from New York, and a couple of ex-girlfriends. Some of my old buddies are sober, some aren't, but all of them have a lasting investment in underground art/music/culture, and that's still of central importance to me. I always had a good relationship with my mother but my relationship with my younger sister has improved a lot. I didn't speak to my older sister or my father for years. Now I talk to my dad a couple times a month and I talk to my older sister nearly every day. It's huge progress for me to be in touch with exes because my old relationships always used to end in flames. They still sometimes now, but it's much easier to salvage a friendship out of it now that I'm sober.

DB: What is your spiritual life like and what do you do on a daily basis to integrate it into your life, and why do you think spirituality is important for growth and sustainability in recovery?

MS: I do not think spirituality is important for growth and sustainability in recovery. I have no spiritual life to speak of. I'm antireligion and antitheist, which is to say not just that I don't believe in gods or religions or karma or soulmates or whatever, but also that I think belief in any kind of deity is harmful to humanity at large. Furthermore, I think the insistence upon a belief in a higher power in AA is opportunistic of the program and alienating for many addicts. I know that this puts me at odds with the recovery community at large, but I think it's important to hit it here and hit it hard because I know there are other folks like me out there. I'll go one step further. What has been incredibly helpful to my sobriety and my overall mental health is hallucinogenics like psilocybin, LSD, and DMT. Every time I eat mushrooms or acid or smoke DMT, I wake up the next day with renewed determination to move forward as an artist, as a sober person, and as a human being. It helps my anxiety, my depression, and my alienation. People tell me I'm not sober because that word has been perverted by AA until now it doesn't apply to anyone not going to meetings and subscribing to their outdated religion. I'm a writer, I trust the dictionary. You look up "sober" in the Oxford English Dictionary and it's two definitions are "not affected by alcohol" and "serious." I absolutely fulfill both of those definitions. Furthermore, the lasting positive effects of hallucinogens on mental health have been documented in clinical trials by institutions like Johns Hopkins and NYU. Scientific studies support what many of us already know, that these are not life-destroying drugs like cocaine, meth, opioids, and alcohol, but powerful medicines to be used responsibly and treated with respect.

DB: What was one situation you found yourself in that confirmed in your mind that you must seek treatment and recovery and why?

MS: I didn't have a rock-bottom that preceded some stunning epiphany that alcohol was going to kill me and that I needed to change. Instead, I realized almost out of nowhere that alcohol was never going to kill me (which was what I had wanted) but that it would just give me such a garbage life that, when my death finally came, it would be a tremendous relief. I guess I finally figured out that I was going to keep living for a while, and that it was time to finally learn how to live. I was right—sobriety has brought me a life I could never have dreamed of when I was drinking. Getting sober is absolutely the right thing to do . . . and there's no one way to do it. This is how I do it but if something else works for you, well, it works for you, and I support it.

LARA FRAZIER

"My family has become the most important relationship in my life. They have shown me the meaning of unconditional love and I am forever grateful."
– Lara Frazier

Bio: Lara Frazier is a speaker and truth-teller, a sobriety warrior, an innovator, and a writer. She is a FIERCE believer in the power of owning our stories and is a strong advocate for addiction recovery. Lara shares a story of healing: in sobriety, through addiction, in life and love, and in all the other big, huge moments of fear and magic that we rarely talk about, but we should. Lara Frazier lives in the Tampa Bay area with her pig, Peaches and her partner, Austin Cooper, The Founder of Sober Evolution. She received her MBA in Marketing & Global Business from Pepperdine University. After many years of working in the entertainment industry, Lara became addicted to prescription pills and left her career to seek help and find her truth. Lara is well known in the digital recovery space as an innovator, speaker, writer, and influencer. Lara's work has been featured in publications such as The Huffington Post, Glamour, AddictionUnscripted.Com, and WorkIt Health. Currently, Lara is the Director of Marketing for Spring Gardens Recovery, an amenity-rich and holistic-based recovery center near Tampa, Florida. Lara continues to document her story of healing in the most authentic and vulnerable way she knows how: through her own eyes and with her whole heart.

Occupation: Writer, Director of Marketing, and Business Development at Spring Gardens Recovery

Drug of choice: Adderall, opiates, Xanax

Length of sobriety: 5 years

DB: What do you do on a daily basis to maintain your sobriety, and what is the most challenging part about it?

LF: On a daily basis, I pray always—throughout the day, to God, to the Universe, to Nature. I express my gratitude and think of what is beautiful in my life. I practice self-awareness. I exercise, take Epsom salt baths, use essential oils, and think of how I can be helpful to someone else. Service. Radical self-care. Boundaries. Saying no so I can say yes to what I really love.

DB: How have you reconnected with your body since being in recovery, and what are some things you include in your daily life to increase your health and vitality?

LF: In the beginning of my recovery, I paid no attention to my body. At about three years of recovery, I started working out on a regular basis and changed my diet habits. I eat clean, healthy food, and limit my sugar and caffeine intake. I move my body through cardio and strength training. I do yoga. Since paying attention to the body as part of my recovery—I have a sobriety practice that is truly holistic.

DB: How have your relationships changed (types of people, length/meaning of relationships, etc.) from when you were actively using to being in recovery?

LF: My family has become the most important relationship in my life. They have shown me the meaning of unconditional love and I am forever grateful. When I lived close to them, I saw them weekly. Now, I speak to them on the phone weekly. I am a much better friend—loyal, honest, committed. I used to suffer from love addiction but after receiving treatment and therapy—I no longer identify as having a love addiction issue. I have a loving, healthy relationship with my best friend—he is my partner.

DB: Who are the top three to five people you surround yourself with and why are they influential in your recovery?

LF: I surround myself with God, first and foremost. I see God in myself and every person I encounter. My partner, Austin Cooper, is sober and is a huge positive influence in my life. I also check in with my sobriety heroes like Holly Whitaker, Laura McKowen, and Glennon Doyle. I am an active member of private Facebook groups for females who I speak with on a daily basis

DB: What is your spiritual life like and what do you do on a daily basis to integrate it into your life, and why do you think spirituality is important for growth and sustainability in recovery?

LF: I found God in recovery. And I found God by reading the poetry of Rumi. It's expansive love and it's unconditional. Marianne Williamson's book A Return to Love changed my entire spiritual practice. I believe in no religion and all religions. My religion/spiritually is kindness.

DB: What was one situation you found yourself in that confirmed in your mind that you must seek treatment and recovery and why?

LF: I was literally dying from drug induced psychosis. I was addicted to Adderall and my brain would turn on me when I used it. I experienced deep, intense, terrifying paranoia. The doctors told me that if I did not stop using Adderall, I would have permanent brain damage. And yet, I kept going.

One day, after several treatment attempts, I just said yes to help.

I didn't fight it. I showed up. I committed to treatment and to recovery. I stayed in my last rehab for almost three months and then lived in sober living for 10 months. I worked a 12-Step program and attended therapy. I joined Hip Sobriety School and started feeling empowered in my recovery. I reframed my thinking and saw how much more beautiful life is in recovery.

JASON SCHNEIDMAN

"I would take a crack hit, and I would hit 9, 1, [on the phone] and I had my finger on 1. I'm lucky to be alive. I smoked $500 worth of crack a night."
– Jason Schneidman aka Mens' Groomer

Bio (via www.chrismcmillanthesalon.com): Jason Schneidman grew up on the beaches of SoCal and has always been the poster child of its carefree, keep-it-simple lifestyle. Surfing, loud motorcycles, and fast cars are Jason's muses, as are rock music legends like Jim Morrison and the intelligent but rebellious actors of Old Hollywood like James Dean and Steve McQueen. This marriage of glamorous, dynamic Hollywood, and the chill SoCal scene is what moves Jason and influences his style, his choices and his life.

But beneath Jason's laid-back surfer vibe lies a fierce work ethic that has led him to make a name for himself far beyond hairstyling to creating fully unified looks for press tours, red carpets, music videos, and editorial gigs. His trendsetting genius and effortless cool have earned him a devoted group of clients including Hugh Jackman, Bruno Mars, Jonah Hill, and Rob Lowe. His editorial work has appeared in magazines such as *Rolling Stone, GQ, Entertainment Weekly,* and *Billboard*.

One key to the magic? Jason cuts and styles hair with extreme energy and passion and is always working to create a look that is visionary, versatile, and authentic for each individual he works with. Jason believes that a properly styled man must look and feel carefree, confident, and stylish. That's genuinely sexy. And that's what Jason brings to every client, every day, no matter who they are.

Occupation: Celebrity Hair Stylist / Men's Groomer at Chris McMillan Salon

Drug of choice: Crack

Length of sobriety: 14 years

DB: What do you do on a daily basis to maintain your sobriety, and what is the most challenging part about it?

JS: I think the best way to answer that question is to, take a look at my behavior. And my situations, and what am I doing to be a good person? Am I spiritually connected, am I in fear, or am I in faith? And do I need to clean up a wreckage from that day?

The most challenging part about it is me. I know that because dude, I have no say. You gotta understand it's a balance bro. I'm out cutting people off, flying to work, and then I'm like, "Oh god, what did I just do." And there's moments when I get grandiosity, and I'm not humble. And I'm like, "Don't you know who I think I am?" And then I'll realize it a couple minutes later, and I'm like, oh fuck. It's a balance bro, it's a little bit of both.

DB: How have you reconnected with your body since being in recovery, and what are some things you include in your daily life to increase your health and vitality?

JS: I hate working out. I fucking hate it. But I manage to stay fit through my dieting. And my addiction is sugar now. So, what I do, is I maintain a balance of not overdoing anything. I love vegetables, and I love meat. A lot of people don't like veggies, but I can live off of the land. Protein and vegetables. So, I eat protein and vegetables three meals a day. And then I'll order four desserts and I'll take one bite of each.

It's totally how I do it. And trust me dude, just like the balance of living, and the yin yang of me being me, and then me trying to be a better me, same thing with my dieting. I'll get off track, and for three weeks, I'll start throwing down. And I'll just like, God food is good, life is good. And I'll start feeling it, and I'll see it. I'll get the man boobs and the fucking muffin top, a little bit. It'll start creeping up. And I'm like, "Dude reel it back in buddy." And I'll cut it way down. I'll go heavy no carbs for three weeks. And then I show up and people are like, "Dude, you look great, you're getting skinny." Instantly, three weeks, no carbs, no sugar. Or low sugar and low carbs. I would say no carbs, low sugar.

And then right now I walk. That's my thing. I have a bad lower back, and this doctor who I see is like, "Dude the best thing you can do is walk." We are driving in our cars, we are sitting at work, we are standing at work. But we never go out and move, like we're meant to. Like we're meant to as humans, to get out and to hunt and that kind of thing. And we don't move. So, what I do, is I walk 20 minutes in the morning, and I try and do 20 minutes at night. But at least 20 minutes a day walking. And then I'm gonna say one more thing. My workouts are surfing. And I don't surf that much because as a kid, that's all I did. From 12 to 20, I was in the water surfing every day. That's why I was a bad student, and that's why I got into trouble. I was ditching school, and smoking weed, and surfing. That's all I wanted to do. So, my workouts are definitely surfing or anything that's fun, that I don't know I'm working out.

DB: How have your relationships changed since being in recovery? Who would you say are the top three to five people you surround yourself with and why are they influential in your recovery?

JS: My relationships changed, a full 180. So, I didn't have friends,

I had acquaintances. My dad, he loved me unconditionally, but they didn't have time for me. Because I wasn't present. So now, like I said, I take a look out on a daily basis, what am I doing to be the best son, what am I doing to be the best friend, where was I lousy, what situation did I do that didn't feel right? And then I go ahead and clean it up. And I give ‘em a call, or I talk to them, and I say, "What do you think about the way I handled this?" You know what I mean? What can I do better? And in the morning, or when I go into situations that I'm in fear. And I don't know if you know what fear is, but I was taught what fear is. This is a really great quote. "Fear is afraid of losing what you've got, or not getting what you want."

"Fear is afraid of losing what you got, or not getting what you want." So, if you're in a situation where you're in fear, and your heart's going, or your heads pounding, and you're like, "Oh my God, I'm nervous." You're like, why am I nervous? Okay. And you're like, well I need this big interview, or I need to make this money, and you're afraid of not making it. So, what happens is, if you can take an action. To better that situation. So, what will give you a better chance of getting the job? Well, go get a haircut. Wear a nice shirt, get a good night's rest, make sure you eat before I show up. Make sure you have eye contact. You can do actions to better your chances of getting the job. But you can only do that stuff leading up, you can't change the outcome. You gotta stay out of the results, so if the jobs tomorrow, you can only take actions leading up to it, but you can't sit there and worry about the outcome. Am I gonna get the job, am I not gonna get the job. Because you're not in the moment. And when you're not in the moment, you're not there for other people, and you're not there for yourself. I'm sorry, this is kind of deep stuff, but it's like am I in fear, or am I in faith.

And then, if there's a situation that you can't take an action in, you have to turn it over to God. And that's the spiritual side of things. And my God isn't Jesus Christ. I grew up Jewish. But the thing is, God to me, is just like karma, it's good orderly direction.

And it's somebody I can turn I over to, or something, and just be like, why am I in fear? Well if there's not an action I can take, I just turn it over. I just gotta have to like be happy with what I got right now. You know what I mean? I was taught there's three kinds of business in this world. There's my business, there's none of my business, and there's God's business. Three businesses. My business, God's business, and none of my business.

Sometimes the results. Like you go to get a job and you go to get the job, and you don't get the job, sometimes it's nothing something you did. Sometimes it's just none of your business. It could be the guy who was hiring you, you look like an ex-enemy or something. You know what I mean, so it's like three kinds of business. My business, God's business, and none of my business. So, if that dude doesn't want to hire me, it's none of my business. You can't force people.

So basically, I'm kind of a solo project. I don't have tons of friends, but I have a couple of good people that I can call to check in with if I'm in a situation that I can't handle. So, I have Jason, who's super spiritual be he's got low riders, he surfs, he's a tattoo artist. I have my boy Taylor who's an actor who surfs. And I helped him get sober. And we bro down. We'll go to breakfast every once in a while. We'll just catch up. My wife's my best friend. She didn't know what she signed up for, but I'm a lot of work. She has to hear what I'm into, 'cause like I said, it's a balance. I'm all about me, me, me, and then I have to reel it back in, and be like, what's going on? And my dad. My dad is just an older version of me. And he's level headed, he's been in service for his whole life, he's still teaching at 76, he does high school biology. And I can literally call my dad and just rap out, it's crazy. So those are my go to's.

DB: What is your spiritual life like and what do you do on a daily basis to integrate it into your life, and why do you think spirituality is important for growth and sustainability in recovery?

JS: Well I do Good Orderly Direction, that is my spirituality. So Good, Orderly, Direction. G-O-D. And it's kind of like that yin yang, what am I doing to be a good person today? I'm taking a look at my actions and my behaviors. I take moments to just sit in silence and reflect. And then I'm going out, and I'm being of service. And I'm constantly looking out through the day, where's god knocking on my door for me to show up. And a lot of times, I just say "God, what would you have me do? What would you have me be? What would you have me do? What would you have me be?" And that's it, that's what I do.

DB: What was one situation you found yourself in that confirmed in your mind that you must seek treatment and recovery and why?

JS: Well, I just knew. I had a good upbringing, and I knew in my heart of hearts that I had so much to offer myself, and the world. And I was dying. I was really dying. I would take a crack hit, and I would hit 9, 1, [on the phone] and I had my finger on 1. I'm lucky to be alive. I smoked $500 worth of crack a night. And my heart was jumping out of my chest, and I'm lucky to be alive. When I had that burning bush moment, it was when I was sick and tired or being sick and tired. And you can quote me on that one. It's not mine, but feel free to use it. I learned it. You have to be sick and tired, of being sick and tired.

LAURIE DHUE

"I started working out more and found that getting the blood pumping was one of the very best things for my recovery."
– Laurie Dhue

Bio: Laurie Dhue is founder of Dhue Together, which provides resources and support for individuals and families dealing with the disease of addiction.

One of the nation's leading recovery advocates, Dhue is in long-term recovery from alcoholism and drug addiction. She has worked closely with the White House Office of National Drug Control Policy (ONDCP), the Substance Abuse and Mental Health Services Administration (SAMHSA), Faces and Voices of Recovery (FAVOR), and the National Council on Alcohol and Drug Dependence (NCADD). Dhue has spoken on behalf of many national recovery organizations including the Hazelden Betty Ford Foundation and the Caron Foundation. She travels coast-to-coast giving speeches, emceeing events, and moderating panel discussions.

Dhue has had the distinct honor or speaking at the White House in 2014 and 2017 on behalf of ONDCP. She was also a featured speaker at the inaugural UNITE to Face Addiction national rally in Washington, DC in 2015. Dhue appeared in the award-winning 2013 documentary "The Anonymous People" and the 2017 documentary "Reversing the Stigma," produced in conjunction with OASAS (New York State's Office of Alcoholism and Substance Abuse).

Prior to her work in the recovery field, Dhue enjoyed a distinguished career as an award-winning national news anchor who hosted shows on all three major cable news networks: CNN, MSNBC, and Fox News Channel. She most recently served as lead news anchor for The Blaze TV. Her 25 years in news has included interviews with numerous world leaders, politicians, entertainers, and prominent newsmakers as well as extensive reporting from the Middle East during the War on Terror. A resident of Atlanta, Dhue is a board member of the Georgia Campaign for Adolescent Power and Potential (GCAPP) and Kennesaw State University's Center for Young Adult Addiction and Recovery (CYAAR). She is also a Strategic Advisor to She Recovers, a national women's recovery advocacy group, as well as a consultant to Shatterproof, a national advocacy, treatment and prevention nonprofit.

Dhue is a graduate of The University of North Carolina at Chapel Hill, where she was a letter-winning member of the women's varsity swim team and an academic All-American.

Occupation: National Recovery Advocate and Certified Recovery Specialist, Former Network News Anchor

Drug of choice: Alcohol, cocaine

Length of sobriety: 11+ years; sobriety date is March 14, 2007

DB: What do you do on a daily basis to maintain your sobriety, and what is the most challenging part about it?

LD: As soon as I wake up, I talk to my Higher Power, who is God. I start off by thanking Him for the gift of waking up sober. That's a pure miracle. Then I ask His protection and care with complete abandon, praying for Him to help me stay out of my head and help others (I have learned that when I get in my head too much, it can take me to a bad place quickly. A friend once said "Don't go into your head without a hardhat and a flashlight, because it's dark and dangerous in there." So very true.). I also ask God to bring love, relief, and joy to everyone in my life, particularly those friends and family members who may be going through a challenging time.

I actually talk to God throughout the day, thanking Him for the little gifts I receive hour upon hour. One of my favorite times to talk to God is while I'm driving . . . not because I want him to help me deal with traffic, but because it provides me 10 or 15 minutes of uninterrupted time.

I reach out to at least one woman in recovery every day. We can do together what we cannot, and should not, do apart . . . so it's essential that we stay in contact with those who are sharing our journey of recovery. Such a comfort to know that millions of other women know exactly what I'm going through!

I go to at least two or three 12-Step meetings a week. When I don't go to meetings, I just don't feel right. I can get off the beam very quickly. When I go to meetings regularly, I just feel better because I am more connected. And when we stay connected, we have a much greater chance of staying in recovery. It's that simple. The saying "meeting makers make it" may sound hokey, but for me, it's the absolute truth. I once went two YEARS without going to meetings (I maybe went to four or five) and was miserable; I became increasingly self-centered, fearful, quick-tempered and not much fun to be around. It was crazy. I went to any lengths to get drunk all those years, right? So why couldn't I simply get my butt to meetings? I think I just assumed that I could coast on all the years in recovery I already had. It was a huge mistake and I am truly lucky that I didn't relapse.

Recovery has been relatively easy for me. I was so exhausted—on every single level—by the time I made my decision to get sober that giving up alcohol and drugs was an enormous relief. I knew for years that I needed to quit, so when I finally did, I was all in (with the exception of the aforementioned two years) and have never looked back. I got sober the first time I tried and even though I know that relapse is possible, I'm going to do everything I can to maintain my spiritual fitness in order to continue living sober one day at a time. My biggest challenge is my own head and the thoughts contained within it. I can go to a dark place rather quickly, but the good news is that now I know how to get out of that place just as quickly. I focus on gratitude, which is everything. If you stay grateful, you stay sober.

DB: How have you reconnected with your body since being in recovery, and what are some things you include in your daily life to increase your health and vitality?

LD: Sometimes I want to cry when I think about how poorly I treated my body all those years. I poisoned it, day in and day out, for the better part of 20 years, and yet miraculously, had never had any major health problems. I guess I can chalk that up to good genes. When we give up drinking, drugs, or any other toxic substance, the healing is multifold. We begin the process of healing not only our minds, but obviously also our bodies. Feeling better can happen in as little as 24 hours. Once I got through the painful detox from alcohol and cocaine, which included sleeplessness, night sweats, nausea, and the worst headaches I've ever had, I started feeling stronger less than a month later. Six months later, people at work started asking me if I had lost weight or if my hair was blonder (No and no, though certainly I was less bloated). They noticed that I seemed better overall, but couldn't pinpoint why. I looked and sounded different on TV. My skin was clear, my eyes were brighter, my delivery so much clearer. My brain and body were working again. A few months in, my mother and I took a vacation to a tiny island in the Bahamas. During a boat trip, I discovered a starfish while swimming and proudly showed it to her before throwing it back. She looked at me holding the starfish, got tears in her eyes and said, "We've got our Laurie back." Wow, right?

I started working out more and found that getting the blood pumping was one of the very best things for my recovery. I was a Division I NCAA swimmer at the University of North Carolina at Chapel Hill and had always loved exercise, but of course my fitness regimen had fallen by the wayside during my many years of drinking and drugging. Several years into recovery, I discovered SoulCycle, which changed my body and my life. The confidence I gained in those spin classes has had a lasting impact on so many levels. When we see our physical strength and improve, our mental, emotional, and spiritual strength increases as well. These days, I pay close attention to how my body feels, and when something is off, I address it immediately.

DB: How have your relationships changed (types of people, length/meaning of relationships, etc.) from when you were actively using to being in recovery?

LD: Because I am not lying or hiding or living in shame anymore, my relations with other people have significantly improved . . . to say the least. Living a rigorously honest life is important to me and my rigorous honesty has become very important to the people who love me. I'm so grateful to have many friends and family members who, through my journey, have learned about the disease of addiction and understand the importance of my staying upfront and truthful. However, my straight talk is not always understood and appreciated. I have to remember that, for many people, complete honesty is threatening. But for the most part, I surround myself with people who are also interested in honesty. Simply put, I like to be with people who tell the truth. I don't have time for those who don't. I also listen more and put myself in other people's shoes significantly more often before I got sober. I also appreciate my friends and loved ones more deeply than before. And perhaps most significantly, the way I love people has also changed; my love for others feels so much more pure and real.

DB: What is your spiritual life like and what do you do on

a daily basis to integrate it into your life, and why do you think spirituality is important for growth and sustainability in recovery?

LD: It's a curious thing to ponder: If addiction is a brain disorder, then why is spirituality an essential part of recovery? Well, it's not that simple. Addiction is a lot more than just a physical thing, it affects every part of our lives. It's also emotional and spiritual, leading us to become dishonest, self-destructive, angry, and self-centered. It's a spiritual crisis, and a spiritual crisis needs a spiritual solution. Spirituality is a very personal thing, but I do feel comfortable saying that, because I communicate regularly with my Higher Power (God), I am in a good place spiritually. I have always been a person of faith, and that has only increased during my time in sobriety. Standing in the sunlight of the Spirit is vital to my daily happiness and increases my gratitude a hundredfold.

DB: What was one situation you found yourself in that confirmed in your mind that you must seek treatment and recovery and why?

LD: So many terrible things happened over the years, it would be difficult to pinpoint one moment or one situation that led to my decision to get sober. I don't think I'm at all different from other people who have suffered through addiction who are now in recovery; I eventually got sick and tired of being sick and tired and knew I was going to die if I didn't stop. My life was pure insanity. I lived many YEARS in a blackout, where things were just fuzzy. There's so much I simply don't remember. I even overdosed one night and was discovered face down on the floor of my apartment after ingesting alcohol, cocaine, Xanax, and marijuana. I almost died, but it wasn't enough for me to get sober. Crazy, isn't it? That's the power of this disease; it makes absolutely no sense.

But if I had to pick the primary catalyst for getting sober, it was my sister Nancy's pregnancy with the family's first grandchild nearly 12 years ago. It was a time of great joy for our family, and as my sister begin to bloom, it occurred to me that I finally had a reason to quit drinking and using drugs. I wanted my future niece or nephew to know me, love me, and be able to count on me. I wanted to be the fun aunt, the aunt who showed up for things; not the aunt who missed her flight home because she was still drunk from the night before. Not the aunt who embarrassed her family. Not the aunt who drank herself to death. Well, that little baby is now 11 1/2 and his name is Robert. He also has a brother named Thomas, who is 8 1/2. They call me Aunt YaYa. My beautiful, bright, funny, and highly entertaining nephews are two of the biggest reasons why I stay sober. And I have a much closer relationship with their mother, my sister, because of the decision I made back on March 14, 2007.

SIMON KIRKE

"No hangovers, no guilt and being able to remember what I did the night before is a blessing!"
– Simon Kirke

Bio: Drummer Simon Kirke kept the beat for two of the 70's most popular bluesy hard rock bands, Free and Bad Company.

Born in London, the Beatles inspired him so he picked up the guitar and then the drums. He joined a local band called the Maniacs, in which Kirke played drums and lead vocals (something quite uncommon at the time).

Kirke worked out a deal with his parents after graduating high school, that if he couldn't "make it" as a drummer in a band within a two-year period, that he would begin a college career.

Just a few months before the deadline, Kirke landed a gig with a group called the Black Cat Bones. The drummer befriended the group's talented guitarist, Paul Kossoff, who in turn convinced Kirke to leave the group with him and begin a new outfit with singer Paul Rodgers. Soon ex-John Mayall's Bluesbreakers bassist Andy Fraser signed on and Free was officially formed in1968. Mixing blues with hard rock, the group would prove to be quite influential, especially on the strength of their classic 1970 release, Fire and Water, and its strutting, anthemic hit single, "All Right Now."

When the band broke up, it didn't take Kirke long to find another gig. Kirke and Rodgers started a new band, Bad Company, which was quite similar stylistically to Free. Joined by ex-King Crimson bassist Boz Burrell and ex-Mott the Hoople guitarist Mick Ralphs, Bad Company was one of the first groups signed to Led Zeppelin's record label, Swan Song. Their debut album, 1974's Bad Company, would go on to become one of hard rock's all-time classics, as it birthed such long-standing rock radio standards as "Can't Get Enough," "Ready for Love," and the title track, "Bad Company," written by Rodgers and Kirke himself. The group hails as one of the all-time top rock outfits. Simon Kirke is the only member of Bad Company who's been in every lineup of the band.

In addition to his work with Free and Bad Company, Kirke has guested on a long list of recordings by other artists over the years, including 4 years with Ringo Starr & His All-Star Band.

Kirke just finished his latest solo album, "All Because of You", to be released on BMG Records in 2016 and he will also be going on the road with Bad Company for their upcoming world tour.

Occupation: Musician

Drug of choice: Cocaine/alcohol

Length of sobriety: Cocaine, 26 years; alcohol, multiple terms of several years . . . to date: 2 years

DB: What do you do on a daily basis to maintain your sobriety, and what is the most challenging part about it (if anything)?

SK: I pray . . . say the serenity prayer . . . and remember how bad it used to be back in the old days. I thank God for my health and the lady in my life: Maria. I go to meetings regularly . . . which is easy living in NYC

DB: How have you reconnected with your body since being in

recovery, and what are some things you include in your daily life to increase your health and vitality?

SK: I was always a fitness enthusiast . . . even when I was using. Being a drummer is very physical and requires a high level of fitness . . . but since I gave up my DOCs life is so much better. No hangovers, no guilt and being able to remember what I did the night before is a blessing!

DB: How have your relationships changed (types of people, length/meaning of relationships, etc.) from when you were actively using to being in recovery?

SK: I recently divorced and remarried. I was not a good husband and lay most of the blame for that on my preoccupation with using. Since becoming sober I have regained the trust of my children bit by bit and the pride and admiration of my new wife.

DB: Who are the top three to five people you surround yourself with and why are they influential in your recovery?

SK: I have several people who I talk to on a regular basis . . . no full names of course . . . but they are my support group. A couple are in the music business like myself and they are the ones I most relate to.

DB: What is your spiritual life like and what do you do on a daily basis to integrate it into your life, and why do you think spirituality is important for growth and sustainability in recovery?

SK: My spiritual life consists of prayer and meditation, vital not only for recovery but for anyone who lives in New York City!

It is vital to rise above the demands of the body on a daily basis . . . prayer and meditation have given me an inner strength impossible to attain otherwise.

DB: What was one situation you found yourself in that confirmed in your mind that you must seek treatment and recovery and why?

SK: My goodness there are many episodes but the most harrowing one was when after a night of bingeing on booze and drugs I nearly died. All the others had gone into the hotel leaving me in my bunk. Had my girlfriend at the time not revived me and walked me around, I would have died for sure.

MAYRA LEAL

"I triumphantly stay connected to an energy that's greater than myself and it gracefully keeps me from picking up again."
– Mayra Leal

Bio: Mayra Leal, born and raised in Houston, TX, graduated from the University of Houston where she obtained a degree in advertising. During her studies, she discovered a passion for film, TV, and digital media and managed to garner the attention of veteran producers, directors, marketing agencies, and a loyal fan-base over a span of 12 years.

Despite some success, she recently decided to step away from the entertainment industry in pursuit of a more fulfilling career. She is currently a social media manager for IMMORDL Nitro Super Coffee. She enjoys learning about natural health solutions, is a self-taught soap-maker, and natural product creator. She currently resides in Houston, TX with her parents, caring for her disabled mother.

Occupation: Product distributor for various health conscious food companies

Drug of choice: Alcohol, but with it came cocaine, molly, edibles, mushrooms, etc.

Length of sobriety: 4 years

DB: What do you do on a daily basis to maintain your sobriety, and what is the most challenging part about it?

ML: Love myself. I do things for me. I work out, I eat healthy, I read, I meditate (irregularly), I pray, I remember to tell myself I love myself whenever possible or that I'm enough. I triumphantly stay connected to an energy that's greater than myself and it gracefully keeps me from picking up again. I just want to return to myself. Eliminate all the layers of conditioning and get back to what I am at my core, LOVE. The most challenging part about it I'd say is that life continues to happen. Life is changing and that often brings up discomfort, which I feel, INTENSELY. But I'm aware now that all challenges pass and that there is no right or wrong way of handling difficult situations. It just is. The goal is to get through difficult situations with grace, but when that doesn't happen, it's totally ok too and knowing that brings me peace.

DB: How have you reconnected with your body since being in recovery, and what are some things you include in your daily life to increase your health and vitality?

ML: I maintain a regular, healthy workout regimen. I enjoy circuit training 4 times a week. I also enjoy hot yoga, though I haven't practiced in a few months. I no longer consume processed sugar, dairy, or gluten. I'm mostly a vegetarian, but listen to my body and if it's craving meat/chicken/fish, I go for it, as long as it's organic grass-fed beef, pasture raised chickens, sustainably sourced, etc. I take zero medication. My only vice is probably my daily coffee. I gave that up for 30 days once and it wasn't pretty. I love essential oils and am constantly diffusing mood oils in my home or smudging my place with sage and Palo Santo. I'm not where I want to be energy wise, but I'm working on it.

DB: How have your relationships changed since being in recovery? Who would you say are the top three to five people you surround yourself with and why are they influential in your recovery?

ML: My relationships are much more mature. There's substance to them and conversations are never surface conversations. I love diving into deep topics like "what's the meaning of life" "why are we here," etc. My family now trusts me, I've become way closer to them since I got sober.

DB: What is your spiritual life like and what do you do on a daily basis to integrate it into your life, and why do you think spirituality is important for growth and sustainability in recovery?

ML: As mentioned previously, I triumphantly stay connected to a power greater than myself. I look for signs from my spirit guides, I ask my ancestors to guide me. I pray. I meditate irregularly, but I meditate. I eat healthy. I exercise. I connect with myself and when I am triggered, I ask "Why?" And do whatever I can to learn from that trigger, pick up a book, take a workshop, see a therapist, etc. Though, I'm not always successful at gracefully getting through adversity. My ego enjoys getting involved entirely way too often, but I'm getting better at noticing when the ego wants to disguise itself as me. Seeking ways to become a better version of myself is a must and to me that's a spiritual practice. Drugs and alcohol no longer serve my highest good and knowing that keeps me from using again.

DB: What was one situation you found yourself in that confirmed in your mind that you must seek treatment and recovery and why?

ML: My last days using got pretty dark. I found myself rocking myself in a corner till the early [morning] after having consumed mushrooms, weed edibles, alcohol, and cocaine and telling God that I'd never ever drink or use again if he just kept me alive through that situation. A few days later I was back at it again. And towards the end of that bender, I didn't want to be alive anymore. I found a small pair of scissors on the floor and romanticized about cutting myself. In that moment . . . GOD sprinkled grace over me and I texted someone I knew could help me. I was in treatment the next day and never looked back.

NATHANIEL V. DUST

"Breathwork helped me connect with my body in a way I'd never experienced before."
– Nathaniel Dust

Bio: Nathaniel Hodder-Shipp, B. Msc. (aka Nathaniel V. Dust) is the founder and president of Breathwork for Recovery (http://breathworkforrecovery.com/) and has worked as a professional healer for almost a decade. Nathaniel uses the power of a person's breath as a catalyst for positive change and works with an arsenal of healing techniques to help people process trauma, disarm negative thought patterns, and maintain healthy and happy relationships with themselves and loved ones. Nathaniel's client base ranges from those seeking relief from everyday anxiety to people suffering from severe emotional and physical trauma and desperate for help. His specialty includes using breathwork in addiction treatment facilities to help accelerate clients' journey to recovery.

Occupation: Healer

Drug of choice: Methamphetamine/alcohol/anything you had

Length of sobriety: 9 years

DB: What do you do on a daily basis to maintain your sobriety, and what is the most challenging part about it?

NVD: I do my best to do breathwork every day, even if it's just for a few minutes. It's the practice that saved my life and it has paved the way for me to remain sober all these years. I think it's also important to put pen to paper, but I find myself not as consistent with it as I would like to be. Making time for writing is the most difficult part. It's tough when you're juggling a business, a marriage, and your own healing. In between groups, I often sit in my car and do a few minutes of breathing or pull out my phone and jot a few thoughts down.

DB: How have you reconnected with your body since being in recovery, and what are some things you include in your daily life to increase your health and vitality?

NVD: Breathwork helped me connect with my body in a way I'd never experienced before. I lived in my head most of the time, trying to avoid the uncomfortable emotions and pain. Breathwork allows you—almost forces you—to get out of your head and truly feel what it's like to live in your body, even if just for a few minutes. After quitting drinking and using, I was skeptical that I was ever going to be able to feel good. Breathwork changed that. I carried so much emotional pain in my body and it was difficult to find a safe way to access, process and release it. Breathwork was what allowed me to confront that pain in a safe and healing way. I've most recently been working with a practitioner to help physically release the residual pain using a series of unique fascial release protocols. It's all connected!

DB: How have your relationships changed since being in recovery? Who would you say are the top three to five people you surround yourself with and why are they influential in your recovery?

NVD: I'm close with my family again. The thing about addiction is that it impacts the whole family; no one within the unit is left unscathed. When I started drinking and using, I pushed them away. Now, we're closer than ever and talk regularly. My brothers respect me, which is something I had never felt from them before. I am happily married. My wife is incredible. I could never maintain any sort of romantic relationship in my active addiction. I attempted but would destroy them. It's remarkable how, when you start to develop a relationship with yourself and respect yourself, it radiates outward toward and helps cultivate healthy and fulfilling relationships with others.

My wife, Anne Hodder-Shipp. She helps keep me grounded and sees things differently than I do, so it can really help shift my perspective. She also makes me laugh and is the smartest person I know. It's good to have someone like that on your side. When the shit gets thick, she's got my back and goes out of her way to do little things to remind me of how special she thinks I am.

My mentor David. He has helped me create the life I have today. He's the one who really made this breathwork technique what it is and has helped tens of thousands of people, so that alone is something. We have a special relationship and I know I can count on him to support me through my struggles and help me reframe situations. Mostly, he holds up a great mirror, so I can see myself for who I am.

The Director of Operations for Breathwork for Recovery, Jeff. When I built Breathwork for Recovery years ago, it was scary and overwhelming. No one else was doing this kind of thing at the time, and as a leader, you don't have anyone ahead of you guiding the way. You're out there with a lamp in the darkness not knowing where the hell you're going. Jeff has proven to be reliable, detail-oriented, and a good friend. I'm more of a big-picture kind of guy and can feel bogged down with the details. Jeff helps with that.

My cats. Harriet, Burt, Lucy, and George. Cleaning up cat shit really keeps you humble.

DB: What is your spiritual life like and what do you do on a daily basis to integrate it into your life, and why do you

think spirituality is important for growth and sustainability in recovery?

NVD: Again, back to breathwork. Along with developing a relationship with my body, it has reconnected me with my spirit. The things I've experienced in breathwork are sometimes hard to fathom, and I'm the one who's experienced them, so it's weird. To me, Spirit is that thing that connects us all. It's the thread woven through all our lives. I would consider myself an atheist; I don't believe that there's a grand creator or puppet master pulling the strings. We are in charge of that as human beings, but Spirit is in all of us. It's part of us, so connecting to that allows us to remember who we are. From that place, you want to harm yourself (and others) a lot less.

DB: What was one situation you found yourself in that confirmed in your mind that you must seek treatment and recovery and why?

NVD: My work-appointed therapist told me that in the 25 years she had been doing that job, I was the worst alcoholic she'd ever seen. It was eye-opening. I had already ruined most of my relationships and was on my way to destroy the career I had built. I had demolished a lot of my life already and hearing that humbled me enough to seek help. This was after many friends had attempted to get me help, after I had created so much chaos in my life; it was this cumulative effect. Her words just struck me.

DAWN NICKEL

"I support other women in or seeking recovery on a daily basis – that is and always has been what works best for me."
– Dawn Nickel

Bio: Dawn Nickel is an accomplished and versatile leader and the creator of She Recovers, currently the largest online platform dedicated to supporting women in recovery from addiction and related life challenges. Dawn started her journey of recovery from drug addiction in 1987. She is a strong advocate for the view that every woman in or seeking recovery must be supported to find the tools and pathways that will work best for her as an individual.

In the summer of 2011, while recovering from a serious case of workaholism, Dawn decided to apply what she knew about recovery to that area of her life. On an extended leave from work, Dawn began to blog and created the She Recovers Facebook page to share her journey and to reach out to other women wanting to recover their lives and their potential. Since 2012, she has dedicated herself to creating and holding space (online and off) for women in recovery to connect with themselves, and with other like-hearted women.

The Verified Facebook page now has over 265,000 followers. Today, in addition to operating her health and social policy research consultancy, Dawn is determined to grow She Recovers and its offerings so that more women (and more women from diverse backgrounds) have the access, resources, support, and freedoms necessary to cultivate individualized and holistic pathways in order to find health, sustain long-term recovery, achieve their potential, and help other women to do the same.

Dawn's youngest daughter Taryn Strong, also in recovery, is a trauma-informed yoga for recovery instructor and an integral part of She Recovers. Dawn and Taryn currently operate a resource-inspired website and blog, run an international yoga & recovery retreat program, and design and manufacture a line of custom recovery jewelry. Their newest and most promising development is the launch of the She Recovers Coach Designation Program, in collaboration with IAPRC, a respected recovery coach training institute. With that program, She Recovers is currently training (50) female recovery coaches who will then apply to become the leaders of She Recovers Chapters in their local communities.

On May 5–7, 2017 Dawn and Taryn hosted She Recovers in NYC at the prestigious Conrad Hotel in Lower Manhattan. This unique and ground-breaking gathering of 500 recovering women was also available by Digital Ticket (Livestream) to thousands more people across the world. Keynote speakers at the event included spiritual teacher Marianne Williamson, *ABC 20/20*'s Elizabeth Vargas, powerhouse author/blogger Glennon Doyle Melton, and author/motivational speaker Gabby Bernstein. She Recovers in LA will be held September 2018. Keynote speakers are still being finalized but so far, Cheryl Strayed, Janet Mock, and Tara Mohr are confirmed.

You can learn more about Dawn via the following recent interviews:

- Recovery Speaks Appearance (2017)
- Interview with Sherry Gaba for Recovery Today Summit (2017): Realizing our Power and Potential After Addiction
- Interview with Erica Spiegelman on Rewired Radio (2017): Building a Healthy Community
- Expert Panel with The Clearing (2017): Holistic Approach to Emotional & Addiction Recovery

Occupation: Founder of She Recovers

Drug of choice: Cocaine, alcohol, pills, marijuana

Length of sobriety: Last drink and cocaine 1987, last marijuana 1989. No mood or mind-altering drugs since 1989 with the exception of two days in 2000 after my mother's death—I took oxycodone for two days.

DB: What do you do on a daily basis to maintain your sobriety, and what is the most challenging part about it?

DN: I have been doing it for long that I truly don't find anything challenging about maintaining my sobriety. I support other women in or seeking recovery on a daily basis—that is and always has been what works best for me. I pray, meditate (not religiously), read a lot, and spend time with people I love. I am a member of a 12-Step program but in recent years, with all that I am doing with She Recovers, my meeting attendance is spotty. I still sponsor three women. My husband is also in recovery, and has been a huge part of my daily maintenance for the last 30 years.

DB: How have you reconnected with your body since being in recovery, and what are some things you include in your daily life to increase your health and vitality?

DN: I like to move my body—mostly by walking in nature. I drink a lot of water, and eat a well-rounded and healthy diet. I drink coffee – but it's decaffeinated. My daughter and business partner (Taryn Strong) is a yoga teacher – so yoga is a part of my life although I do not have a daily practice.

DB: How have your relationships changed (types of people, length/meaning of relationships, etc.) from when you were actively using to being in recovery?

DN: I feel fortunate in that I still have a handful of friends from way back when, although I don't see them often. I have two groups of nearest and dearest friends – the first is made up friends I have made in the 30 years of recovery in my anonymous program. The second group are the women in our She Recovers tribe over the past seven years. I spend a lot of time with my daughters, grandchildren, husband. As much time as I can with my sister and her family, and my dad. I love spending time by myself. The biggest difference between relationships in addiction and relationships in recovery is that today my relationships are healthy, authentic, and reciprocal.

DB: Who are the top three to five people you surround yourself with and why are they influential in your recovery?

DN: My husband, primarily, he has always been by my side in recovery and keeps me accountable. My two daughters, and two of our grandchildren. They are the most influential in my recovery because they are my world. I also spend a fair bit of time with my business partners in She Recovers and one or two dear, close friends

DB: What is your spiritual life like and what do you do on a daily basis to integrate it into your life, and why do you think spirituality is important for growth and sustainability in recovery?

DN: Daily prayer and meditation. Prayer morning and night, meditation at least once a day. Currently into guided meditations using Insight Timer.

DB: What was one situation you found yourself in that confirmed in your mind that you must seek treatment and recovery and why?

DN: It was so long ago—but the defining moment that always comes to mind is when my daughter (who was six at the time) told me that I made her sick when I was pleading with her to get her baby sister a drink because "mommy is sick, I need your help." She had just had it with me, and she let me know it. I decided that morning that I would seek treatment. And I did. I've never looked back, and I've always credited her and her baby sister (who grew up to be Taryn) for getting me into recovery. Grateful, always.

TOMMY ROSEN

"A body is the thing that goes to the wayside in addiction quite often, so the reconnection method is critical."
– Tommy Rosen

Bio: Tommy Rosen is a yoga teacher and addiction recovery expert who has spent the last two decades immersed in recovery and wellness. He holds certifications in both Kundalini and Hatha Yoga and has 25 years of continuous recovery from drug addiction. Tommy is one of the pioneers in the field of Yoga and Recovery assisting others to holistically transcend addictions of all kinds. Tommy is the founder of the Recovery 2.0 Global Community, the Recovery 2.0 Online Conference series and the Recovery 2.0 Group Coaching Program. He leads Recovery 2.0 retreats and workshops internationally and presents regularly at yoga conferences and festivals.

Tommy's first book, *Recovery 2.0: Move Beyond Addiction and Upgrade Your Life*, was published by Hay House in 2014. Tommy and his wife, yoga teacher, Kia Miller, live in California, where they teach yoga and grow organic vegetables in their backyard.

Occupation: Founder of Recovery 2.0

Drug of choice: Everything

Length of sobriety: 27 years

DB: What do you do on a daily basis to maintain your sobriety and what's the most challenging part about it?

TR: On a daily basis, it starts with my sadhana practice. Sadhana is a Sanskrit word that means spiritual practice, and there's a morning practice that I try to do every day, so my day is centered around the effort to attain the state of yoga, which to me is the opposite of addiction. Yoga just simply means union, addiction means, to me, disconnection. So, I start with a little bit of yoga, some breath work, some meditation, some chanting. Sometimes I journal. I eat really healthy and incredible food throughout the day to keep me energized. I just basically live in recovery. It's just part and parcel of my life, so sometimes I'll hit meetings. Sometimes I go to therapy. I'll speak with my counselors, and my teachers, and my sponsors, and I have a lot of people around me that I consider to be teachers and who help me, and that's pretty much my day. And I'm always working to help whoever I can help who struggles with addiction of any kind, so that's the work of Recovery 2.0, and I just do that. That's my vocational focus, my energetic focus.

The challenge is to be a human being in this crazy world, and to be centered, and to be kind, and to be compassionate, and to find the lesson in all the challenges of life. None of that stops because you get sober. Getting sober, you know, getting sober allows you to feel. Allows you to experience. Allows you to penetrate the experience of life a little bit more deeply in my experience, so getting to do that, not only are you going to experience life more fully, but you're also going to feel things more fully, both joy and difficulty.

When you lose somebody, for example, or you lose a job, or you lose an opportunity, or you lose something that's meaningful to you, you're going to feel grief. And the beauty of it is you get to feel grief and process through that feeling and have a full spectrum human experience, so life becomes rich. It just becomes unbelievably rich in every way when you're sober.

The difficulty I'm working on right now in my life is simply to go more deeply into the state of meditation and the state of yoga and that takes time and commitment and practice, and not just the practice of mediation and yoga like getting on a mat. But, the practice of yoga in your entire life, in everything you do, even like this minute with you right now, this has to be a conscious practice for me, so I'm working at that all the time. There's a billion ways to be distracted, a billion ways to get caught up in thinking. Infinite ways to be in an addictive frequency any given day, whether that's drugs and alcohol or you're binge watching some Netflix show kind of avoiding the things you should be looking at.

DB: Now how have you reconnected with your body since being in recovery and what are some things you include in your daily life to increase your health and vitality?

TR: A body is the thing that goes to the wayside in addiction quite often, so the reconnection method is critical. For me that, again, that's going to be yoga, also though for me, I love to train. I love to train in the gym. I love to work with trainers. I love tennis. I love mountain biking. I just love movement in general, so connecting with my body is really important for me and it's something that I do every day.

In terms of health and vitality, of course diet goes along with movement, so remineralizing the body, staying really hydrated, these are things that people who are stuck in addiction never do. In fact, most people on the path of recovery, especially early in recovery don't do this well, either. Most of the guys that I work with are hitting the caffeine like there'll be no caffeine left in the world tomorrow. That's how they hit it.

So, we gotta hydrate and remineralize the body, energize the body with the food that we eat, and then we find the sense of comfort and ease within the body, and then things get really, really good.

They are two of the most underutilized tools. Fitness and diet. In fact, it's upsetting that the first place many people turn for the solution to their discomfort is some kind of pill rather than looking at diet, rather than hydrating, rather than moving the body which in many, many cases can take care of depression, mild depression, it can take care of some of the discomfort, it can take care of so many conditions in the body if you just start moving, and you start filling up your body with good nutrition.

DB: How have your relationships changed since being in recovery? Who would you say are the top three to five people you surround yourself with and why are they influential in your recovery?

TR: Well, interestingly, I'll just start on the romantic side of things, I'm married for 15 years with my incredible wife, Kia. We have an amazing relationship, super present, super loving, super awesome, and like all relationships, not without its work that has to be done and not without the challenges that keep people relating to each other regularly. But, if you had understood me as a man in active addiction, you would not believe me. You would not believe that I've had a successful relationship for 15 years. You literally would challenge me, say Tommy, frankly, knowing where you're coming from, I don't understand how you would be with anybody for 15 days, much less 15 years. So, that right there has spanned across all kinds of relationships from family to friendships to my business relationships.

I say this with great humility, but people have come to trust me, and rely on me, and count on me, and they've done that because I've shown some consistency over a period of time. Something I was never able to do in active addiction. So, the building of trust, and the building of connection between people becomes truly possible when you can finally show up consistently over period of time.

My wife, number one. She's a source of seamless strength and connection for me. She's ground zero. We live together. We eat together. We work together. We're together, so that's going to be big.

Number two, my teacher, Guru Prem, who I've written and spoken quite a bit about. This is the man who gave me the advanced user's manual to wealth of the human body and human life. He became my life teacher in 2003, and he's been there with me ever since and I've been with him ever since, so he's somebody that's just there. There are some key friendships that I have. There are too many to name. There's probably, off the top of my head, 10 people that I am regularly in contact with just to stay current. Then there are other teachers of mine, nutritionists that I see, acupuncturists, Chinese medicine people that I see, a rolfer that I see. These healers just keep my mind and body together. They constantly are helping me. And one of the ways I love to spend money is to spend it on health and well-being. And so those are the folks that I mostly keep around me and stay close to.

DB: What is your spiritual life like, and what do you do on a daily basis to integrate it into your life, and why do you think spirituality is important for growth and sustainability in recovery?

TR: Spirituality is simply part of the human experience. It's not something that once achieved is again achieved. It's impossible to separate the spiritual side of your life from the physical side of your life. It's one and the same. This is one of the great misunderstandings of people. "I'm choosing today to be more spiritual." You can't be. You can't be any more spiritual than you are. What you can choose to do is to pay attention to that side of your life, and I think that's what people really mean when they say, "I'm on a spiritual path." Meaning I'm aware of the connection between mind, body, and spirit, and I live in an attempt to be aware of that on a daily basis.

So, the spiritual side of a human being is just there. To cultivate it, to nurture it, to become aware of it, that's the work of your life. That will be the most meaningful work of anybody's life. Whether they think so or not, it doesn't matter. It's not "I said so, so it's correct." It's not about that. It's just the way that it is. A human being is, in essence, a marriage, and internal marriage of body and spirit, and when that marriage is doing well, your life is just expanding in every direction and it's just amazing.

When that marriage between body and spirit's not going well your body and your spiritual need, your heart's pulling at odds with each other, that's that inner conflict that so many human beings feel, and one of the reasons that people become addicted to things, trying to solve that problem. Trying to solve that internal marital problem if you will, between body and spirit.

But it's the same, you know, to imagine that there's a world that exists without the undercurrent of spirituality is just simply a misunderstanding of how things are. I'm not trying to put anybody down, it's just a misunderstanding. You have to slow down long enough to sit down and close your eyes and understand that there's more going on than what you can see, and what you can feel, and what you can taste or touch. And the more you work with that, the more is revealed, as it says in the Big Book and another 20 or 30 spiritual doctrines that will quantify this point for people. But, it's very important to nurture that connection between body and spirit. It's where your fulfillment and your happiness are going to come from.

DB: What was the one situation you found yourself in that confirmed in your mind you must seek treatment or recovery and why?

TR: I ultimately sought treatment out of desperation, as many do. There was no spark of genius to it, just, I have no next move. I have nothing I can do. I can't see my way forward. I'm going to die, and I'm going to die like this. And so without having any plan of what to do next, I did the only thing I could think to do, which was just to call my family and ask for help, essentially. Which, I did in a very round-a-bout way, but thankfully my father, on that phone call, was able to sway me to getting help. The asking for help in that moment of bottom, where you are finally willing to tell the truth.

I don't have this. I don't have this thing. I need help to move forward. Can you help me? That's a beautiful, sacred, incredible moment. I wish that moment for everybody who struggles with addiction because from that moment everything can become possible.

TIM COLLINS

"There's no denying there is something greater than myself when you are on top of a mountain, or you're walking on the beach, or beneath the ocean."
– Tim Collins

Bio: Tim Collins is the founder of the Canyon Ranch Recovery Program, ADD DAILY MEETING a nonclinical 12-Step community that features guest speakers from around the country and offers major recovery events every year at both the Tucson, Arizona and Lenox, Massachusetts properties. Tim was the cofounder of the Boston Managers Group, the Collins-Barrasso Agency, and the sole founder and director of Collins Management through which he oversaw the comeback of the highly celebrated rock band, Aerosmith, as well as many other prestigious music projects. Celebrating sobriety since 1986 from multiple addictions, Tim has served as a board member and advisor to recovery programs across the nation including the Caron Foundation, Victory Programs Inc., The Wilson House, the Grammy's MusiCares recovery assistance program for musicians, and more. He is honored to have been a featured speaker at multiple conventions including the International AA Convention in Minneapolis (2000), MAAD Dog Daze in Palm Springs (2015), and Bid D Round Up in Dallas (2015). Tim is devoted and passionate to 12-Step service and has had the good fortune to travel globally working with the recovery community.

Occupation: Collins Management, Inc.

Drug of choice: Alcohol/sleeping pills/cocaine

Length of sobriety: 32 years

DB: What do you do on a daily basis to maintain your sobriety, and what is the most challenging part about it?

TC: I get out of bed each day, and just for that day, I make a decision to rejoin a trusted 12-Step fellowship. I take Steps 1 through 3, which is basically "I can't, he can, and I think I'll let him." I turn my life and my will over to my higher power as I understand him. Then, I do a little meditation, a reading, some prayer, and journaling.

I pick up the phone and call at least three other recovering addict/alcoholics. Sometimes they're my sponsor, sponsees, or even somebody brand new. Often somebody calls me. Most days, I attend a 12-Step meeting.

Every day is a challenge in a subtle way. The further we get from using, the closer we are. It's easy to lose our humility. We can start to take it for granted. There's an old 12-Step saying: "If you think you have humility, then you probably don't."

Sometimes, I might think I kicked it, but for me, it's a daily reprieve based on the maintenance of my spiritual condition. I can very easily put many things before my recovery. My experience is whatever I put before my recovery, I eventually lose.

When I was managing rock and roll bands, I could easily have prioritized that over getting to a 12-Step meeting or returning a call to a fellow addict, and I often did. But nothing is more important. It really comes down to that connection that makes it all possible. I learned I cannot keep it, unless I give it away.

DB: How have you reconnected with your body since being in recovery, and what are some things you include in your daily life to increase your health and vitality?

TC: I'm grateful that I hit my bottom at a place called Canyon Ranch. I went there in the middle of making an Aerosmith record. Everyone was fighting. Band members walked out of the studio in the middle of the project. It appeared the band was breaking up. It was chaos and I left to clear my head. It was my first time visiting the desert. I went to the dining room for dinner, and it was 110 degrees I asked myself, what am I doing here?

They asked me what I wanted to drink. It was August 1985, and I said, "I'll have a Tom Collins. Nice summer drink." They said we don't serve alcohol. I had an anxiety attack. It was in that moment that I experienced undeniable powerlessness. Ordinarily, what I would have done in the old days was have a drink. There was nothing to drink. It was very humbling.

Being at Canyon Ranch, I was surrounded by health and vitality. Without the booze, I was lost, confused and angry, but I knew I had to do something. I went to the medical department and got a physical. I went to the gym and got a trainer. They came up with a manageable plan for me that made it fun and challenging. It was like teaching a child to brush his teeth. Slowly, I lost my resistance to exercise and it became like a game. I was loving it.

Now on a weekly basis, I have an exercise plan. I don't do the exact same thing every day. I love to hike all over the world which is something that, since I was once 305 pounds, to be in a manageable body is such a delight. It just feels incredible being in nature. There's no denying there is something greater than myself when you are on top of a mountain, or you're walking on the beach, or beneath the ocean.

Meditation helps to slow down my mind and get in touch with what's going on in my body. After getting sober, I learned that nutrition and sleep were crucial. Food itself is a drug, and my body needs good nutrition in order to live its fullest life. I had more energy, clearer mind, and consistent moods. As a rock and roll manager, I rarely slept. Three, four, five hours a night at best. But I learned that without having the right sleep, my body couldn't function. It didn't have the right fuel.

DB: How have your relationships changed (types of people, length/meaning of relationships, etc.) from when you were actively using to being in recovery?

TC: My career was putting me in touch with people all over the planet, and unfortunately when you're using, you tend to gravitate to those that are using. When I got sober, I learned that the right people, places, and things made all the difference in the world. There were a lot of people around me for the wrong reason and vice versa. Once I let them go, I realized those relationships were shallow. Some of them were dear friends, but as the disease of alcoholism progressed they got sicker and I got sicker trying to help them. Most of them weren't willing. As a result I decided to leave that circle. It was bittersweet. I knew I would never stay sober with the same old crew. If nothing changes, nothing changes.

I discovered that underlying all addiction was dysfunctional relationships with others. I wanted to fix them but you cannot help anyone who doesn't want help. As a result, all I did was drive people away. When I first got sober, I returned home and immediately relapsed. I would get sober and relapse probably thirty times that fall, and finally wound up at a 12-Step fellowship on January 2, 1986. I realized that lack of power was really my dilemma and I needed to find that power. The 12 Steps led me there.

Now I have a community of people who really get it. It's funny that people who gravitate to me, do so now with the hope of changing, which is something that didn't happen before. I'm very open about my recovery and have no shame about it. For me, it's a disease. It's a brain disease. It's a physical allergy coupled with a mental obsession that eroded my spiritual values. I found my mind craved what my body cannot tolerate. It was killing my spirit. If my best friend and my dealer were in the same room, I'd go hang out with the guy with cocaine. That's how sick it got.

DB: Who are the top three to five people you surround yourself with and why are they influential in your recovery?

TC: Well, the most influential person in my recovery is no longer with us. His name was Bob Timmons. He was the guy who really helped me understand I was sick needing to get well, not bad needing to be good. I spoke to him every single day. It was hard to lose Bob, but I carry what he taught and like him, I pay it forward. Today, I have a sponsor and guys who I sponsor who I have taken through the 12 Steps.

I made an unlikely dear friend who's a Catholic priest. His nickname is the "Drunk Monk" and he was the Chaplain at the Caron Foundation, one of the world's best treatment centers. We have spoken almost every day for the last 30 years. He could tell after about two or three minutes of hearing my voice how I was doing, and eventually I could do the same with him. He helped me to embody this program and practice it in all areas of my life. To develop rigorous honesty . . . because if we don't develop that on the recovery journey, we're going to lie to ourselves at some point and think we're cured or immune. But everybody in my recovery is important to me. No matter where I go in the world, I'm able to find that community.

I also always have a spiritual guide who is outside of my day-to-day world who I can share with without having to hold back. I know I won't be judged or told what to do unless I ask for direction. These are the kind of people that I surround myself with now. People who want to make a difference in the world by living in the recovery solution and freely passing it on. Together we can do what we could never do alone. There's a bond that connects us to something far greater than ourselves.

DB: What is your spiritual life like and what do you do on a daily basis to integrate it into your life, and why do you think spirituality is important for growth and sustainability in recovery?

TC: To find spirituality, I do my best to be present and willing to live in the solution. I do service every single day. I do whatever needs to be done. I take quiet time and I block the world out for a few hours, especially when I start to feel disconnected and unsure. I now look at what I can give instead of what I can take. As a result of that, I get to live a life I never thought possible. You're either busy living or you're busy dying, and finding a spiritual path has opened up a whole new world of experiencing and seeing things that I would never have cared to do before. I find my church when I engage fully in the world living authentically, developing and maintaining relationships, hiking, traveling, scuba diving, and seeking continued growth. It allows me to live my best life, but only one day at a time. The food I ate yesterday doesn't nourish my body today.

DB: What was one situation you found yourself in that confirmed in your mind that you must seek treatment and recovery and why?

TC: I knew something was radically wrong after being told there was no alcohol at Canyon Ranch. I had an anxiety attack. In that moment I had no power to control my mind or body. I knew right then I had to get help. I needed to find a power greater than myself.

DOUG'S TWO CENTS ON RELATIONSHIPS

Relationships are often one of the first things we destroy when we are suffering from addiction. This is true whether it's our relationships with family, friends, or anyone else. A well-known benefit to entering recovery is an improvement in relationships. As recovering addicts, we can be impatient. But we have to keep in mind that damaged relationships take time to heal. It will be a process to get things back to where they were. While, we are all capable of being forgiven, there will be many who don't forget. Keep in mind that actions will speak louder than words. Be patient, focus on the things you can control, and try not to take things personally. Remember, you can only control what you can control and unfortunately that doesn't include other people and their emotional processes.

From my personal experience, my relationships changed completely. As an addict, I focused solely on what I could take from people, who I could con, steal from, or lie to. And incredibly, I thought that was normal behavior.

Today, I am more focused on giving, being honest, and staying grateful. This is not to say that I am perfect, far from it. But, now I know when I am doing something that isn't right, whereas before I could care less about who I was hurting, lying, or scamming.

The types of people I choose to hang around with have also changed. When I was using and selling drugs, I only wanted to hang out with people who were cool with me snorting pills or coke and had no issue with me rolling around with a pound or two of pot in my car. If you weren't buying drugs or doing them with me, I didn't want to be around you. Plain and simple.

These days I try to surround myself with people that bring out the best in me. These are people who are living healthy lives, focused on growth, and willing to tell me things that I don't want to but need to hear. With that said, helping others who are still struggling is a big part of my recovery.

JENNIFER GIMENEZ

"You know why they're influential in my recovery? Because they're truthful to me. I don't need people to lift me up and give me bullshit. I'm all about no bullshit, and they give me honesty, and they give me truth, and they give me direct love."
– Jennifer Gimenez

Bio: As one of the nation's leading experts on addiction, Jennifer Gimenez has become a regular fixture on TV and across the media. Upon moving to the U.S. from Argentina as a child, Gimenez was discovered by famed photographer Bruce Weber at 14. The exotic beauty quickly ascended to international stardom, appearing on 100's of magazine covers from Vogue to Bazaar & Marie Claire, and was the youngest model ever to appear on the cover of American Elle. As a sought-after runway model, Gimenez walked the catwalks of Paris, NY, Tokyo, London, and Milan for the world's top designers such as Chanel, Armani, and Prada, and shot campaigns for Calvin Klein, Guess, St. John, and Paul Mitchell.

Named one of *Maxim's* "Hot 100" and *Esquire's* "Women We Love," Gimenez went on to appear in videos for artists such as Mick Jagger, Prince, 2Pac, Lionel Richie, and Babyface just to name a few. After landing roles on *The Young and The Restless* and *Bold and The Beautiful*, Jennifer scored her first major film role in Ted Demme's *Blow* starring alongside Johnny Depp. She followed up with the blockbusters *Vanilla Sky, Corky Romano, Charlie's Angels,* and more. Surrounded by a fast-paced Hollywood lifestyle,

Gimenez soon found herself at the mercy of her own drug and alcohol demons.

Now over 12 and a 1/2 years sober, Gimenez has used her own recovery to help others, starring on VH1's hit *Sober House* Seasons 1 and 2, *Celebrity Rehab* Season 5, and 2012's *Rehab With Dr. Drew*. She's also appeared on *The O'Neal's Show* on OWN, as a judge on *Model Latina* for SiTV, *Celebrity Wife Swap*, and *The Real Housewives of Beverly Hills*, as well as an expert on top tier media including *The View*, CNN, HLN, *Today Show*, and *ENews*.

Jennifer has become an advocate in the recovery world by sharing her story so openly. She's passionate about helping others battling alcohol, addiction, eating disorders, mental illness, or any of life's challenges. In 2013 Jennifer launched SoberBook.com, a site that allows everyone to be the writer by sharing their stories anonymously. Gimenez is also the spokesperson for Royal Life Centers, a rehab program with 15 centers nationally.

Occupation: Model/Recovery Advocate

Drug of choice: Cocaine (tried everything)

Length of sobriety: 13 years

DB: What do you do to stay sober on a daily basis and what's the most challenging part about it?

JG: Oh my God. Well, it's so different. Through time, through the last 12 and a half years, almost 13 years . . . wow, wow, we're in September—yeah, I'm four months shy of 13 years—there's been different stages and right now what I'm doing is I pray a lot, thank God. I tell on myself. I think telling on yourself . . . that was something I was taught by my sponsor. If I'm having a really tough time, I reach out . . .

Like, today in my life, everyone in my circle, they're good people whether they're sober or normies, as we call them, and I tell on myself, I'm not having a good day . . . it's not okay, and I need help with this.

DB: What's the biggest challenge?

JG: Honestly? Not blowing my brains out. And why?

Life is full, and I'm so grateful. I so appreciate my life. I never thought it would be this kind of life, but I don't even know if I even imagined the kind of life I would've had back then when I was out using. You know, I have a lot of responsibilities. Not that I'm complaining about it. I appreciate my life. I love my life. I do what I love and I think it's so important for us to find things that we love to do and live those dreams, and then there's more dreams that come on and we keep adding on to more goals or more desires of things that we want to be, become or do.

DB: How have you reconnected with your body since being in recovery, and what are some things you do on a daily basis to increase your health and vitality? Injuries aside, you know?

JG: Well, I've had every eating disorder from my modeling days on. I've been from anorexic to obese. I got really heavy in my early sobriety this time around because I was on medication and I dwindled off. I dwindled off doctor's orders and I wasn't allowed to do a lot of things. I did a lot of things that weren't necessarily in the program as well as doing the program, but some of the things I couldn't do was look at tabloids or tabloid shows or magazines and kind of look on the outside.

I remember when my sponsor said to me, nine months sober, like, "Are you ready to dig deep?" I was still trying to do it my way and she was like, "Okay, if you want to do it the program way, this is what it looks like. Get pen and paper; get ready to dig deep. You cannot use, you cannot drink, you cannot hurt anyone, you cannot hurt yourself, you cannot be in a relationship and no sex."

And I was like, “Hold up. What?” I couldn’t act out?

I didn’t look in the mirror very much the first two years of my sobriety, and I gained a lot of weight due to some complications and weening off the meds, and I moved out of Hollywood. I thought I had moved to Egypt, but it was just an hour away and I didn’t know who I was going to be or what I was going to do. I ended up getting—after applying at two jobs, Target and Starbucks, which they turned me down—I got *Sober House with Dr. Drew*.

When I was on that show I always felt like my dresses shrunk or the scale was broken, and then when I came into clarity and acceptance of where I was, I was at, like, 267 pounds, and here I am doing the show and I’m very, very heavy, for me, for my body, and I was bashed non-stop on that show, being called fat all the time.

I remember when I finished that show I wanted my mind, body, and spirit to connect, and it was so important because my spirit and my mind was connecting but my body wasn’t. The journey of losing weight . . . I think that’s harder than anything I’ve ever done in my life.

And what do I do? There’s been different phases, again, different phases. I try to do the cleanse. I think it’s called the Master Cleanse, or whatever, for 21 days. I drank water and cayenne pepper and all this stuff, and I literally lost six pounds and then gained 18 back, and that was my heaviest. And not eating wasn’t working. Like, my God has a sense of humor, and when I don’t eat I start gagging, so I had to learn to eat correctly. I got trainers. I had different trainers, and I always had male trainers until I had this one woman, Darlene Berg, and she was the changing point for me.

It was so weird ‘cause I remember going, like, “How haven’t I had a female trainer? Wow, it doesn’t make sense.” She got me, and she taught me how to eat. I had to keep a journal and I had to write down what I was eating, when I was eating, why I wasn’t eating what I was supposed to be eating and how I was feeling. And so I do this thing where I don't emotionally eat. I try not to. I like food. I'm from South America, from Argentina. My family, we love bread, meat, pasta. I don't not eat and I don't deprive myself, as well.

And then there's different people. I remember doing *Sober House* the second season, and Dennis Rodman was on the show, and he gave me the greatest gift in that show. He taught me how to work out; he worked out with me every day. But he told me things like always be active. Like right now I'm on this call with you and I'm pacing, or I'm standing instead of just sitting. I just do things, like always be moving.

For me, because sometimes I have bodily injuries, my neck or back hurts or whatever, I can't always work out and lift weights, but I do cardio. Or I'll do what I can, really light weights or bands or yoga. I do different things, but I'm constantly asking my body questions. You know what I mean? Like I'm always in connection with my body as best as I can possibly be to know, am I hungry? Am I really hungry? Am I feeling like I need fruit? Do I need salad? Do I feel like I need meat or chicken or something? It's kind of like I hit a lot of walls in my body regimen, but then I'm like, okay, now it's time to do something else.

DB: How have your relationships changed from being in addiction to recovery?

JG: Oh my God. Do you have 15 hours? They've changed from night to day. I'm a big advocate that I don't believe people change until you change, and you got to do the work, and by doing the work . . . I do the program and the program has taught me and the steps have taught me to have a personal relationship with . . . you know, learn to have a relationship with somebody else such as my sponsor, right? And then it was with myself and with God, as I like to call God, say, a higher power. And from there I applied it in all my affairs.

It took time. It took a lot of time for some people. The ones that I thought were going to be easier to get back, like my mom's trust, it took a long, long time. In relationships, I try to pick healthy people in my life. I think it's all about vibrations and where we're at and what we think and how we believe, and in the beginning I didn't have any of that. People just loved me and I didn't understand that until years later.

If it wasn't for those people, like I call them my old-timers, loving me and nurturing me back to health, I don't know what I would do in my life, and because of them I was able to give to people in my life. And now I have honest relationships with people in life, and I'm a little too honest. Like I can come out kind of rough and blunt at times, but I don't mean to.

DB: Who are the top three to five people you surround yourself with and why are they influential in your recovery?

JG: Miranda Mangiaterra
Peter DeRosa
Brandi Glanville
Adrienne Janic
AJ Cortez
Heidi McGuirk
Paul C.
Amanda Marino
Ryan Flaim
Amy Hall
Aung
Katie B.
Rubina
Doug Bopst

You know why they're influential in my recovery? Because they're truthful to me. I don't need people to lift me up and give me bullshit. I'm all about no bullshit, and they give me honesty, and they give me truth, and they give me direct love.

I was taught universal love by my sponsor. I was taught kind love, compassionate love, understanding love, "save your ass not your face" love. You need to learn love. There were so many layers of love. I really do believe there's so many layers of love. And my friends keep me accountable, and they know me, and they get me. And they love me in spite of me being crazy, you know what I mean?

DB: What is your spiritual life like, and what do you do on a daily basis to incorporate it into your day?

JG: Okay, I trust and I believe in a God that I don't fully understand, and I learn who God is on a moment to moment basis. And I say God, because I know some people may get all weirded out that I say God 'cause that's what that is for me. I don't know if you need to put that in there, but I've gone from thinking what this program and what recovery is about a spiritual malady. It's not about a religious malady. I don't suffer from a religious malady, I suffer from a spiritual malady. And I get to create the God of my understanding and, like I say, I trust in that God that I don't fully understand.

But I see God through so many things. I see God when I'm at the ocean. I see God through you when we're having a conversation. I see God through people's eyes. I feel love and compassion. And another thing I like to do is I've been meditating.

I've been meditating and I've been meditating a lot lately. I thought I needed to kind of be in this weird position and do this like humming noise or something. Sometimes it's not that. Sometimes it's just either laying on the floor somewhere or my bed or sometimes on planes or sometimes just like as I'm walking, I can meditate and talk to God. I learned to talk to God. I'm that crazy girl that looks like the crazy lady walking down the aisles totally talking to God. Today, I was shopping and I found myself talking out loud to God. What do I do? I need those 15 minutes no matter what. I feel the more sober and the longer I stay sober and the more sober I get, the more I have to rely on God. Just three months ago or what not,then something else happened. I'm like, "Oh my gosh. I got to go even deeper." I need that spiritually because we all are spirits. We all have souls. I want my spirit to grow.

DB: Why do you think it's important for sustainability and growth and recovery?

JG: Because if I don't have something bigger than me to believe in, then I'm doomed. You know, a lot of people have problems with calling something or believing in a god. I believed in drugs and alcohol for a while until they stopped working. My sponsor, again another time in my early sobriety, said to me, "I need you to believe in something bigger than yourself. Do you think that's possible? I don't give a shit what it is as long as it's not you. Can you do that?" I was just like, "I guess." Just kind of being like that little bratty girl. I started believing in the "rooms" and I started believing in the fellowship. I started believing in the program. I started believing. Little by little I started believing. I go back to that God I didn't know and that God that I don't fully understand— He hasn't let me down yet.

DB: What was the one situation you found yourself in that confirmed in your mind you must seek treatment recovery and why?

JG: Well, I mean I guess I'll talk about this last time because I was a relapser. I thought I got it together, but I never did the steps and I never worked inside. I didn't do an inside job. I did just some outside job and I call that making it shiny and pretty on the outside. But this last time when I went to treatment, it was my first time going into treatment and I went because my best friend and my mom told me I had no other option. They were the last two people left in my life. I went on a two-week run after I kicked them out and it got very ugly and dark. After that two and a half week run, I went into treatment. I went under my terms. My terms were five days. I ended up staying from July 12 until the 2nd of November.

I relapsed in treatment. When I left, I left for 10 weeks and it felt like one long night. I remember that I didn't feel high. I just remember I was coming to and I remember I was thinking about Dr. Drew's little smirk he does. I was thinking about Bob Forrest who's one of my counselors in treatment. I was thinking about his red hair and who was hooking up with who in treatment and what was happening and who was leaving. For a girl like me that wants to numb and sedate herself, it was a really fucked up place to be because I was trying to get high and I was thinking about people in treatment. Such a bad place, you know?

I remember, I mean, I just went into my mom's room. At this point, I was staying at my mom's house. She just wanted to be there for me and she said I had to come to her house. It was pretty dark and I could hear her cry and pray every single day as I was using in my room, in my old childhood room. I remember one day I just went into her room and I said, "Alright. Take me back to treatment."

That day was it. It was just, that was it.

LINDSAY CHRISTIANSEN

"And even if working out was not good for my body, I would still do it because I need it for my mental state, for my sanity."
– Lindsay Christiansen

Bio: Lindsay is an Orange County based yoga instructor, fitness model, and health coach and mom. She's known for bringing a combination of playfulness and mindfulness to helping others achieve their goals. Lindsay was born and raised in Iowa.

She moved to Boulder to attend the University of Colorado and fell in love with the active, health conscious city. While studying for her degree, Lindsay began teaching group exercise classes at the fitness center on campus.

After graduating with her BA in psychology, she continued working in the fitness field and found that her degree in psychology was a valuable tool in being able to better help clients reach their goals and move through obstacles.

Lindsay began practicing yoga in 2007 and fell in love with the practice and the physical and mental wellbeing she found through yoga. She became a certified yoga instructor in 2014. Lindsay teaches group classes, works with corporate and private clients, and leads yoga retreats.

Occupation: Yoga Instructor/Recovery Advocate

Drug of choice: Benzos and alcohol

Length of sobriety: 2.5 years

DB: So what do you do on a daily basis to maintain your sobriety, and what is the most challenging part about it?

LC: So I'll just tell you what I did today. I'm super big on having a morning routine. And it's a quick one, because I'm usually kind of up and running and gotta get my daughter to school so it's not some big drawn out thing. But this morning, I honestly woke up super on the wrong side of bed, just kind of feeling stressed out and like I haven't had much time for myself lately. And so first thing I did, it's funny, I always had kind of an issue with getting on my knees to pray, but there is something magical about it. So, I kind of grit my teeth and I do it and I get on my knees and I pray. And my prayer is either the third step prayer, I love the third step prayer, or kind of almost like some variation of it.

So, this morning it was really simple and it was like, "Hey, let me be present for my life today. Let me stay out of my own head. Let me help people wherever possible. And let me take it moment by moment and day by day." And so, a super quick prayer. I usually say it out loud, which, is something that used to feel really forced to me but I think that there is something powerful about not only just thinking something but saying it and hearing it. It just helps me kind of integrate that into my day.

And then of course 12-Step meetings are a big part of my life. I try to hit at least three a week. And checking in with my sponsor and my sponsee. These are basically big ways of saying I just try to get out of my own head from the beginning of the day and my day tends to have a better trajectory when I do that. And there's not as much struggle when I do that, when I do feel connected. So, prayer is first, meditation's second, and I have a meditation app on my phone that I love and it's a 10-minute morning meditation. So, I sit on the couch. And a lot of times I'll have just a word that

I bring to mind. And today it was gratitude because I just needed to be in gratitude today. I was kind of getting into feeling sorry for myself. So, I'll tend to pick kind of an opposing word to where I'm at... if I'm feeling really flustered, I'll pick grounded. Today it was gratitude. And it's literally just I sit there, my mind wanders off, I'm thinking about random stuff, I notice it, and then I come back to the word gratitude and just sit there and rest and sit with it.

At first of course the challenging part of your sobriety is literally just staying sober day by day, not putting alcohol or drugs into my body. Now the day to day struggle is gone, and I'm super blessed for that. It's easy to take your eye of the ball when that happens. Things are good, my life is going great. I have a lot of really amazing things on my plate. I have my job and I'm a parent and then I'm going back to graduate school. So, all super awesome things, all things that take up time. So, the struggle now is always remembering that sobriety has to be number one. Because it's super easy to wanna blow off a meeting because I have to do stuff for school or stuff with my daughter that I wanna be present for. So, keeping sobriety is number one.

And one thing that I hear over and over from people who have had years of sobriety and then have gone out or gone back to drinking or drug use, those people, first off, and it's scary, those stories are scary as hell, what I hear people saying is, "My life got good, I got busy, and I didn't put sobriety first." So, my challenge now is just through it all remembering why I have all the things that I have, and keeping my sobriety as my absolutely number one.

DB: How have you reconnected with your body since being in recovery and what are some things you include in your daily life to increase your health and vitality?

LC: Okay, so it's super funny because even while I was in my gnarly drug use, I was super jacked up on Xanax, benzos, even alcohol sometimes, I was a fitness instructor. I would've told you I was really into fitness and really into my body. But, of course, I was slowly poisoning myself. And I maybe looked okay, but dude, I was super unhealthy and had a super unhealthy relationship to my body. And I think my relationship to my body was really a reflection of my relationship to my deeper self. I didn't really like myself very well. So, I used fitness to almost punish my body, so it would be like I was kind of beating it into submission. I was burning the calories on the freaking elliptical machine. I was lifting the weights to look a certain way aesthetically. But it wasn't from a place of self-love. My fitness has changed a lot because it now comes from a genuine place of loving myself. And sometimes that looks like taking a lot more rest days. Sometimes that looks like freaking eating an ice cream cone with my daughter. I'm happy with the way I look now. And I'm not as lean as I used to be. And I was at 8% body fat and somebody would've said, "Wow, that girl looks really amazing and fit and healthy," but I was at my least healthy for sure.

But here's the other side of it, I love going to the gym now, it feels good to me. I like the endorphins. And even if working out was not good for my body, I would still do it because I need it for my mental state, for my sanity. So, my relationship to my fitness now looks more like me smiling and happy and celebrating my body.

DB: How have your relationships changed since being in recovery? Who would you say are the top three to five people you surround yourself with and why are they influential in your recovery?

LC: I actually have real ones now. I actually have people now that I'm real with and honest with and vulnerable and raw with. And when I was drinking and using, so much of my life was really built around putting on a persona because a lot of it was just I was literally hiding the fact that I was drinking and I was using. So, I was a liar. I lied a lot. And I lied about stuff that wasn't even necessary I guess because I really wanted to manage the way that I was seen in the world. I wanted to be seen as a good Mom at preschool drop-off. I wanted to be seen as a good employee and honestly, I wasn't those things. So, there was a shit ton of lying. So, if another mom at pickup would ask me, "Oh, what'd you do last night?" I'd make up some crap because I didn't wanna say I sat home and pounded a bottle and a half of wine and took all the pills that I could get my hands on.

So anyway, what I'm trying to say is there's this big bleed-over effect into the rest of my life where it wasn't literally just lying about like, "Yes, I'm not drunk. I'm not on pills." It was everything. I was this totally fake person that I thought I was supposed to be. And so, I had friendships, but they weren't very fulfilling because it was based on a totally false reality. I didn't ever really let anybody get to know me. I was just always like this caricature. So, they weren't fulfilling. Now what I'm trying to say is my relationships are so much more fulfilling because they're not based on lies. They're people that I'm real with, they're people that know the real me. There's a lot of people in my life that hold me accountable. And there is something so freaking beautiful about telling somebody the truth, the real raw, not pretty truth, and having them still love you. There's some amazing power in that.

And I think the other side of that power is that I didn't accept myself when I started working my program and started being honest. And one big turning point came when I was working the fourth step, which if you don't know what the steps are, the fourth and fifth step are you write down all the gnarly bad things that you've ever done, and you don't leave anything out, and then you tell another human being, somebody you trust. So, for me it was a sponsor, but basically somebody that you trust, somebody that gets it. And there's such a freedom that came with, with just looking somebody in the eyes and telling them the really bad stuff, and then having them, nod and be like, "Me too, I get it," or we'd laugh about the absurdity of it. But it ended with a hug. And it was like, "Oh man, all this stuff that I thought was just so shameful that no one could ever love me through, she loves me more because of it. And that's cool." And that really started the process of rebuilding my ability to love myself.

DB: Thoughts on top people?

LC: Great question. Funny enough, one of them is my ex-husband. We got divorced kind of when I was in my back and forth of getting sober, and we're co-parents now. And he knows me better than anybody, and he's a great one to keep me accountable. And he's become one of my best friends. And this was literally a person that there was just so much conflict, obviously. We were in a marriage, been married 10 years, going through a divorce. There was so much conflict there. And I would've told you at the get go that because there were lawyers and all this junk, that we could've never been friends. And our romantic relationship wasn't one that was meant to be saved I don't think. But our friendship and our ability to co-parent has been a really beautiful gift of my sobriety.

Another person that I surround myself with is my sponsor. I respect her, I love her, and I do what she says. Because a lot of times, my ideas about what would be the best course of action to take are not great ones to be honest with you. It's hard to see the picture when you're inside the frame they say. And I don't know if that's the best thing to do. And so, I trust her, and she's somebody that if she tells me to do something, I'll pretty much go do it. And she hasn't led me wrong. So, she is an important person.

This is a funny one, but my daughter. I really think that I enjoy every single minute with her all the more because of the minutes that I lost with her. And there was a lot of guilt surrounding that. I think one positive way to look at it is "Oh my gosh, I am so present now for that little girl." And that doesn't mean I'm perfect and that doesn't mean that I'm not in my head and that doesn't mean that I'm not snappy and irritable sometimes with her, but for the most part I have this really beautiful perspective that has come with the lost time that makes me treasure the time that is right now with her.

DB: What is your spiritual life like and what do you do on a daily basis to integrate it into your life and why do you think

spirituality is important for growth and sustainability and recovery?

LC: Okay, so when I first go in to sobriety, everybody talked about spirituality and I wasn't a particularly spiritual person. I maybe sort of kind of believed in God. I was an agnostic I would've told you. It's changed, and it's changed gradually. It didn't have to all change at once. I didn't have to have some huge awakening moment right at the beginning. It was suggested to me at first that I pray. And I kind of met that with resistance, but I did it anyway. And at first it didn't bring me a lot of relief, and slowly over time I just kept doing it because I was told to, multiple times a day. It started to work for me. And it started to make me feel a lot better. Anyway, what I'm trying to say is it's been a really slow progression. It's super-duper crazy important to me today, and prayer is a huge part of my life. And, I do not know what I would do or where I would be without my personal connection to God, and it doesn't look like a religion, it's my own understanding of a higher power that I connect to all day every day pretty much.

But man, I'll tell you something, God to me now is what Xanax was to me back in the day. It drops my shoulders. It softens the area around my heart. Lets me breathe easy.

DB: What was the one situation you found yourself in that confirmed in your mind that you must seek treatment and recovery and why?

LC: Okay, so you would talk a lot about a rock bottom. And I had a lot of things that from the outside probably a sane normal person would've been like, "Oh yep, she just hit rock bottom." Literally I've OD'd, I've had to be resuscitated, I've had to go to the hospital, I've had multiple overdoses. So, all these really, really bad consequences and I didn't stop because of them. And there was this "straw that broke the camel's back" moment where I had just gotten home from a trip and my daughter was really excited to see me, and I couldn't see her because I couldn't stop drinking and using and I felt like crud and so I woke up and I kept doing it. And this was that Monday and my daughter had been so excited to see me, she's a little one at this point so she didn't have much concept of time. But dude, I did. I couldn't see my daughter because of it. And that was it. It was an emotional rock bottom I would say. I wasn't homeless. My teeth weren't chipping out of my mouth or anything like that. If you didn't know me and you looked at my life, you might've been like, "Oh yeah, she's doing pretty well for herself." I wasn't man. I was miserable. And it was an emotional rock bottom.

And I'd gotten sober before, and I'd have a little bit of sobriety, kind of stop working my program, basically get the heat off me, get people to think I was doing better, and then I'd go back to my old ways. I'd be like, "Yeah, I can have a glass of wine, right?" Yeah, it was an emotional rock bottom. And the next day I woke up I don't even remember doing this, but I wrote this really gnarly journal entry about how I was feeling. And it was so raw and real and honest, and I wrote it in basically a black out. But I woke up the next day and I still had that feeling. And I couldn't leave my house I was so sick that next day. But, the day after that I showed up at a 12-Step meeting. And then the day after that I showed up at a 12-Step meeting. And the day after that I showed up at a 12-Step meeting. And I found that after I went I felt better. I felt like I was doing something productive to make my life better. So, I just kept showing up and doing what people told me to do that were smarter and had been doing this more successfully for some amount of time. And that's where I started rebuilding my life from my version of a rock bottom.

DUANE BETTS

"Gratitude is huge. I'm not religious, but I try to be grateful for my life and pray to something no matter what it is."
– Duane Betts

Bio: As a teen, Duane Betts cut his teeth sitting-in regularly with Rock and Roll Hall of Fame inductees The Allman Brothers Band. A consummate musician, Betts led Malibu rock-n-roll outfits such as Backbone69 and Whitestarr, then ascended to a near-decade stint playing guitar alongside his father, Dickey Betts, in his group, Great Southern. Whether as a touring guitarist for folk-rockers Dawes or sharing the stage with luminaries from Kid Rock to Jack Johnson and Phil Lesh, Betts' six-string stories and impassioned songs portray a life, and a history, steeped in blues, rock-n-roll, and country music tradition. Currently, Betts is dividing his time between recording his first solo album, and playing in JAMTOWN, a supergroup featuring G.Love, Donovan Frankenreiter, and Cisco Adler.

Occupation: Musician

Drug of choice: Opiates and cocaine

Length of sobriety: 2 years

DBopst: What do you do on a daily basis to stay sober and what's the most challenging part about it?

DBetts: I try to get some sort of exercise every day if I can. If I'm not in an airport all day, I try to do some sort of movement like yoga, hiking, running, or even just a walk if that is all there is time for. Eating healthy food and surrounding myself with good people that lift me up. Living in gratitude is also something that I try to practice. Gratitude is huge. I'm not religious, but I try to be grateful for my life and pray to something no matter what it is. You don't even have to know what you're praying to, but just to keep conscious contact with something outside of yourself is key.

DBopst: What would you say the most challenging part about it is?

DBetts: For me, this time, it hasn't really been as challenging. I mean, it's always challenging in a way, because it's right there. I can always make the decision to go do it and I know it's always going to be there. It's such a cut and dry thing for me. I know that if I make that choice, NOTHING is possible. All the stuff I have in my life right now, all the love, the relationships and my career. None of that is possible if I'm using. Right now, it's a pretty clear-cut decision. I like the way things are going right now, and I am riding this natural high. I want this positivity to continue and that is really what keeps me from going back.

DBopst: How would you say you've reconnected with your body since being in recovery, and what are some things you do on a day-to-day basis to increase your health and vitality?

DBetts: I love yoga. I try to get outdoors and get in touch with nature. I jump in the ocean when I'm home, even if it's really cold. That's actually a really good thing for me. I try to get in contact with my surroundings and breathe the fresh air. All that stuff is just imperative, you know, to kind of feel amazing.

The idea is that you want to feel really good, so you have to do things that put you in that place. Drugs make you feel good in an artificial way, so when you take that away you have to do other things to take the place of that. Which is exactly what we're talking about. Running, hiking up a mountain, running on the beach, jumping in the ocean, doing yoga. Drinking green juice, eating a bison steak. Stuff like that, you know. All that stuff, when you stay really regimented that's kind of it for me. I am feeling my best when I stick to a regimen.

There are those times when you're on the road, I'll let myself fall off it a bit. If I am in Italy, I'll eat pasta. If I am in Macon, Georgia, I love to eat soul food. I love to eat barbecue, anywhere. But on the average day, I try to go back to my regimen that involves eating clean and eating a lot of protein and veggies and stuff like that.

DBopst: How have your relationships transformed from when you were actively using to now being in recovery? And then, who are the top three to five people you surround yourself with and why are they influential in your recovery? If you care to share who they are.

DBetts: Yeah, I mean, my relationships have completely transformed. Everybody wants me around and now I can really be present. If you're under the influence, you might be there, but it's not the "real you." So, they're happy to have the "real me" back. My relationships with my Mom and my Dad are much better. Everybody knows they can trust me now and the faith they had in me to carry the torch is there.

That's an important thing to me, is knowing that they trust me. The top people would be, my Mom and my Dad. They obviously mean the world to me. I have a lot of good friends that have helped me and guided me through. One of them is Jose Hernandez. He has helped me a lot in my recovery. Khalil Rafati is another. He has guided and mentored me and helped me out a lot when I've had problems. My girlfriend Lisa is a huge support source. She's amazing, and I trust her opinion greatly.

DBopst: What do you do on a day-to-day basis for your

spirituality, and why do you think it's important to integrate it into your life in recovery?

DBetts: I try to pray. Sometimes I go through phases where I'm good at it, and other times, not as good. I just try to give thanks and remain aware of the fact that I have an amazing life. Sometimes the small things that go wrong can really get the best of me, but in the grand scheme of things, they are so minute. When that happens, I am learning to absorb it and then try and brush it off. Remembering the things that really matter. I am not always good at it, but I am trying. Not everything is going to go my way all the time and I try to remind myself to be grateful and aware of the beauty in the world. That is so important to my recovery. Staying grounded.

DBopst: What was one situation you found yourself in that confirmed in your mind you needed to seek treatment and or recovery, and why?

DBetts: There were so many, although the first one that comes to mind was the first time I went through withdrawal. It was terrible and I swore to God that I would never touch that stuff again. But I did. This pattern happened over and over to the point that I just accepted the fact that I was screwed.

At one point, I was living on a beautiful piece of property in Malibu at a friend's house. It would have been so shameful to be seen there in the state I was in, so I opted to stay closer to my dealers at a storage loft. That kind of thing was happening a lot. The shame and guilt of it all. Now, thankfully, I can see whoever I want and not be afraid of having to act like I am "fine." It is very liberating. I am finally at a place where it just seems perfectly natural to get out of that life and really live it at the other end. This is the time I am going to be free of it. That's it, you know what I mean? It's always going to be a day-to-day thing and it's not a cakewalk, by any stretch of the imagination, but I don't have the temptation to do it this time. There was a point in my 20's where it was fun, but I always knew I had a big problem. It just snowballed from there and the fear of facing the reality of withdrawal was a big deterrent to getting clean. I am so thankful I kept trying and that my friends and family stood by me. I am so much happier where I am now.

IVANA GRAHOVAC

"Addiction robbed me of the ability to have close, intimate, meaningful relationships with anyone and everyone."
– Ivana Grahovac

Bio: Ivana Grahovac, is the Director of Advancement for the national nonprofit Facing Addiction with NCADD. She is a woman in long-term recovery from addiction, with a proven track record in the nonprofit addiction field. Prior to that, she served as executive director of Transforming Youth Recovery, a strategic grant program for school-based recovery support. Ivana began her career as director of The Center for Students in Recovery at The University of Texas, where she led the expansion of collegiate recovery programs to all eight UT System schools; a measure unanimously approved by the UT Board of Regents. Ivana received her MSW at University of Michigan, where she created their program "Students for Recovery."

Occupation: Recovery Advocate for Facing Addiction

Drug of choice: Heroin

Length of sobriety: 14 years

DB: What do you do on a daily basis to maintain your sobriety, and what is the most challenging part about it?

IG: It has evolved over the years. In the first few years I would go to an AA meeting every day (I had an incredible 7 a.m. meeting a few miles down the road) and would sometimes go to meetings twice a day. It helped me entrain into the frequency of recovery energy and focus, thereby allowing me to harmonize into a group conscience. Nowadays I meditate first thing in the morning, I stay connected to the Source, and pray and practice mindfulness throughout the day. I try to adhere to a path of spiritual principles as I make my way through the day, and everyone in my support system is either in recovery or any ally to recovery. There is nothing challenging about staying away from drugs or alcohol today. I have devoted myself mind, body, spirit to this lifestyle and revere and venerate the feeling of being fully present and embodied naturally in this world. The most challenging thing was when I was new in sobriety and stuck in struggling and suffering and thinking this was how I would have to feel for the rest of my life—that was an illusion. Trying to illuminate others who are new to recovery that they too have the capacity to heal and overcome their perceived limitations can be very challenging as well.

DB: How have you reconnected with your body since being in recovery, and what are some things you include in your daily life to increase your health and vitality?

IG: I also had an eating disorder I was recovering from while getting off heroin. I started by playing tennis with senior citizens because they were so friendly, encouraging, and gentle. Being around people my age felt scary because I would anxiously imagine all the judgments from my peers. At 1 year sober I found yoga and dove in headfirst. During grad school while other students were partying, I was doing back to back yoga classes as a way to unwind and heal from the stress of academia. I have run marathons, been fanatic about barre classes, and now practice kundalini yoga every day as well as hike and swim. I am a huge fan of Epsom salt baths!

DB: How have your relationships changed (types of people, length/meaning of relationships, etc.) from when you were

actively using to being in recovery?

IG: Addiction robbed me of the ability to have close, intimate, meaningful relationships with anyone and everyone. It took many years for me to learn how to be able to be in authentic relationship with others, but most of all it took me a long time of healing, introspection, and learning lessons of all shapes and sizes before I could have a beautiful relationship with myself. I have had incredible teachers and mentors in my life, mostly women in recovery who have guided me to a higher vision of recovery.

DB: Who are the top three to five people you surround yourself with and why are they influential in your recovery?

IG: I call my family every single day, no matter what. We say "I love you" on the phone every time we hang up. The experience of going through the harrowing addiction process and having unwavering support as I managed the upheavals of early recovery and beyond has solidified and amplified our bond. My beautiful boyfriend and I are constantly side-by-side with our three pups. I have incredible friends in recovery who I call on anytime I need a sounding board or constructive feedback on handling perplexing situations.

DB: What is your spiritual life like and what do you do on a daily basis to integrate it into your life, and why do you think spirituality is important for growth and sustainability in recovery?

IG: A spiritual practice is definitely key for me. Just like people use drugs/alcohol to cope with stress or numb themselves from feeling certain emotions or heighten experiences, so too does a spiritual path help me navigate and transcend moments in life that are baffling to me. I truly like to glean spirituality from multiple sources, and currently kundalini yoga as taught by Yogi Bhajan has been helping me overcome anxiety issues. In addition, plant-based eating (veganism) has truly elevated my consciousness. To be free from the karma of eating animals that have been tortured and slaughtered while others continue to eat them with impunity is honestly such a shocking thing to witness today. Once you connect with the amount of suffering that animals are forced to endure just so someone can have the convenience of going through a drive-thru to grab a burger—it's beyond astonishing how blind and unawakened they are to the plight of another being who feels love and pain just like humans do. Since people in recovery have to do a lot of awakening to overcome their addiction, I am confident we are going to see a huge influx of people in recovery joining the vegan movement. We've suffered while shackled to addiction, now that we are free we should avoid causing further cruelty at all costs.

DB: What was one situation you found yourself in that confirmed in your mind that you must seek treatment and recovery and why?

IG: Withdrawals! The bone-crushing pain of heroin withdrawals had me scrambling to go to treatment. And knowing that I was hurting my family. The lies of the addicted mind were trying to convince me that my family had been hurt beyond repair due to my addiction, but I was able to feel how they were not going to give up on me no matter what, so therefore I couldn't give up on myself. They kept giving me another chance to heal, and so I finally accepted help.

JEFF BRISTOL

"Having gone through recovery has shown me just how amazing the human body is."
– Jeff Bristol

Bio: Jeff grew up in Temecula Valley and was heavily involved in sports. As a child, Jeff played soccer, baseball, football, and basketball, but wrestling is where he really excelled and found his passion. In high school, Jeff was named an All-American wrestler and went on to wrestle at University of California Davis, a Division I college via scholarship. While at Davis, Jeff placed in the Pac 10 Conference and continued his education, ultimately graduating with a Bachelor of Science in Sociology and Organizational Studies.

Jeff's lifestyle in high school and college led to him have a major battle with addiction throughout most of his 20's. He spent nearly a decade in and out of rehab and jails before moving to San Diego where he got sober and discovered Fitness Quest 10. He joined the Fitness Quest 10 team in 2011 as and started in a part-time front-desk position. Shortly after joining the team he felt like he had discovered his purpose, so he got his training certification and set out to change peoples' lives. Sports and fitness had undoubtedly always been a huge component of Jeff's life and a career in the health and fitness industry was a natural fit.

Jeff thrived in his role as a trainer under his boss Todd Durkin, the owner of Fitness Quest 10 and an internationally recognized trainer, speaker, and writer. In 2017, Jeff grew into a management role and now splits his time between training clients, leading the team, and growing the business. He believes that discovering Fitness Quest 10 and pursuing a career in fitness were a couple of the main contributing factors that led him to the path of recovery.

Jeff lives in Scripps Ranch right down the street from where he works at Fitness Quest 10. He is married to Samantha Wilson, and they have a son Knox who was born in November 2016. He encourages anyone who is ever in San Diego to please come and visit him at the gym!

Occupation: Personal Trainer

Drug of choice: Heroine

Length of sobriety: 5+ years

DB: What do you do to stay sober on a daily basis and what's the most challenging part about it?

JB: Okay, well I'm a firm believer that one reason that I was able to number one get sober and number two stay sober is that, mainly through my job, I have the ability to be of service to others on a daily basis. You know, I think that through working in our industry, it's a job where technically you're really just being of service to people that are coming in and trying to live healthier, happier, even if it's a performance standpoint. So through my job I have the ability on a daily basis to get outside of myself and to be of service for others because I think that for recovering addicts, alcoholics, it's a dangerous space to be in our mind, in your own stuff, on a day in day out basis, and that's where you start getting a little squirrely. You start thinking a little crazy. One idea doesn't seem so bad. The old saying of the idle hands are the devil's playground.

People ask me sometimes what changed or how I got sober and it was kind of a crazy deal that led me to work at Fitness Quest 10 where I just moved out of my old hometown and moved to San Diego and answered a job opening on Craigslist for a front desk position when I didn't know anything about Fitness Quest 10 or Todd Durkin. But that was the beginning of the change for me when I started to work towards recovery. And I think that what really helped me is just that on a day in day out basis I am able to get outside myself and be of service to others through my job.

DB: So how have you reconnected with your body since being in recovery? What are some things you do on a daily basis to increase your health and vitality?

JB: First of all, being having gone through recovery has shown me just how amazing the human body is. I tell my clients this just from a standpoint of just from a comparison of when you stop exercising and then you start exercising again. Because I grew up as an athlete playing multiple sports and was in high school, college wrestling, and went to go wrestle Division 1 in college on a scholarship. At one point in my life, I was training really hard and in great shape.

During my high school/college career that's when I started drinking and using heavily which led into my 20s [as] a long five- to 10-year battle with drugs. When I'm talking drugs, it wasn't that I was smoking marijuana a couple days a week. It was that I was injecting heroin and meth into my body, so those just wreak havoc on the body. I remember times where I was so skinny and my face broken out and having staph infection on my face from picking it all night long. I mean I've seen my body really deteriorated.

Getting into recovery, and then in addition to getting into recovery, getting into the health and fitness industry, I had the opportunity through my job again to work out on a daily basis or on a regular basis and to eat clean and to promote that not only within myself but with the people I'm around. I like to treat my body like what they say, "Your body is your temple. You only get one of them." At one point in my life, I was so reckless, I was so addicted that I didn't care what I did. I was just chasing the high it didn't matter if I was shooting up a bunch of chemicals of crystal meth or whatever it was. I've gone a complete 180° now where I'm really thinking about what I'm putting into my body from a nutrition standpoint. I exercise on a regular basis. It just feels really good to be feeling good, looking good, and having good energy and just to see how amazing the body is and everything like that.

DB: How have your relationships changed since being in recovery? Who would you say are the top three to five people you surround yourself with and why are they influential in your recovery?

JB: Yeah. Well, I will tell you that addiction, alcoholism . . . that just wreaks havoc on relationships. I was someone who grew up with an incredible family and had a great childhood and upbringing and had great relationships with my family and loved ones. Then as my addiction got worse as I went into my 20s, those were the people that really took it the worst. I mean really hit the hardest was my family, so my parents. My poor parents they suffered more than anybody, almost more than the person who is actually in the battle of addiction.

They call it a family disease for a reason. My relationships with my parents suffered so much. They were just devastated for the better part of a decade. They suffered a ton, visiting me in jail, trying to get me to go to rehab, paying for multiple rehabs. The financial and all that other stuff is just nothing in comparison to the emotional damage that addiction and alcoholism can do because it turns a person, somebody who my parents raised to be the kid they want them to be and it turned me into a completely different person, somebody who was lying and stealing, lying to my family, stealing from them, just completely destroying my relationships with them. Thank God, I was able to turn things around and get sober. Now, it's normal to not have the insight to appreciate your parents as much when you're younger. I think common for being younger and immature but that's nothing in comparison to getting into addiction where it's like you don't care about anything besides your next high.

I did a lot of damage to my relationships in those years of drinking and using but thank God I've been able to repair those relationships. My wife was with me. We were together before we got married during some years where I was still using. We went through some real terrible years. But, I was able to get sober before we got married. Our relationship is better than ever and the relationship with my parents and my siblings is definitely just the best it's ever been.

Well, I have to say that my wife is first and foremost has been the most influential person in my recovery. She is somebody that's very familiar with substance abuse and recovery. She's a social worker and a therapist and experienced some of the same issues within her own family. So, when her and I got together she was no stranger to the disease, no stranger to addiction. So, she rode the storm out and helped me a lot in the beginning getting sober by setting the right boundaries and really doing anything and everything she could to help me get sober. So that's my wife who basically sees right through my bullshit.

Then I want to say my immediate family would be the next ones. My mom and my sister are two people that fought for my sobriety early on. Then my brother and my dad who I've always really cherished their relationship as a son and a brother but during those times of drinking and using I wasn't the son to my Dad. I wasn't a brother to my brother. I would say that my immediate family would be that next group of people.

Then the next people that I surround myself regularly that help maintain my sobriety are so huge, goes back to my job here at Fitness Quest 10. It's my clients and my co-workers. These are people that I day in and day out get to come in. These are all people that are encouraging me and our community. We're a community that supports being your best self. So, I have clients and co-workers that I get to be surrounded by on a daily basis that we're all lifting each other up. So that's another thing.

Then finally it would be my friends that are in recovery. So, I've made a good amount of friends in recovery over the years through going to AA and NA and my sponsor and other co-workers that are in recovery and other friends that are in recovery and just always having that connection with people that are in recovery. It's just like a look. You just look at each other and you just have to nod at each other and you know. It's a mutual respect and something that definitely keeps me grounded and reminds me that I'm not the only crazy one out there.

DB: What's your spiritual life like? How do you view spirituality and why do you think it's important for sustainability and growth in recovery?

JB: Definitely. Yeah totally. That's being in the rooms of AA for a long time and being in recovery, being a lot in multiple different recovery homes and what not. That always is the topic that is more controversial or seems to be difficult for people in the beginning to wrap their head around. I don't know who, maybe it was my sponsor that early on, told me do not get caught up on that idea. I'm definitely not a very religious person. I wasn't raised in religion. So, would I call myself a Christian? Maybe but I think it's more just the understanding or identification with a power that is greater than yourself.

Whoever it is you speak to at night. I think that just really grasping that concept and maybe not being okay with not knowing exactly what it is but identifying with a power that's greater than myself, which I know that there is. There's been times in my life over and over again where I've been shown. I have no idea why I'm still alive today or I'm not in prison and the blessings that have been given upon me and the things that have happened in my life that I know that there is somebody or something working through the people in my life and working through myself that and just understanding that.

It's also almost comes back just to gratitude, attitude of gratitude basically. I think that relates to that spirituality thing. I guess maybe it's the disease of alcoholism or addiction is such a selfish disease where it's everything is surrounded by the individual. The whole world revolves around me. Well it's me getting out of that idea that the whole world doesn't revolve around me. There's a lot of things going on in the world that's out of my control and it's in somebody else's hands and just I think identifying with that has been a huge thing for me because I didn't get caught up in that higher power dilemma in the beginning.

DB: What was the one situation you found yourself in that confirmed in your mind you must seek treatment or recovery or why?

JB: That's really a hard question to answer just because I do remember realizing at some point during my college career where it was pretty hard for me to really grasp the idea that I needed help when I was younger and I was doing really good in sports in school. I was ranked top in the country for wrestling and I was getting offers for colleges and I went and wrestled on a scholarship. So, during that time, those were the beginning years of me drinking and using where I developed my addiction.

So, it was hard for me to grasp it but there was a point in my college career where I remember where I was coming off a bender, been up for several days and just hit an incredibly low just like that just helpless, hopeless. I was so helpless and so hopeless that I realized that I needed help. I actually flew home to tell my parents that I needed help but then it's the way the addict mind works is that I slept for a couple days. I got up and I felt better and I remember going back up to college and telling my parents,

"Never mind. I'm fine. It's going to be okay."

I went back up and went back right to my old lifestyle. Then the years went on and things got worse and worse and I was going in and out of jail and overdosing and going to hospitals. There was a night that I overdosed and got woken up by the paramedics with Narcan, or whatever, and went into the hospital. I remember getting out of the hospital that night going back over to the same house I was at and using again. So, it was like the rock bottom was really hard to grasp because I was aware for a long time that I needed treatment and that's why I went and got treatment multiple times. Thank God this last trip was my last trip to treatment and it stuck but it's tough.

MEGAN MORRISON

"My music has also helped me stay sober. Writing songs is how I express a lot of emotion."
– Megan Morrison

Bio: Megan Morrison is an American singer, songwriter, actress, and model. She performed initially in musical theater, appearing in high school and college plays, and studied vocal performance at the University of Massachusetts and Hunter College before dropping out to pursue a musical Career. Her debut album *Late Bloomer* with her band Dorothy's Surrender was a success in the underground rock market. The band received recognition for their single and music video *Dirty Stayout*. Megan is currently working on her solo career with a single release coming in the near future. She is also fronting her new band Revlover, who released their debut single *The Legend of Johnny Brown* last fall and are working to complete an album. Megan is also a professional fire performer and can be seen dancing in music videos with Pitbull and Elvis Crespo as well as on stage with Jessie J. www.meganmorrisonmusic.com

Occupation: Singer/Songwriter, Model, Fire Performer, Actor

Drug of choice: Alcohol

Length of sobriety: 2 years, 7 months (Sober date: 9/6/15)

DB: What do you do on a daily basis to maintain your sobriety, and what is the most challenging part about it?

MM: I try to stay as grounded as I can. When I am connected to myself and my surroundings, I can live a more peaceful life. When I am in touch with my feelings and emotions, I have a better grasp on reality and how to deal with life. I try to meditate every day, even if it's only brief. I do a lot of deep breathing, not even so much consciously anymore. I've learned that what happens around me is out of my control . . . it's how I react that makes a difference in my well-being. I'm able to deal with situations at ease now that would have given me a lot of anxiety before. I will always have anxiety, I know this about myself. The difference now that I'm sober is that I can recognize when it's starting and I can stop it using the tools that I've learned in recovery. Stressful situations are just a part of life, but I've learned there is a better way to deal with them than drinking. Drinking may temporarily relieve stress, but it never makes the problem go away. It only makes it worse.

Another thing that helps me stay sober is helping others who are struggling with addiction. I speak at meetings and sponsor women who are following in my footsteps. I want to help them see that there is a better way to live and that they have something to live for. I attend meetings every week to listen to speakers who share my same journey in sobriety. There are so many of us and it's so important to connect with others that share the same disease. My music has also helped me stay sober. Writing songs is how I express a lot of emotion. Having a passion gives me something to put my energy towards. Even though the music industry can be very stressful, making music is what truly makes me happy. Every day it pushes me to open my mind and be creative. It is my outlet for everything. I don't have any struggle with wanting to drink again, but some days life seems like too much to handle. Those are the days when I have to be extra good to myself. I don't mean go to the spa or buy myself something nice. I mean take extra deep breaths, exercise, make sure I eat well and enough, drink lots of water, take a walk, read a book, don't put too much pressure on myself to finish everything on my to-do list . . . because there is always tomorrow.

DB: How have you reconnected with your body since being in recovery, and what are some things you include in your daily life to increase your health and vitality?

MM: My body thanks me on a daily basis in sobriety. I mistreated it for years and I'm amazed how good it is to me after all of that. I was really sick towards the end of my drinking career. My liver was starting to fail on me and rightfully so. I was in and out of the hospital and I still couldn't stop drinking. This disease is a powerful thing. I didn't want to die, but I just couldn't stop. All of the things I mentioned above are included in my daily ritual. If I'm not feeling well or feeling uneasy I stop and think, "Have I drank enough water? Have I eaten enough? Do I need more vegetables today?" It's so simple but it's something I never did before. I was only concerned about when I was having my next drink and what it was going to be. I try to do some kind of exercise every day, whether it's yoga, going for a run, swim, or working out, as long as I do something.

I'm able to listen to my body much clearer now without alcohol being in the way. I know when something's not right and instead of just pushing through, I try to figure out what is making me feel bad.

DB: How have your relationships changed (types of people, length/meaning of relationships, etc.) from when you were actively using to being in recovery?

MM: My relationships with close friends and family, especially my husband, have gotten so much stronger. I've been able to get a lot more honest with people and I've learned that it's ok to be vulnerable. I think because I've showed people this side of me they've been able to do the same thing. A healthy relationship is all about honesty and feeling comfortable with who you are. A lot of people I considered my "friends" really dropped off the map after I stopped drinking. I realize now that drinking was possibly the only thing we had in common. I've also learned to keep negative people at a distance. We can't always choose who we have in our lives but we do have the choice to keep their negative energy at an arm's length away. I no longer invite these types of people into my life. It's amazing when you start putting out positive energy you start getting it back in return. Some incredible people have come into my life in sobriety!

DB: Who are the top three to five people you surround yourself with and why are they influential in your recovery?

MM: My husband. He motivates me every day to be a better person. We have built an amazing life together. In the last three years since I've been sober, our life has become so incredible I am grateful every day for it. We have both grown together in a beautiful way. My mom. She has been my supporter through all of this and has always believed in me. She went through it once already with my dad so I am motivated to never have her go through it again. Not only is my mom my creator but she's also my best friend. She's seen me through a lot over the years and never loved me any less. I only want to give her the same love in return. My sponsor. She is someone who has been through it all before and there is nothing I can't tell her. We are able to laugh about things that most people wouldn't find funny. I trust her and truly value her as not only a mentor but a true friend. She's been there for me when I need her the most.

My sober woman friends. It is so important to stay close to other women in sobriety. We support each other and lift each other up in times of need. Friends that have stood by me through it all. My friends that weren't scared off by my troubles and me getting sober I really value. They knew the real me and stuck by me though everything. Our friendships have only blossomed since then.

DB: What is your spiritual life like and what do you do on a daily basis to integrate it into your life, and why do you think spirituality is important for growth and sustainability in recovery?

MM: Spirituality is so important in recovery because you need to understand that most of what happens in life is out of your hands. When you can accept this, you can truly live a happier more peaceful life. To say there is not a power greater than yourself puts a lot of pressure on oneself. To be able to let things go and realize you are out of control is when you can really start to focus on what's important in your life.

I personally am very spiritual. I know that this universe is too amazing not to have some greater force out there. I am not religious, but I do pray to a god of my understanding every day. Praying has become something different to me. I try not to pray for certain things. I've realized if there is a god, it is not Santa Claus. I try to pray for other people more than myself. I usually just say general prayers for the well-being of people I know and the planet. Of course there are some prayers that are about things I want in my life. But instead of praying "please make this happen" I try to pray for strength, courage, and wisdom to help me achieve what I am praying about.

I've made dedicated spaces to pray and meditate in my home. Peaceful places where I can really feel connected to god and the universe. I look forward to taking a few minutes to sit, breathe, and pray in these places every day.

DB: What was one situation you found yourself in that confirmed in your mind that you must seek treatment and recovery and why?

MM: The situation where I knew I needed help happened five years before I actually got sober. I was in my apartment in Miami Beach alone, my boyfriend (husband now) was traveling for work.

I finally got the call that I had been waiting on for years. My dad was dying. He struggled with alcoholism most of his adult life. He had gotten very sick years before because of liver failure, but had a very strong will to live. Unfortunately, he was never able to seek the help that saved my life and ended up with cirrhosis of his liver. At this point there was nothing else they could do. As I sat on the floor of my apartment sobbing, phone calls went back and forth with my family up in Maine. I felt like a giant stake was being stabbed through my heart. On the last phone call my family held the phone up to my dad's ear and I told him I loved him and said goodbye. I could barely catch my breath through the agonizing fear and stream of tears. So, I dealt with this the only way I knew how. I drank and drank and drank until I passed out. I probably went through ten bottles of wine that night. I remember at one point thinking, ok, this is my warning sign. I thought to myself I will stop soon, I have to stop, I don't want to end up like him. But eventually that possibility seemed like a distant not so probable future. I maintained my drinking for a few years, but after that it started to go downhill. Fast forward five years and I'm in the hospital with the beginning stages of the same thing that killed my dad, and I'm powerless. I can't stop it on my own. I knew I needed help back then, but I was too scared to acknowledge it. Not just too ashamed to admit it, but too afraid to live a life without the comfort alcohol gave me. I didn't think it was possible. But it is . . . and it's so much more. Here I sit almost eight years after my dad's passing, still crying with these memories, but I am peaceful and happy, and it's not because of alcohol. It's because I've discovered who I am and how to live the life I want without it. I am grateful recovering alcoholic and if my story can help just one person I'll have done my part.

ALISON HAASE

"I'm challenged because I keep thinking I've arrived and God humbles me immediately."
– Alison Haase

Bio: Alison Haase is a functional amateur athlete, business woman, and constant seeker of personal development and growth. Getting sober at 18 has afforded her infinite opportunities in life, be it professional as a successful business owner or sales person, athletic pursuits in competitive bodybuilding, and now obstacle-course racing and running, and being a walking example of how abundant life can really be when lived well and without substance. Alison finds tremendous joy in helping others, using her experience to benefit their distrust that life really is an amazing adventure worth living.

Occupation: Business Executive

Drug of choice: Heroin and ecstasy

Length of sobriety: 15 years

DB: What do you do to stay sober on a daily basis and what's the most challenging part about it?

AH: Well, my morning always starts with rolling right out of bed right onto my knees and asking God to help me with myself and free me from the bondage of self. It sounds very cliché but it's true. The first thing I think about when I wake up is me. And I'm the only thing that's ever gotten in my way so I ask God to relieve me of that.

I read a daily affirmation to get my mind right. I train in the morning. I go to the gym most of the time unless I'm too tired. I walk my dog. I eat a healthy breakfast. I go to work, talk to sober people on my way and call my sponsor. Again, just trying to inject myself with positivity and the right mindset so that I can be of service to others probably because I think ultimately that's why we're here, to be of maximum usefulness.

I work. I try to go to a meeting every day. I'm blessed to belong to more than one fellowship so I have three to bounce between but I'd say I probably go to five to seven meetings a week. I talk to a lot of people that are sober during the day, whether it's people that help me or that I help and sponsor but I have a network of people that I'm in touch with. I pray a lot. It's more of a continuous conversation as opposed to a set ritual at certain times.

I eat really well so I feel really well. I don't go around shit that I'm not supposed to go around. And people that I'm not supposed to go around, whatever that means. I read. I write. And that's just kind of become part of who I am.

I'm challenged because I keep thinking I've arrived and God humbles me immediately. Like my ego is the biggest part of me and that's the biggest part of the disease. For me it's that balance. It's a constant ebb and flow. The pendulum's always swinging and I'm trying to get it to swing less drastically. And I've struggled with eating disorders and body image my entire life and it really plagued me through most of my recovery from alcoholism and drug addiction.

Because that for me was easy. It was cut and dry. If I didn't want to be around it, I didn't have to be around it. It's not a requirement for living. Whereas food, it's a requirement for living. You need to eat several times a day should you choose to do that. You have a body. It's not negotiable. And so getting out of my way and being of service to others is my greatest challenge.

I love being of service but getting out of the way so I can be present for others has been hard because I'm all I think about. And my body is all I've thought about and what it looks like. And it's a mind-fuck. I mean it, really. And being honest about it. Like calling people and sharing where I'm at and learning to just pick up the phone until it goes away and just listen to other people.

DB: How have you reconnected with your body since being in recovery and what are some of the things you do daily to increase your health and vitality?

AH: Well, I've learned that I have one right. It was like this separate entity for me for so long. I had no connection. I didn't appreciate it as a living organism. I really believe that it has been gifted to me to experience this life. It's my vehicle through this journey. It's how I physically feel, see, hear, touch, smell and it's my job I think to take the best care of it. And it's my house.

It houses my soul. It houses my heart and it's my job to keep it as well as possible. As somebody that does have trouble with body image and an eating disorder it's even more important that I put first things first. I don't eat certain things that I know don't work for me whether it's a mental or a physical thing. I can't be the judge of that. I'm crazy left to my own devices on that topic. So, I move every day in some capacity.

I work harder than others but I derive a lot of empowerment from lifting and being strong as a woman. It gives me a lot of purpose. I got into obstacle course racing because there's something really validating about that and satisfying. And for me I learned where to find God in nature. You know, when I was out . . . I believe in the fundamental energy that we're all guided by and I found that outside through movement.

Meditation hasn't been a quiet thing for me. It's been an active thing for me and a pursuit in seeking through that kind of movement. So, you know every day I eat really well. I drink a lot of water. I try not to drink coffee after noon. Like all those things we're like "Oh you take such good care of yourself" is a discipline. And ultimately feel connected and more present for people when I'm not polluting myself with additional substance.

DB: How have your relationships transformed from being in active addition and now being in recovery? And who are some of the top people you hang out with and why are they influential in your life?

AH: I'm laughing because I told you my story the other day and it's like I slid down further in the relationship category sober because I was so young getting sober at 18. I feel like I was a kid and I wasn't ready to be well yet or something and so I had to attract really low people. And I think a challenge for me has been getting sober so young I learned to love anonymously. And that's amazing. Allow your heart to speak to you, connect with other people energetically, then go from there.

But I took it very literally, oh like fuck it, you gave me a hug. Good enough. Come on home. You know what I mean? And that just isn't a good barometer for the character of people. And so, as I've worked on myself and gotten closer to God, I've found that the people around me are getting better in that they're succeeding in their life whether it's financially, whether it's physically, whether it's spiritually. And the people closest to me are women.

That was not the case. I had a lot of guys in my life but my closest core group are women and they hold space for me. And most of them are sober. Not all of them but most of them because it's just a different language and it's an automatic communion that you share with another person when you've been through that and you can relate it. And it's like an unspoken understanding. And that's why I love 12-Step recovery because it's a group of people in that same energy.

But women that hold space for me and don't try and fix it. I call and I'm struggling and they listen. "How can I help?" Not "I think you should do this." They hold up the mirror. They may tell me things I don't want to hear but because they care about me. They want me to get better and I do the same for them.

DB: What is your spiritual life like and why do you think spirituality is important for sustainability and growth in recovery?

AH: Oh, it's the answer. Like for me, and I denied that, and I struggled in recovery for so long because I wanted to be God. I couldn't have articulated that at the time but I was really hell-bent on being the answer, being independent, being self-sufficient, and figuring out myself. And I just kept getting hurt and abusing myself for lack of a better word.

And so, until I admitted defeat, like I can't do this alone, something beyond me can. And what happened for me is I watched other people get better and I borrowed their experience until I had my own. And I still do that. Like I go through situations that I don't have experience with but somebody else does. And I think that's the power of what you're doing and sharing it because if somebody else didn't share their story somebody else wouldn't know that they could get through that.

And that's the power. And being vulnerable and sharing weakness is half weakness. So, what do I do? I said I roll out onto my knees in the morning. I read a spiritually-aligned book. I pray constantly... constantly. I recently have gone back to church although the jury is definitely out on that.

But my fundamental belief is that there is an ever-loving guiding energy between all of us in this world and it is aligning all of us for our best version of ourselves with the choice of becoming that or not. And for me the third step is about having a relationship with that greater being or whatever energy. And understanding that that presence cares for me. And I think that was the turning point when I realized that this thing, this energy cares for me. It was like, I'm worth caring for. And that really changed the game for me.

DB: What was the one tell-tale moment that confirmed in your mind that you must seek treatment or recovery or both and why?

AH: I have a disappointing entry into sobriety because I really didn't have anything crazy happen. I've never been arrested. I've never been to jail. I never went to rehab. I was threatened to lose the horses and I was like, all right, game over. But, I will say in recovery I have hit way more painful bottoms than not. And it all was through food and body and men. You know, that constant external seeking was very "vanilla," for lack of a better word.

And I don't want to paint a picture that other people can't, like you need this crazy story to get well. If you want to get well, get well. But, I guess I needed some more pain sober and so what comes to mind are a few things. One was hitting my head and getting another concussion sober and almost losing the ability to talk and function. And that's when my bulimia really came back and it forced me back into AA, so that was a blessing.

But I was driving 20-mile radiuses from store to store as a sober woman so . . . that people wouldn't see all the food that I was getting and then I was throwing it all up and clogging pipes. It was pretty horrifying. I did that for a long time. And then another was coming out of a relationship with a heroin addict that I met sober. He was sober and then he relapsed and for the first time in my life I realized how strong love is and how heartbreaking it is when your love isn't enough to save another addict.

And I had a very up close and personal account for how it works. Some of us are constitutionally incapable of getting honest with ourselves and that was that man. And I've had a series of other bottoms sober and I think it's all necessary to bring us closer to God.

KYLE WHALUM

"You know, the gratitude thing is huge. I think a lot of people don't realize that gratitude is a muscle that you have to work out like any other muscles."
– Kyle Whalum

Bio: Kyle Whalum spent his childhood in Los Angeles before moving to Nashville, TN where he would go on to pursue music, inspired and championed by his Grammy winning father Kirk Whalum, an acclaimed Jazz saxophonist. He started touring professionally at the age of 17 while studying music at Belmont University. He has performed with such diverse talents as LeAnn Rimes, Steven Tyler, Kelly Clarkson, Zac Brown, and Brett Eldredge. Hoping to shave a little weight for stage, he began running at the age of 24, after recovering from a traumatic ankle injury and has continued to run ever since. Kyle—age 35 at the time of this writing—has competed in distances from the 5k to the 100-mile ultramarathon. He has completed 12 ultras, including 300-milers, and is in training for his fourth 100-mile attempt.

Occupation: Bassist for major pop star/icon

Drug of choice: Alcohol

Length of sobriety: 5 years from active addiction, still use in moderation

DB: What do you do to stay sober on a daily basis and what's the most challenging part about it?

KW: Yeah. So, on a daily basis, for the most part for me is really important, someone that's more in the moderation type of lifestyle that's I don't drink in the day or in the morning for the most part. Like there are days where we'll have an off day or I've finished a very long run and like a noon beer is okay with me. But for the most part nine days out of 10 I don't partake in anything until it's the evening or whatever. That's big for me. That's just my own personal approach. Because again, for me, I'm trying to live moderately. Like I do enjoy having some beer or whatever. But it's important to me that I'm never intoxicated. That's a huge, huge thing for me because I used to be intoxicated on a daily basis.

So, that's one kind of technique I use. Another one is . . . the active lifestyle is really important for me. I get more of a thrill from being outside, or pushing my body, or going up a mountain than I do from previously when I used to get drunk, I didn't exercise at all. All I had was going to the bar and chasing girls and getting drunk, and I get more of a thrill from the opposite side of the coin now. So, I need to make sure every day, which this kind of falls into the spiritual side, but I need to make sure every day I'm doing something that elevates me. Because a lot of times that's through physical activity, through running. And sometimes for me it can even be work challenges, just really trying to rise and be better at what I do. That can be family. That can be waking up and trying to go the extra mile with my daughter or for my wife.

So those things thrill my brain in a way that formally when I was living more of the active addiction that's all I had. I didn't have those other avenues to channel that energy through.

DB: Now how have you reconnected with your body since being in recovery and what are some things you do to increase your health and vitality?

KW: Number one for me is running. I got into running actually in active addiction, so I was a running alcoholic, which is kind of funny to me. And I'm not the only one by the way. There's a lot of runners that drink too much and probably some that are on the spectrum. But yeah. I got into running and you know I remember I signed up for my first ultra-marathon, and there's a long story to get there. It started with, I started to jog for fitness trying to get my weight down. And then kind of learning I kind of like it, and then signing up for a 5K. I'd run a 5K almost every day. I could smoke this thing, you know? Then being humbled by that because it was harder than I thought. Then down the line I'd do a half marathon, I did a full marathon. I did several of those.

And then I read a book called Born to Run talking about ultra-marathons, and how a lot of us think 26.2 is the physical limit of endurance, and that there's a whole communities and cultures throughout history that have run much further than that and lived healthy lives and lived to tell about it. So, I was fascinated by that whole thing. And right around the time I got sober actually I ran a 50K, which is a 31-mile mountain trail race. I remember finishing that race and thinking to myself, "God. I don't even feel like I need or want to drink." That was such a thrill for me, you know? Like I could live this kind of life. I could be a sober guy who's active and I don't think I would really look back.

And it wasn't too long after that race that I actually went to treatment. So, things did kind of spiral back down off that high. You know, actually in treatment and after treatment running was a huge part of me reconfiguring and rewiring my brain, my spirit, my body. It gave me something productive to do every day that I can feel good about. So yeah. To this day running is still my main physical method of mitigating some of my symptoms of this kind of ailment, you know, that is addiction. So yeah, running's huge.

You know, not everybody can run. Not everybody has two legs even. So, I can't go ahead and say that running is a cure for addiction, but there's other ways to do it, you know? If I'm injured and I can't run I'll practice yoga, I'll get more into my meditation, do push-ups, you know whatever it is, calisthenics, or start lifting weights, or hiking, rafting, anything that gets me outside in nature and moving my body makes me feel good, and it tends to be better for the overall picture as far as symptoms.

DB: How have your relationships changed from being in active addiction to being in recovery? And who are the top three to five people you surround yourself with and why?

KW: Yeah, man that's a great one. First and foremost is my family. You know I didn't have a family when I was really drinking, alcoholically. You look back on it and you kind of see why. I wasn't living in a way that was conducive to being a partner. And I was also surrounded by people who drank just as much as I did, so nothing was weird about that. I think that's probably a common theme.

So, when I got sober, that's when my wife and I got married. We had been friends and lovers previously for the past 15 years before that. And when I got sober and was really clear-headed was when it dawned on me that she was the love of my life. And she stuck with me through that whole process too, when you get such a weird transition, change everything. But really for a while it was just me and her. And I had to figure out who my new friends would be. Because of the running and stuff I started really being attracted to people that led more of an active lifestyle. For a lot of them, drinks . . . take it or leave it. Or if they did drink, it was way more moderately than I used to. The run was the focus, you know? So, between my family and just finding friends in the active community that really were just living a more healthy lifestyle, as cliché as that sounds, that helped a lot.

And then even professionally, I started saying no to gigs as a musician that were heavy drinking gigs. Party gigs. I've done that before, and I don't want to be on a bus with people who are abusing alcohol and drugs every night. So, I'm really lucky that I'm where

I am in my career right now because I have a pretty healthy crew. It would be kind of frowned on to be really drunk. You know what I mean? Like over the top wouldn't really go down well in this crew. And so that's also a really healthy place for me to be. Everybody has a positive attitude, and a lot of the guys in the group and the band are spiritual. And so that helps as well. It's that whole cliché thing about surrounding yourself with positive people.

DB: Absolutely. Now what do you do for spirituality? How do you integrate it into your day and why do you think spirituality is important for sustainability and growth and recovery?

KW: Oh yeah. Okay cool. So, for me, I hate to put everything back on running, but you know being outside and using my body is kind of a way I tap into it. I always consider it like a prayer. So, like that's my way of getting out and sort of worshiping whoever made all this, whoever saw to put me here in this great job with this wonderful family, with a healthy body. You know the best way you can celebrate that I think or worship is to go out and use it. So, for me, the running itself is an act of prayer and I rarely run with headphones, especially if I'm in the trails or on a mountain or anything. That's all I need. I don't need any other distraction.

Another component spiritually for me is just mindfulness. I really try to be mindful of how I'm spending my time. I practice a lot of gratitude, which is something I did . . . that has stuck with me. And that is not a negative thing, you know? So, I don't want paint . . . It's had mostly a positive effect on me. I don't think I wanted to stay there forever, but I learned a lot of real useful nuggets in there that I've been able to kind of maintain.

You know the gratitude thing is huge. I think a lot of people don't realize that gratitude is a muscle that you have to work out like any other muscles. And a lot of times you're not going to feel like doing it. So, like when you need to be grateful the most, say like somethings gone bad and you need a perspective on really how good you do have it, that's when it's the hardest to practice gratitude. So, that's a part of my mindfulness is just waking up and literally practicing and having to be very purposeful about thinking about the things throughout the day I'm grateful for, helps me keep a positive attitude at work. Where things get shitty on a run, it helps me think about the big picture, like the fact that I have all my limbs, and I don't have ALS, or you know, I'm not hungover drunk right now laying on my couch and can't get off the couch. So that's a big part of it.

Meditation's been huge for me. I wish I could claim to whoever's going to read this, that I'm an avid meditator and that I do it every single day. But it tends to come in seasons. Usually after my focus race I'm able to dedicate a little more time in the morning to at least get in 10 minutes of actual sitting and actual . . . like a mindfulness meditation. So, those are big for me.

And I would say probably the fourth component of my spiritual practice is really mountains. I just don't know, sometimes selfishly how other people don't get it. If you can go to a mountain and sit there for a second and pray at the peak, for me that's something I have to do. The mountains, the ultra-running, I run a 100 miler every year. And for me I tend to do them around big events in my life. So, like the first one I ran was . . . I was about to get married. So, I got married two weeks after my first 100 miler, and I found that as a really useful way to pray and process and wrap my head around the whole event, right? Because you have 24 to 30 hours out there in the woods, on the mountains, and the trail basically alone to ponder, right?

And then I ran my second one right as my first child was about to be due. So, I prayed about her a lot. And still think about all that, how I was praying so vigorously out there on the trail for this baby that's now my daughter and that I know very well. For my third 100 I had just gotten the job with a well-known pop band and I was very nervous about that. And that was a big step up in my life and I knew probably a game changer for me and my family.

So, I was able to have this 100 mile race where I could process all of it and come in ready to work. And so now I'm training for my fourth 100 in November [2018], and I'm due for the birth of my son in early January [2019]. So, it's a way for me to kind of pray about that.

So, I would say those are my four kind-of blatant spiritual practices. I'm not much of a church goer and I don't really have a hard, traditional religion that I follow.

DB: Perfect. Now what was the one moment that you found yourself in and confirmed in your mind you had to seek treatment and recovery and why?

KW: So, and this is what I love about recovery folks, this is why I wanted to take the interview with you and chat with you is just because we can get real. So, what my reality looked like when I went to treatment was I had grown up in a party environment, like college years were, I tended to kind of gravitate towards the people that were just cheery, and drinking all the time, and still got up and nailed their shit. Romantically, that was who I wanted to be was the party animal that can still like nail it. And years and years and years after this lifestyle I kept going. I was starting to not nail it anymore. I was gaining weight. I was having hangovers so severe . . . I would have panic attacks and have to go to the hospital, or I'd have to isolate for two days to recover, or two or three days really be back on my feet.

I identify as a hard-up addict, not necessarily any particular discipline. So, for me, I was having a lot of unprotected sex, and I was being really sexually reckless. Hooking up with friends, hooking up with good friends' ex-girlfriends, you know? A lot of one-night stands when I was on the road and back home. I hit personal rock bottom was I'd just wrecked my car. And you know rock bottom is kind of a cliché, so take that or leave it. But for me, when I'd had enough was I'd just had a car wreck that was totally preventable. I was texting on the way back from the bar.

I still maintain that I don't feel like I was that drunk. I've been a lot drunker than that. I didn't think I was particularly tipsy that night, but the fact that I was texting kind of lets me know that I just was probably not firing on all cylinders.

So, I ran head-first into a light post and totally banged my car up and I was able to kind of shoddily drive it home. It was clanging and banging and making all this noise. It was hard to drive it straight. I knew I had like cracked an axle or something. Get my car home and what else do I do? Of course, I keep drinking. Like that's what I did at that point. It's like, "Oh this sucks. I'm going to have a few more beers and go to bed." I wake up the next day, my car doesn't work. I need to be at a job. This is before Uber. I'm having to do taxis, and having to ride my bike, get rides with friends.

And meanwhile this whole week I was experiencing the worst hangovers and the most consistent . . . I was starting to drink in the morning to just kind of cover the hangovers up so I'd have Irish coffee. I would pepper drinks throughout the day. And it started to be by the time 6:00 p.m. rolled in, it was really time that most people would start having drinks, I was already tipsy and that would end up in a blackout that night. I was getting drug home from the bar a lot. I was waking up the next day hungover, with a bottle of whiskey by my bed and calling girls over to kind of numb the . . . I knew something was going on that was really odd and not healthy and I was scared. But I was medicating with my girls and you know . . . when I look back on it, it was sort of a head. It was like a month, I think it was vaguely a month-long kind of bender that pretty much I think ended, chopped the chapter off that came before the period I'm in now. It's like the end of that way of life for me.

There's one particular morning where the day before I'd laid in bed all day and I'd had sex with four different girls unprotected, and I was drinking all day, and I woke up the next morning, started to drink again. I just kind of broke down and called my parents and just told them. I was worried. I felt, I guess you would call it suicidal. I felt like I didn't want to live the way I was living, but I didn't know how to not do that. So, it kind of felt like I just didn't want to live. And I called a buddy that I knew had been sober for like six, seven years. And I was like, "Man. I don't know if it's forever." I remember saying this to him. "I don't know if it's forever, but I need to get sober like right now. And I need to really take a hard look at this and I'm willing to go to treatment if you can get me in." He was able to get me a bed in Nashville at a place. I did the whole month-long treatment. And I did go to AA meetings for the first year. And the second year I was kind of off on my own. But it all helped me. I can't knock anything that happened the way it happened.

SARAH ROBERTS

"And so, for me, I don't have a choice when it comes to my nutrition. I prioritize it the way you've got to put gas in your car. It's as simple as that for me. And moving my body is a non-negotiable as well."
– Sarah Roberts

Bio: Sarah Roberts battled alcohol addiction for over a decade and got sober at the age of 29. She went on a personal journey towards wellness and now shares what she's learned with others in order to help them create a lifestyle they love. She is a wellness entrepreneur and the host of her television talk show, *REALTalk With Sarah*. She is also the founder of the sobriety podcast, *Sobriety Starts HERE*, the author of *The 28 Day Kick The Sugar Challenge* and the founder of the popular blog SarahTalksFood.com. To connect with Sarah, find her on Facebook, Instagram and Twitter @SarahTalksFood or send an e-mail to Sarah@SarahTalksFood.com.

Occupation: TV Show Host, Wellness Entrepreneur, Author, Blogger

Drug of choice: Alcohol

Length of sobriety: 16 years

DB: What do you do on a daily basis to maintain your sobriety? And what's the most challenging part about it, if anything?

SR: I mean for me it's all about just taking care of my body and taking care of my mind. So, for me, I start every morning, I like to think I have this amazing morning practice and I know that it's so awesome when I do my morning practice, but I don't always get to it.

I think the most challenging thing of all of it, is trying to get everything in that we want to get in. And sometimes I do and sometimes I don't. And so I think the other challenging thing is just having some self-compassion and understanding that not every day is going to be perfect, and that's okay.

Every day I wake up, I say, "Thank you." It's a small little prayer that I say as soon as my eyes open. I learned it from Oprah, and I took it. I heard her say it about 15–20 years ago and I've been doing it ever since. I love opening my eyes and just having some gratitude for the fact that I'm here, and that I'm alive and that I have this opportunity and a new day to serve.

I wake up, and I immediately drink lemon water. It's a huge part of my morning. It's the first thing I do, is hydrate. I do that, about a tablespoon of lemon, usually about a half to a whole lemon and that in warm water. I sip on that and I make myself my morning smoothie. I'm very much into whole foods. I don't do the supplement thing. For me, it's just packing a smoothie full of as much nutrition as I can get into my body first thing in the morning. Then, I sort of let that digest a little bit, and then I do my work out of the day. Usually, lately, because things are so crazy, my workouts have been Tabatas just because they're fast. And I just don't have the time. Yesterday, I hit the gym and I was able to do a longer workout. I think that's another, you know, that's kind of the hardest part, like when you're busy, what do you choose to keep and what do you choose to leave?

And so, for me, I don't have a choice when it comes to my nutrition. I prioritize it the way you've got to put gas in your car. It's as simple as that for me. And moving my body is a non-negotiable as well. Like you were saying earlier about the antidepressant and the overused drug of choice, I choose to put in really good food so that I can crowd out the temptation for the other kind of food that's out there that I won't even call food. But, that's kind of the way that I set it up for my day.

DB: How have you reconnected with your body since being in recovery, and what are some things you include in your daily life to increase your health and vitality?

SR: Meditation. I love the Insight Timer App. Sarah Blondin is one of my favorites. Definitely taking some time to just get quiet. But, I also don't always have that time to sit down and do a 20-minute guided meditation, or even just a quiet meditation on my own. And that's okay. I find too many people are putting pressure on us to, "You got to have the accoutrements, you have to have the altar, you got to lay down on pillows, and you have to have the music, and the incense." No. I mean, if I'm waiting for a coffee in line, I will just sort of quietly zone out and focus on my breath and just take a minute to just be in the moment.

I think that's really one of the biggest lessons that sobriety's given me, is realizing, and I'm not somebody who did AA at all, but that concept of one day at a time, for me it's one moment at a time sometimes. You know, if we're just stressed and something's not going the way we want, just taking that minute to reconnect with my breath and just take some deep long slow breaths and remind myself that right here, right now, all is well, I am safe, I'm okay, and that this too shall pass. You know, whatever it is that I'm going through.

That's kind of like my daily meditation that I do regularly. If I'm in a scary situation, where I'm about to go on TV, if I'm about to be interviewed by somebody, or if I'm about to go and speak in front of 500 people, I often will do that. I just get recentered with my breath, and that really, really helps me.

Reconnecting with my body, first and foremost, and I'll just keep saying, it's going to get boring for you, but not using my body like a trash can. I certainly did for many, many years. I smoked cigarettes, I took drugs, I drank alcohol, and I ate food. You know, I would eat pizza at 2 a.m. I mean, that happened. That was something that was part of it.

I really did not care about my health at all. I really treated my body like a trash can. I allowed people into my body that should not have been there. I allowed thoughts into my body that should not have been there. I surrounded myself with people that were not people that were uplifting to me. They were also heavily in addiction, I just couldn't see that. For me, it was just surrounding myself with other people who weren't going to judge my drinking behavior.

So, definitely reconnecting with my body through food and through movement, through mindfulness, meditation, yoga, and just really serving others. Really connecting with other people.

Especially since I started my blog in 2015. Prior to that, I was so rife with shame that I could not tell anybody the truth, and what I've learned since coming out publicly is that I can only serve in a bigger way if I'm willing to take the mask off and say, "Here I am, this is the truth about me," and just to live more authentically.

And I find what is beautiful about that is that other people feel like, "Maybe I can do that too. She's done it, maybe I can share." And I'm seeing so much inspiration on the internet and just in my social circles and connections where it's like people are finally saying, "You know what, I'm scared but I'm going to let people know that this is the truth of my life." Because we're seeing so much gray-area drinking. As we know, alcohol use disorder is on a spectrum. And so many of us have that preconceived vision of what an alcoholic is or what a drug addict is. And they have to have lost everything, they're on the side of the street, they don't have a car, don't have a home, have no relationships. And it's like, "No, they're the doctors, the lawyers, the CEOs of companies. They're the entrepreneurs, the people doing the grind like everybody else. They've got kids in mini-vans. And everybody's drinking and everybody's doing drugs." I mean prescription drug use is getting out of control.

And, so I just think, "There, but for the grace of God, go I." I mean, I'm no better than anybody that has to hit a rock bottom like I'm describing, like the people on the street, but that is not the only way to have to finally feel like "turn a corner or die." That's just not the way it is. I'm glad many people are starting to wake up and realize that, I don't have to lose everything to realize that alcohol's just not serving me, or drugs are just not serving me anymore.

DB: How have your relationships changed since being in recovery? Who would you say are the top three to five people you surround yourself with and why are they influential in your recovery?

SR: So, my relationships have changed in every way. So, first off, the people I am in a relationship with have changed. Instead of having drinking buddies and people that weren't even necessarily friends, they were really people that I was relying on to be around me because I could gauge my drinking behavior against theirs, and judge whether or not I was in the middle, below, or above them . . . those relationships have fallen away. I just no longer have those relationships anymore at all. The ones that I have now cultivated are just beautiful, authentic, genuine relationships. So many people in the recovery space that I'm now connected with. That I feel like I can truly be my real, genuine, authentic self with. I can share with them my rock bottom, we can hear each other's awful stories, and yet that other person is never ever going to say like, "Oh my God, you did what?" Like, it just never happens. Even as bad as we think our story is.

And that's what I love about the website Sobriety Starts Here, that my partner and I started, where we have these amazing conversations with people. And it's like . . . sure it might be jaw dropping for a moment like, "Oh my God!" But, then it's just like, "Oh my God, you went through that, and then you came through that." And that's what's just so incredible.

So, for me, my relationships have just evolved and grown and changed into really wanting to get to the meat of the person. I'm sick and tired of superficiality, of always staying on the surface, being really fake and just really being vapid. I'm done. If you want to talk about weather and who won the game, I get it. That's fine for the elevator. But, if you're going to be in my sphere, you're going to be somebody who goes deep. And we're going to talk about real shit. And we're going to get really into shame and grief and loss, and authenticity, and all of that messy, dirty stuff that we often don't want to bring up like mental illness, and mental health, and how we're feeling about ourselves, and all of that. Those are the kinds of relationships that I now cultivate, and I cannot live without. They're amazing.

Top three to five influential people in my life. From a personal perspective, my partner Roger Deveau is the love of my life. He is amazing, and he has supported me throughout my entire recovery since he's met me, and I've supported him. He got sober when he met me, and we've been in relationship since. It's been amazing. I spend a lot of time with Roger. We work together, we live together. We do business together. He is by far number one.

I've got some great close friends, specifically one who is, she's a healer and an intuitive. She's a beautiful friend who loves me and supports me exactly as I am and is never looking to change me. I absolutely love her. Then other friends like that as well.

Mostly, the people I surround myself with are people in recovery, or they are people who I coach in my program. I'm surrounded by amazing (mostly) women who struggle with either alcohol addiction, very little drug addiction, but some. I do coach some people with drug addiction as well. All of those people have sugar addictions, or just issues with food, weight, and body image. Those are the clients that I coach. I definitely surround myself with those kinds of people because I love nothing more than to serve others and to help share how I have been able to be 16 years in a lifestyle that I don't need to escape from. I want to teach other people to have that same kind of freedom.

DB: What is your spiritual life like, and what do you do on a daily basis to integrate it into your life. Why do you think spirituality is important for growth and sustainability in recovery?

SR: I believe that we are spiritual beings having a human experience. Whether or not people believe or not, that's entirely up to them. We're all allowed to believe whatever we want to believe. For me, for sure, connecting with my deeper self, my true self, my higher self, it's been instrumental. I can't even imagine how. I really can't, and this can be off the record or on the record. I mean it like I really don't know how atheists or people that really believe that we literally die, and that's it, and it's over, I really don't know how they have the same level of joy as people who know that there is more out there. For me, it's just the truth of what I believe so deeply in my soul.

Death is the evolution of our soul. It's not the end of anything. It's the end of a physical presence, but it's not the end. I truly believe that. For me to be able to connect with my loved ones that have passed on, I do that regularly . . . as woo woo as that might sound. I rely on them. I lean on them for support. In fact, it's going to sound crazy, but my maternal grandmother came through in a session that I had with one of my healers. She is the one that was asking when am I going back on TV? I was like, "What is she talking about?" I finally kept listening and listening. My healer just kept saying, "Your Nana is back." She keeps saying, "You better get on TV, and she's pissed off that you're not doing it."

I'm like, "What is she talking about?" I've been on TV, but I don't have a TV show. This woman, my healer, said to me, "Apparently, you're going to write one e-mail, and it's going to be done." That's exactly what happened. I wrote one e-mail, and they invited me in. I pitched the show, and it was done that day. For me, it's like I can't ignore these kinds of signs. I believe wholeheartedly that we are spiritual beings, and we need to tap into that. Meditation, definitely, helps me to really stay grounded and stay connected to my higher self.

DB: What was one situation you found yourself in that confirmed in your mind that you needed to seek treatment?

SR: I didn't seek treatment, but for me I got sober when I got a DUI when I was 29-years-old. I'm now almost 46. That was about 16 years ago. I was out for dinner with a friend, but really dinner was mostly just wine. I made a bad choice. I got in my car and decided to drive. There was an accident, and I was charged. I really knew in that moment that I could not keep doing the things I'd been doing, and yet it was terrifying. I had no idea how I was supposed to live my life without alcohol. It was extremely shameful. I spent the night in jail. I had to do the whole court thing. I had to take courses. I had to get a pardon. I fought for that after the fact. It was such an emotional roller coaster for so long.

At the same time, I look at my rock bottom as the beginning of everything. I feel that with so many rock bottoms. When everything falls away, we have nowhere else to go but up. We have to push off from somewhere, so rock bottom was the place I was able to push off from, and finally realized that this was not the life for me. Four years though after I got sober, I relapsed. It was after moving to a new city. I was all alone in a brand-new city, and I felt the pressure of people pressuring me to drink. Because I was so mired in shame all that time, I had never told anybody that I was sober for a reason. I was like, "No, I just don't drink because I'm into health and fitness." Part of that became true.

I got into health and fitness because I got sober and figured I had no other choice. I was like, "What else do I do? I can't keep drinking, so I've got to do something else." So, I started hitting the gym, and I started learning about nutrition. I started learning about sugar addiction and food addiction and really learned strategies to change that. Yeah, it was a crazy time, that rock bottom. That definitely was the greatest lesson. I look at my addiction as the greatest teacher and my recovery as the greatest blessing of my life. I don't look at it in any other way. There are no negatives here, none, and there are no regrets.

If I didn't have every single experience that I did have, I would not be sitting on this call with you right now, so, no regrets. I feel really grateful to it all, but I stayed so mired in shame for those first 4 years that when I moved to that new city, it was like I didn't have enough tools around me. I didn't have the support of any type of community at all because I hadn't told anybody that I was sober. I faltered under the pressure, and I drank. It was about a two-week period, and it would just be a glass of wine. I'd be like, "Okay, see, I can do that." The next night it was two glasses of wine. I was like, "Okay, I can do that." Then it went on like that.

It was within two weeks, and it was New Year's Eve. Everyone was going out, and I joined them. I got drunk, and I blacked out. I woke up the next morning. I could barely look myself in the eye in the mirror in my bathroom because I was like, "Are you going to throw away everything you've worked for?" I had gone back to business school when I got the DUI because I couldn't drive, and I needed my car for work. I quit my job, and I was like, "What am I going to do for three years?" I lost my license for three years because I had had a charge when I was 20, so they added that on. So, I lost my license for three years. I was like, "Where could I hide for three years? What can I do that no one will notice that I'm not driving and not in the world?" That's what I did. I went back to business school, and I got really serious about my education. I graduated at the top of my class, and I spoke in front of 2,000 people on graduation day.

I had that relapse 4 years later, and it was like, "You worked your ass off to become this whole new person and look at all you've done." You got sober, and you busted your ass. You got that fucking pardon. You've gone through all these things, and you got your license back, which was a whole ordeal in of itself. I did all of these things, and I was like, "Oh my gosh, I cannot throw this all away." I really saw it as two roads. It was like, I can either go backwards on that road where I know where it leads, and it's shame, and it's hell, and it's a nightmare, and it's being drunk all the time, or it's continuing on this journey. Thank God I took the latter.

MATT BUTLER

"My life goes really well when I'm holistically engaged in living sober and living in a way that I put living by spiritual principles first."
– Matt Butler

Bio: Matt Butler is a folk artist, a rock n' roller, and a storyteller. Weaving personal experience with a timeless style, Butler brings honesty and openness to his classic approach to songwriting. Matt Butler first gained notoriety as the lead singer of the New York based band Reckless Sons, who signed a development deal with Island Def Jam/Mercury Records and released two EPs, the latter with legendary record producer David Kahne (Lana Del Ray, The Strokes, Sublime, Paul McCartney). The turning point in Butler's career came, however, when he confronted his lifelong struggle with alcoholism and substance abuse. After getting sober, Butler recorded his debut solo album Reckless Son, a poignant confession of his battle with addiction and his inspiring path to recovery. Butler's debut album Reckless Son was released to critical acclaim on September 9, 2016. Immediately following the release, Butler wrote and performed Just One, the original song for the feature length and nationally distributed documentary Generation Found. Butler has spent the past year on the road supporting both the film and the album, performing everywhere from The Paramount Theater in Los Angeles to the steps of numerous State Capital buildings. Butler's credits recently expanded to include his first ever Behind The Walls Tour, where he performed exclusively in State Prisons across Ohio. More recently, Butler was honored as a 2017 Leader In Mental Health Awareness by the National Alliance on Mental Illness (NAMI) alongside Pulitzer Prize Winner Ron Powers and Super Bowl Champion Keith O'Neil. @MattButlerSongs

Occupation: Musician

Drug of choice: Alcohol

Length of sobriety: About 6 years

DB: What do you do to stay sober on a daily basis, and what's the most challenging part about it?

MB: What do I do to stay sober on a daily basis, and what's the most challenging part about it? Well, I'd say that one of the primary things that I do is to remain connected to other people who are staying sober on a daily basis. I try to be in communication with other people who have chosen that lifestyle for themselves. I find that being part of a community is really big for me. I find that the opposite of that is sort of like this state of isolation, and separation, and disconnection. That's kind of what I feel is sort of a thing my disease would want. So, I would say, first and foremost, I just stay in contact with people. I believe in prayer, meditation, and exercise. I think the mind-body connection is super important to be aware of. I try to eat right. I try to just have self-respect for myself, I try to take care of myself holistically. I attend recovery support meetings. I have a meditation practice that is very important to me as well.

I think what's challenging is my life when I'm not doing those things. My life goes really well when I'm holistically engaged in living sober and living in a way that I put living by spiritual principles first. When I'm not living by spiritual principles, that's a challenge. Because that's when I get consumed with fear, and anxiety, and anger, paranoia, things like that. My life, I think the easiest way to say it, if I'm sober and living by spiritual principles, my life is very fluid. It's when I'm not doing that that its challenging.

DB: How have you reconnected with your body since being into recovery, and what are some things you do to increase your health and vitality?

MB: When I first got sober, I had the opportunity to join a marathon team to raise money for where I went to treatment, at Caron Foundation to raise scholarship funds. I'd say that I started running, and I found out running was very meditative. Marathon running became a big part of my early sobriety.

I've also experimented with different types of diets to see what kind of foods my body responds well to. I think nutrition is a pretty overlooked thing. Nutrition is just as important as whatever exercise routine you've got going on.

DB: How have your relationships changed since being in recovery? Who would you say are the top three to five people you surround yourself with and why are they influential in your recovery?

MB: My relationship with my family is totally transformed. With my parents and my siblings. I'd say that having them in my life in a way where when I'm being honest with everybody, and I'm engaged in a life that's service-oriented, I just have this incredible ability to look my family in the eyes and speak to them in a way where I just know I'm not hiding anything. As a result, I feel this tremendous support from them. I would say that the people that I surround myself with that are most influential are my family. That includes Mr. Mario Diurno. He's family at this point. He's my best buddy, and my tour manager. I'm with him 24 hours a day. We hold meetings in this fucking car, just the two of us all the time. I'd say the people that are like Mario and I, we do work that is service. We're engaged in a form of service work. We're kind of in alignment in that way. We're both working to stay sober, and we're both working to help other people. We have a good influence on each other in that way.

DB: What's your spiritual life like? How do you incorporate it into your day, if you do? Why do you think spirituality is important for growth and sustainability in recovery?

MB: I think that the most important thing for me, to define spirituality for myself, is living with the understanding that we're all connected to each other. That everybody is connected, and that idea if someone's in pain, we're all in pain, and that if our planet is in pain, we're all in pain. I also think that spirituality is about living honestly. It's about living, that rigorous honesty component is this integral thing. So, I try to live through faith. I try living on my faith rather than on my fear. I don't necessarily have a particular religion or religious denomination that I am a part of, but I actually feel comfortable in a church, in a temple, in a mosque whatever. I enjoy all of that stuff. The idea of separation is why we have so much pain in the world. Spirituality, to me, means understanding that we're all on this ship together, you know?

DB: What was the one situation you found yourself in that confirmed in your mind you must seek treatment and recovery, and why?

MB: I just had given everything up. When it occurred, I traded in my music career, I traded in my relationships with my family, I traded in a very important romantic relationship. I would say that the moment where I needed to seek treatment was when I fully admitted that I had no chance of success of any kind in my life if I was using drugs or alcohol. I already wasn't able to stop. It wasn't the fact that I knew I couldn't stop, it was the fact that I could not sustain any form of relationship with anybody if I was using drugs or alcohol.

MAEGAN KENNEY

"I wanted to not only keep myself busy, but make my life exciting again by engaging in things I was passionate about."
– Maegan Kenney

Bio: Maegan Kenney is the creator/host of The Addictionary podcast, an ambassador for Shatterproof, and a clinical psychology doctoral student at William James College in Newton, MA. She has a master's degree in clinical mental health counseling and is the founder/chair of the school's Opioid Crisis & Advocacy student group. She is a recovered person from opioid addiction who implemented a self-managed program that included Vivitrol and psychotherapy to achieve her goal of assimilated harmony. She is an advocate for individualized recovery programs and has shared her experiences with addiction and incarceration on various public platforms, including *WBZ News Radio, NBC Boston, U.S. News & World Report, Metro International, Shatterproof, O'Connor Professional Group, MassINC*, William James College, and many others.

Occupation: Clinical Case Manager, Clinical Psychology Doctoral Student

Drug of choice: Opiates, which began with Oxycontin. It morphed into oxycodone use comprised of 30 mg Percocet pills after the brand name Oxycontin (80 mg pills) were discontinued. This eventually graduated to heroin. My use began when I was

20-years-old and continued steadily until I was 27-years-old.

Length of sobriety: 6 years

DB: What do you do on a daily basis to maintain your sobriety, and what is the most challenging part about it?

MK: I maintain mental stimulation. I would say that this component of my recovery has been the most beneficial and is a piece that is present in my day-to-day life. This is why I enrolled in a master's program. I wanted to not only keep myself busy, but make my life exciting again by engaging in things I was passionate about.

The most challenging part of my recovery is that the things that keep me sober are also the things that can exhaust me, which has been counterproductive in the past. I often add a lot to my plate, which benefits me by keeping me engaged in things I find meaningful, but I also overload myself to the point where I burnout. I am still learning how to set boundaries and limitations, especially with work demands, so I am not over-extending myself, which I know is unhealthy for me.

DB: How have you reconnected with your body since being in recovery, and what are some things you include in your daily life to increase your health and vitality?

MK: I never used to hike or spend a whole lot of time in nature, despite always wanting to. Now, I make it a priority to breathe in clean, crisp air and check out of my busy life by finding peace and solace in the woods. It helps restore me and reset how I perceive and experience the stress I feel in my daily life.

A daily routine for me includes meditation and laughter. I find ways to laugh about lighthearted stuff, which can sometimes come off as immature. Yet, I use meditation to help regulate my emotional response to perceived judgment so I can continue living my truth. Right now, my goal is to meditate twice a day, but

I don't always achieve it.

DB: How have your relationships changed (types of people, length/meaning of relationships, etc.) from when you were actively using to being in recovery?

MK: My relationships today are far more meaningful because I am authentic and genuine with who I am and the life I once lived. I think my down-to-earth approach to life that has taken shape during my recovery means that I attract the same type of people.

I am convinced that if I continued spending time with people were using, I would have continued to relapse and likely would have never made it out of the darkness still breathing. I isolated a lot during the later years of my use so it was actually enjoyable to find new friends, or friends at all for that matter. I lacked social connection in such a way that it was incredibly gratifying to enroll in a master's program and spend time around others who had the same interests as me. I am still friends with many of those same people.

DB: Who are the top three to five people you surround yourself with and why are they influential in your recovery?

MK: My dad is a huge part of my recovery and has been my biggest advocate, aside from my mom. I am an only-child so my parent's support has been crucial to my healing. The fact that my dad has already experienced the same challenges as me has been vital for me figuring out how to help myself and maintaining hope that I can not only get better, but thrive in life. He achieved recovery in an unconventional way, which modeled a great message for me: You can still make this work despite failing when using the most common means (Suboxone/Methadone and 12-Step programs).

My aunt is also influential because she supports my journey, is interested in knowing more about my experience of addiction/ recovery and produces my podcast!

My two best friends because they appreciate my struggle and why I have the knowledge I have about addiction. They do so without judgment!

My boyfriend because he is the type of guy who just says it like it is! I truly appreciate that because this was something I always had difficulty doing. He helps me remain grounded and most of all, keep it real! He also values and respects me as a person and likely has every reason to judge the crap out of me, but never does!

DB: What is your spiritual life like and what do you do on a daily basis to integrate it into your life, and why do you think spirituality is important for growth and sustainability in recovery?

MK: I meditate, which has become a big part of my recovery program. It's a massive part of my healing because it has allowed me to feel okay in my own skin. I started meditating to try and achieve serenity as my anxiety was surmounting to an intolerable level. Once I began working out of the heart center and practicing self-compassion and nonjudgmental love for myself, I noticed a big shift in how I operated in the world. I started to let go of my need to control my feelings and how others perceive me. Since then, I have been able to give speeches in front of thousands of people; something I could never have imagined. I can trace my debilitating social anxiety back to infancy so speaking in front of large crowds was always a dream of mine, but nothing more. Meditation and continued work in my own recovery has made that dream a reality.

DB: What was one situation you found yourself in that confirmed in your mind that you must seek treatment and recovery and why?

MK: My best friend practically died in my front seat after we shot up. This was right when fentanyl hit the streets so no one had ever heard of it or knew what it was, myself include. I was fortunate that I was still a novice user at the time and missed my vein when we shot up. Otherwise, I would have certainly died that day because my tolerance was a fraction of my buddy's and he barely made it through this situation. I just remember talking to him as I was driving back home and realized that he wasn't talking back to me. He was turning blue right before my eyes and there was nothing I could do about it other than drive 115 mph with my hazard lights on, zooming down side streets, trying to get to the nearest emergency room. When I pulled up to the hospital, he miraculously woke up. He asked me why the hell we were at a hospital and I explained that he was just dead in my front seat! Unfortunately, I still used after this incident took place, but it was scary enough that I decided to get help soon after. I consider this experience one of the building blocks towards my commitment to sobriety that eventually took shape in 2012.

DOUG'S TWO CENTS ON FITNESS

Fitness saved my life. If it wasn't for my cellmate forcing me to exercise when I was in jail, I probably would be back incarcerated or dead. It wasn't the pushups or sit-ups that saved me, it was the way they made me feel about myself. As you read these stories, you'll notice fitness is recognized as an important and instrumental tool for recovery. Exercise is known to release "feel good" endorphins. Many people in recovery compare the feeling of a great workout to the feeling of being high. Hence the term "runner's high." Aside from the physical benefits that we all know it provides, exercise helps to boost self-confidence, energy, and cognitive thinking. These things are all vital to recovery, especially during the early stages. Remember if you feel good physically, it will pay dividends in all other areas of your life. Exercise also helps build structure, whether it's goal setting, sticking to a workout schedule, or being committed to meet a friend at the gym. Having structure can be a life saver in recovery. Just like recovery, exercise doesn't have to be the same for everyone. Do things that you enjoy. Whether it's going for a run, lifting weights, doing yoga or Pilates, or anything else that you will keep doing. A combination of modalities is best. But, what's important is that you do something that you can consistently incorporate.

As far as what I do now to get my fitness fix . . . I lift weights four to five times a week and run regularly. My goals now are just focusing on being the strongest and healthiest person I can be without being overly regimented.

After training hundreds of people in recovery, I am often asked the question "How do I get started?" or "I am not in as good of shape as he or she is."

My answer never changes. You have to start with where YOU are at. You, not your neighbor, not your coworker, not your BFF, but, you. Take it slow and remember safety first.

Getting started could be as simple as going for a 10- to 15-minute walk three times a week or doing a few sets of calisthenics when you wake up in the morning or during your lunch break.

There are plenty of resources on how to begin. If you can't find one or are still a little apprehensive, please reach out to me directly and I will point you in the right direction.

CHRISTOPHER POULOS

"During prison, a guy that I was in prison with, offered to train me for free, and started really slow, it just started with literally just walking."
– Chris Poulos

Bio: Attorney Christopher Poulos was appointed Executive Director of the Washington Statewide Reentry Council (Council) on October 1, 2017 by Department of Commerce Director Brian Bonlender and the Council. On March 8, 2018 he was unanimously confirmed in this role by the Washington State Senate. Previously, Christopher served as Executive Director of Life of Purpose Treatment at the University of North Texas, where he was also an adjunct professor of criminal justice. During law school, he served at the White House Office of National Drug Control Policy, The Sentencing Project, and was selected as law student of the year by National Jurist magazine. While at the Office of National Drug Control Policy, he worked to reduce discrimination by reframing stigmatizing language used by the federal government regarding addiction and justice system involvement. Christopher also served as an advisor to U.S. Sen. Angus King (I-Maine) on addiction and justice policy, and served on several task forces related to criminal justice policy and reentry. He graduated cum laude from the University of Maine School of Law, where he was president of the American Constitution Society and represented children facing criminal charges as a student attorney in the Juvenile Justice Clinic.

Christopher openly identifies as a person in long-term recovery from addiction who has also been incarcerated. Over a decade ago, he made a decision to seek help and has maintained his recovery since. The U.S. Department of Justice selected him to consult for a project documenting the nation's most successful people to have reentered society following incarceration. His work and story have been featured in the *New York Times, Washington Post, NBC, The Hill,* and other outlets. He also gave a TED talk on reentry and his personal journey in 2015.

Occupation: Lawyer

Drug of choice: Alcohol, cocaine, opiates, benzos, amphetamine

Length of sobriety: 10 years

DB: What do you do to stay sober on a daily basis and what's the most challenging part about it?

CP: I'd say that I used to do a much better job just being completely frank. I used to put a lot more into my recovery than I do now, and so I'll share that for the first several years when I wasn't in prison at least, because I was sober in prison and meetings were very limited. I started meetings in prison, but right away when I got sober I got into a 12-Step program and worked the 12 Steps with a sponsor, thoroughly, and started sponsoring people and still sponsor people to this day. Well, there is at least one person I'm currently actively sponsoring, and some others that are technically sponsees but don't actually call me so I don't know if you want to count that or not.

I think that the hardest thing is continuing, as my life gets better and things continue to improve in my professional and personal life, is to just still actually work a program, a personal program, of recovery which is independent of any type of advocacy work or professional work that I do. That is the most challenging thing and that is something where I need to work harder on.

DB: How have you reconnected with your body since being in recovery, or what are some things you do daily to increase your health and vitality?

CP: I actually lost about 80 pounds of body fat in recovery. I initially gained weight when I first got sober. During prison, a guy that I was in prison with, offered to train me for free, and started really slow, it just started with literally just walking. He didn't ask me to do any diet changes, or go the gym, or certainly not run or anything like that. He just had me start by walking, and so for a few months I just committed to walking every single day, and then he added weight training and then I went to walking and weight training and then finally after I was getting pretty comfortable with that he suggested some changes for my eating and my relationship with food. And that, when all of those things came together, that's when my body really started to change and I learned about what to eat, when to eat, when my body needs certain foods and when it doesn't need certain foods, and I've basically kept that weight off. I'm probably 10 pounds heavier that I'd like to be right now. But, it's been seven, eight years since that process started and I went from 250 to about 175 [pounds]. I'm probably 185 right now which I'm relatively comfortable with, and what I do, every single day I get to the gym so I have to say that it's probably not the healthiest but I miss a lot more 12-Step meetings than I miss workouts. That's just being completely honest. It's become part of my recovery making it to exercise every day whether it's lifting weights, running, or doing something, some combination of the two.

DB: How have your relationships changed from when you were actively using to now being in recovery, and who are the top three to five people you hang out with and why are they influential in your recovery today?

CP: Sure, so I mean I think that while I was actively using I was unable to form true relationships. I didn't know how to let people in, really, and be honest with people and I didn't really know how to listen either. I remember more so waiting for my turn to talk than truly listening to who the other person in the conversation, or people in a conversation, were doing. So, short answer is learning how to listen and forming true relationships really for the first time, I think, in my adult life.

And the kind of top people in my life have really, even though I'm not as close to all of them right now, it's basically the same group of people since I got sober. My Uncle Tom, who is in recovery, I know it's kind of funny that his name is Uncle Tom but, anyhow, who else, let's see, my sponsor, Kevin, and my partner Angela . . . and they're people that I bounce ideas off of, spent time with. When I'm taking care of myself I have a group of people around me kind of like my core board of directors that I like to bounce ideas off of because something I'm thinking may be totally out of line or it may be great and it's always good to get a second opinion.

And I do have a relationship with a higher power now. The strength of that depends on my own willingness to pray, and to meditate, and to just do the next right thing. And I think that my spiritual condition improves the more willing I am, I'll just leave it at that. To do the next right thing and to pray and to help other people without expecting anything in exchange.

DB: What would you say your spiritual life is like, and what do you do on a daily basis to integrate it into your life, and why do you think spirituality is important for growth and sustainability in recovery?

CP: So, for the first several years I hit my knees every single morning and asked for a day of sobriety and at the end of the day I hit my knees and thanked God for that day of sobriety and that was, initially, that was really the entirety of my prayer life. It grew from there to actually praying for people. Really going through more of a ritual in prayer, and it probably reached its peak, at least to date, was when I was in prison, and then I had another good, probably solid connection with my higher power, with the universe when I was practicing a lot of meditation-based yoga for a while after prison. And now, the honest answer is I pray a lot less than I should. I know that if I was more willing to pray and meditate on a daily basis I would be healthier, so I'm not going to blow smoke and say that I'm at having the best quality of actual recovery right now.

I have an amazing professional life, but as far as the program that I'm working right now, it could use quite a bit of work and I think that it's good to have this call for me to be able to say that. I am not perfect. I know that when I'm healthiest is when I am starting my day in prayer and meditation, praying and meditating throughout the day and quickly as needed, really, and then also ending the day in prayer and meditation. Even if it's like a minute of something. That's when I'm able to find the most peace in my life and in my relationships and really be at maximum service to other people. Recently, I have not been as willing as before to do that and who knows maybe this call will serve as the catalyst for me to become more willing.

DB: What was one situation you found yourself in that confirmed in your mind you must seek treatment and recovery and why?

CP: I mean my life had fallen apart entirely, so I was not working, I was not going to school, I was selling drugs and using drugs professionally. That's all I did. I was basically, completely in the late stage, chronic substance use disorder where my life was so small. But, the catalyst that happened was actually accidentally discharging a firearm in my apartment. I had this one-bedroom basement apartment and I accidentally shot a gun and thank God no one was killed, but they could've been. That was kind of a wake-up call, and after that happened what really was what happened for me was I tried to continue to seek relief. So, for me substances were always kind of like helping me out because I couldn't deal with myself. I didn't know how to exist in my own skin and I had a ton of unresolved trauma.

So, I think that gun going off may have been partially the catalyst, but I think that the real thing, what really, really, fundamentally happened with me is that the alcohol and drugs stopped providing the relief that they once had. I'd try to get high, try to not feel anymore, or feel differently and I couldn't find the same relief, and it was at that point, that's, that's what really did it, that made me seek help.

TRAVIS BARNES

"Everybody's rock bottom is different. Mine was incarceration and suicide. I don't know if it gets any lower than that."
– Travis Barnes

Bio: If you fear you may be about to hit rock bottom—whether compounded by personal tragedy, inner turmoil, or drug abuse—then fitness entrepreneur Travis Barnes will give you the hope and inspiration to never give up.

Barnes not only picked up the pieces of his life but also set out to build his dream of making a highly successful personal fitness business.

Travis Barnes is an author of two books, a nationally recognized speaker, and now a franchisor of his own fitness business, Journey 333. When you read his story it should give you hope that you can go from less than zero and still have success in life

Occupation: Fitness Business Owner

Drug of choice: Meth

Length of sobriety: 15 years

DB: What do you do on a daily basis to maintain your sobriety, and what's the most challenging part about it?

TB: Well, here's what I'd like to say about that. If you can identify that sometimes addiction is actually a symptom of a greater problem, I would say that what I do on a daily basis now, now that I've solved that problem, it's just continuing to self-validate, continue to live with purpose. I was a kid that came from a broken home, grew up missing that love and acceptance that some kids have in their life, and I chose to start using drugs to fit into certain situations, and have that love and acceptance that I was missing, but when I learned that it was possible to validate yourself, it's funny how the addiction begins to heal, and when you identify those past hurts that you were trying to mask with a drug, and you have a little encounter with them, suddenly, it's not so much about me. I don't have to talk myself off a ledge on a daily basis. I just have to keep on living inspired and living with purpose.

DB: How do you think you've reconnected with your body since being sober, and what do you do on a daily basis to increase your health and vitality?

TB: That's another good thing, too, because throughout my life, I've exercised, and it was interesting that I found addiction by the time where I wasn't really working out anymore. I wasn't working out. I was a bartender in Vegas. It was just different things like that, and, now, you're high on life all the time. They say, "There's a 50% greater recovery with exercise," and I believe it because I really wouldn't want to mess up the way that I feel all the time on a regular basis with a drug or anything.

DB: How have your relationships changed since being in recovery? Who would you say are the top three to five people you surround yourself with and why are they influential in your recovery?

TB: Selfish to more selfless. That's the big thing. When we're caught up in addiction, it's very much about maintaining that addiction, and maintaining that addiction usually means ignoring a lot of other very important things because that's your priority. In the beginning, I would say that things that mattered most were at the mercy of the things that should matter least, a drug or something, and, now, today, being a healthy person who motivates people on a regular basis and tries to provide breakthroughs and inspiration to people definitely helps me to recognize what is important in my life.

I had a wife who stuck behind me for almost a decade of incarceration, and that's amazing in itself because, typically, it just doesn't happen that way . . . 98% of people, they lose their marriages during that kind of thing. Really, just being appreciative for the wonderful family that I'm still blessed to have and recognizing them as being most important.

DB: Thoughts on top people?

TB: That's a very big key. Everybody needs a strong circle. Everybody needs a super strong circle. I am always on the lookout for people that are motivated and pursuing excellence and positive and going someplace with their life, and I guess because of who I've become, I really don't like it when I know that I'm going to be around people that are going nowhere and are going to bring me down. I look to my mastermind. The Todd Durkin mastermind, and I try to associate with those members or fellow business owners or pillars of our community.

It's so funny because, now, I've been asked to speak to different leaderships things in our local Chamber and whatnot, and there was a time where you were the downtrodden of society. You were the castaway. It's funny how we can change our thinking and change our life, and you can also change your circles and change your life. I'm very focused on always spending time with people who align with where I'm heading.

DB: What is your spiritual life like, and why do you think it's important to have a spiritual component to maintain a solid recovery?

TB: It was interesting. My spiritual life, other than going to Catholic school, began while I was in prison. At first, they brought by a book cart, and they had Louis L'Amour and the Bible on there, and I chose Louis L'Amour at first. I think God probably laughed, but, eventually, getting bored in my 8 × 8, I decided, "Okay, I'll read the Bible," and I read these stories, and I read these stories about Jonah getting caught up in the belly of the whale to get his mind right, and I realized I was kind of in the belly of a whale right now, and then about Joseph getting sold out by his brothers and being humbled so he could be exulted, and I was going through such a humbling experience that I learned to look at life differently. I learned to look at life as the gift that it is, so I do things to stay in touch with my spirituality, like church regularly, but more so just conversations with God, just asking God about my plan, believing that God had a plan for me, believing that He could take all the bad and use it for good, which He does on a regular basis now when people are struggling and trying to have breakthroughs, and I can share my struggle and my breakthroughs.

If you look for evidence, you will find it. If you look for the evidence of God and look around at creation in this life, and you look back on your lily pads and you see like, "Okay, God, you were trying to prepare me," a good father will correct his son, and, sometimes, you need to get put into a timeout to get your mind right so that you can become the person, the husband, the friend that you were meant to be.

DB: What was one moment that confirmed in your mind that you must enter into treatment and/or recovery and why?

TB: When I first got locked up, they didn't even know whether I would get 25 years. Drug quantities in the federal system are just nuts, and I remember one time getting a phone call. I called home, but they had had a phone call, and it was from my attorney talking about . . . 25 years being a possibility, and so I actually thought about suicide because I was like, "I can't do 25 years." Prior to that, I had never even done 25 days in jail, so 25 years,

I felt like life was over, and I did. I thought about different things, like could I kill myself by hanging myself in my bedsheets and just different things.

Going through that, I realized that I had been so selfish for so long in my addiction. Was I going to continue that selfishness right into a suicidal event? I decided that no matter what happens to me, that my daughter would deserve a father that she could always at least come visit or talk to and get answers from. I switched from being selfish to being more selfless because I was going to live 25 years if I had to just being at least a place where she could come and get some fatherly advice if she ever needed it.

It turned out that we got a decade instead, but that was a big shift, just hitting that rock bottom and saying, “Who are you gonna be with the rest of your life? Are you gonna be a father, a good husband,” and so I did things, like writing home daily, creating an Easter map for Easter. I started recognizing, what is it that I can even still do from inside this cell to just be a good father? What can I do to be a good husband?

That was a big switch for me. You got to hit rock bottom. Everybody’s rock bottom is different. Mine was incarceration and suicide. I don’t know if it gets any lower than that.

WES GEER

"Body mind and spirit. It's all synced up."
– Wes Geer

Bio: Wesley Geer is a professional guitar player, songwriter, recording artist, and producer who signed his first record deal to Jive Records with the band he founded, (Hed) P.E. Wes toured the world for nearly a decade, and the band sold over 1 million records worldwide. Their music was on high rotation on MTV, radio stations, as well as having numerous placements in popular feature films, TV, and video games.

What many didn't know at the time was while he was masterminding and leading his band to the member's first-ever record deal, Wes was a full-blown drug addict, using alcohol, meth amphetamines, and other drugs, daily, for years. As a progressive disease, no matter the efforts to quell his addiction and control it, things continually got worse. After a nearly a decade of touring the world, with the biggest names in rock, Wes' life was imploding, and he finally left in 2003, for a "lifestyle change" that ultimately ended him up in rehab in 2004.

In rehab he learned tools for recovery and latched onto the stories of others that had overcome their addictions, stories of people being so far down in a deadly hole, but somehow not only got sober, but achieved great things. "These stories of hope were the guiding force that lead me out. These people had a tangible program of recovery proven to work, so I gave it a shot."

The following years found Wes as an instructor at Fusion Academy & Learning Center, an alternative school where he taught music to 6th through 12th graders who had struggled in more traditional academic settings. These same troubled students often succeeded in Fusion's adaptive one-on-one learning environment. Geer's love of teaching blossomed during his time. His classes served as the earliest prototype for R2R; he and one student at a time would write and play songs together. Geer said he quickly noticed "the engagement and the buy-in" the students had in these sessions was much greater than a typical "lesson" as the student's energy was transformed with hope and self-esteem while songwriting and playing music together.

In 2010, Wes decided he wanted to get back into music, and started praying and meditating on what that would look like. Not long after, and only because he was sober, Geer was offered the gig as guitarist with the legendary rock band Korn. He traveled the world performing in more than 40 countries with the multiplatinum stars, as well as appeared numerous live televised and studio recording sessions.

Geer was moved to give back, wanting to create something that could help people who struggled the same way he had. He founded Rock to Recovery (R2R), a non-profit organization created in late 2012 with the purpose of providing those in various types of treatment and recovery programs the cathartic, uplifting, healing experience of connectivity through playing music.

It's a therapy Geer himself turned to after years of abusing drugs and alcohol. During his stay in rehab he admits that music was his "most intimate friend" during his darkest days, allowing him to cope with the rollercoaster of emotions that consumed his early days in treatment.

"I remember being so raw, newly sober. I picked up my guitar and I just started strumming, and that simple act of strumming a few chords had an impact on me like never before. The whole milieu would write these silly songs and we'd forget everything, and even the most dark, shy personalities would start singing and dancing. That always stuck with me."

Rock to Recovery, with Geer and his staff of nine fellow sober musicians, now partner with over 100 treatment programs across Los Angeles, Orange, and San Diego counties, providing more nearly 450+ sessions each month to people struggling with addiction, mental health, eating disorders, at-risk youth, and Wounded Warriors.

In 2016, the Department of Defense granted Rock to Recovery® an official contract for their years of impactful work with the Air Force and Army Wounded Warriors that sees the charity travel nationally to various bases to work with these injured veterans.

That same year, Wes co-created the Rock to Recovery Award Show and Concert, a unique and important event in the community that honors sober icons in the music community. The sober events help raise funds for the organization as well as help destigmatize the disease of addiction by showing those in recovery that recovery is cool and is supported by a growing community of sober rock stars and other artists. Past performers and honorees have included Corey Taylor, Chester Bennington, Wayne Kramer, Mike Ness, Steve Stevens, Fred Durst, Mark McGrath, Dean & Robert DeLeo, Franky Perez, Matt Sorum, and Billy Morrison amongst others.

On Mar 3, 2017, in appreciation of the work Wes and Rock to Recovery do with the Air Force's Wounded Warriors program, the USAF Thunderbirds offered him a ride in an F16 fighter jet—a privilege few people ever get.

In December 2017, Rock to Recovery celebrated its 5th year anniversary whilst Wes celebrated 10 years sober.

Moving into 2018, exciting things lay ahead for Wes. Rock to Recovery Radio launched its first show on February 16 and the long-anticipated book is finally in the works. With an ever-growing team and their 3rd annual Award show and Concert in September 2018, Wes and Rock to Recovery have become an undeniable force in the world of addiction and recovery

In Wes' own words "No gig has been more enjoyable, no high better, than the work we get to do with Rock to Recovery!"

"Music is the Medicine"

Occupation: Musician/CEO Rock to Recovery

Drug of choice: Drug of choice = more

Length of sobriety: 10+ years

DB: What do you do on a daily basis to maintain your sobriety, and what is the most challenging part about it?

WG: I have a routine, and I improvise. I wake up, make my bed, pray, give thanks, and asking for help very specifically on the things I am working on at the moment, asking to be *shown* the right way to do them, asking to have fear and ego removed, and show me how I can grow to a higher vibration, and help more people. I drink coffee, get all jacked up, then I meditate. I ask the angels, guides, ascended masters, God, my Highest self to bring forth the information and the energies I need to grow, expand, and learn what I need to learn. I get told things, I have so many crazy stories. I like to hit the gym on most days, and/or run. Stay active, and I work on my projects, Rock to Recovery. I hit a meeting in the eve's more nights than not. I try and read spiritual literature, or things that help me grow.

DB: How have you reconnected with your body since being in recovery, and what are some things you include in your daily

life to increase your health and vitality?

WG: I think diet is huge. I don't eat fast food, nor junk food. I like to limit the meat. I don't need much. Mostly fish, occasional chicken and I really don't dig beef at all anymore. Too hard on my body. I like to eat oatmeal in the morning . . . steel cut organic, with tons of blueberries, strawberries, almond milk. I go through cartons of berries each week. Lots and lots of water too! Your body is mostly water. Water helps it do everything, carry out waste, etc., etc.

I must stay active. Running, surfing, yoga, hiking, swimming, anything that keeps me going is a must. I can't be happy without being active regularly (even though my mind *always* tries to talk me out of it) and eating well, resting well, and hitting meetings. Body mind and spirit. It's all synced up. But I definitely lift weights and run a few times a week, with some good stretching.

DB: How have your relationships changed since being in recovery? Who would you say are the top three to five people you surround yourself with and why are they influential in your recovery?

WG: Well, I'm single a lot. That's my final frontier. But who's to say if I should or shouldn't be? But I've learned that meeting the sick girls is about me, not them. I've learned to not paint red flags white, and to be okay alone. I used to really have a problem with needing validation from women. Weirdly enough I can date the most amazing girl and, like cocaine, [she] will never satisfy my need for validation. That has to start within. So self-work and going deeper constantly and never stopping trying to grow and call myself out on behavioral patterns that are selfish or don't serve my highest good is a constant. Still, I'm a man and I'm not perfect, nor trying to be, but I must also couple that with the *willingness* to work on *all* my character defects and not just the ones I'm okay with fixing. So, as I get better, my dating, my circle gets better. My frequency elevates, and I meet people that resonate where I do. I used to never want drama in my life, and still don't, but I used to want to make sure everyone liked me even people that mistreated me. I needed to learn to be okay letting people go. But that's slippery too . . . you don't wanna start cutting everyone out each time you get mad. I know people that do that under the guise of "boundaries." I try to always find my part in issues with friends, and make prompt amends so I can have peace of mind and keep in the energy of love over being right. But, sometimes some people are just toxic, and will never meet you where you are. Sick people make healthy people sick. I try to avoid those scenarios.

DB: Top people?

WG: My Rock to Recovery "employees" are also my best friends. We are all sober, 12-Step dudes, musicians, and REALLY passionate about self-work and deepening our spirituality. You know everyone loves to claim spirituality but it's not a state you reach, it's a state you work on. It's unending, so fun, and so much magic there.

DB: What is your spiritual life like and what do you do on a daily basis to integrate it into your life, and why do you think spirituality is important for growth and sustainability in recovery?

WG: Prayer, meditation, humility, reading, learning. It's a fun place to be. I literally started getting "messages" from who knows where God, Higher Self, Spirit Guides, that come to me, and I can get readings on friends now, sounds weird to read I'm sure. But the point is there is magic out there, a frequency that all things are a part of . . . ONE thing we all are, everything is. And when I work on connecting, and work on learning how to not get disconnected so much by fear, anger, resentments, I can also work on ways to go deeper, it's amazing.

DB: What was one situation you found yourself in that

confirmed in your mind that you must seek treatment and recovery and why?

WG: When I went from a respected musician, and friend, who was healthy, and doing well in life to 123 pounds, sucked up, no one wanted to hear a word I had to say. I lost my career in music, cars repo'd, was spiritually bankrupt, hopeless, and couldn't figure out why I kept destroying my life, why I kept crashing and burning. I raised the white flag. Best thing I ever did, ask for help and let people TEACH me what to do. They knew. I didn't. And wow, were they right. Miracles happen.

NANCY CARR

"I started doing hot yoga as soon after I got sober, and it was a life changer."
– Nancy Carr

Bio: Nancy Carr began writing short stories and essays in her free time over 15 years ago. Inspired by writers she admired for their honesty and grit – Joyce Maynard, Augusten Burroughs, Anne Lamott, and Kelly Corrigan to name a few. In 2004, Nancy embarked upon her journey of getting clean and sober and thus started writing as a therapeutic channel in helping her recovery. By early 2005, Nancy had compiled a 250-page manuscript for her own Memoir, "Last Call." Her memoir has garnered 5-star reviews and has been in the top-selling Kindle, self-help recovery genre, since it was launched. Her recovery memoir is raw, honest and inspiring as she's very open about sharing her alcoholism and drug addiction. Nancy's work has appeared on The Fix, Medium, AfterParty, XOJane, and Ravishly, as well as numerous recovery blogs. Nancy is hoping her story will help others, specifically young woman. Nancy has a blog www.lastcallblog.me and keeps busy by working from home with a corporate job that pays the bills and likes to spend time at the Beach with her husband and Bailey, their rescue dog and constant companion.

Occupation: Business Consultant

Drug of choice: Alcohol/Cocaine

Length of sobriety: 14+ years

DB: What do you do daily to stay sober and what is the most challenging part about it?

NC: I have a routine; I get up about 6.30 am and do about 10 minutes of yoga stretches, and so some prayer during that time. I then take out my dog, Bailey, and focus on her during our walk. Then I talk one of my girls, the same girlfriend (in recovery) every morning and we have a mini-meeting. Then I start my corporate day job and get on with my day – and I try not to live in my will and turn it over to God; which is easier said than done most days. About 4 days, sometimes 5, I go to meetings to hear the message or help spread the message to others. I have a sponsor and do step work with her and I also sponsor a couple of women and work with them. This is what has been working for me for a while now. At night, I journal and say some prayers and sometimes do a guided meditation – that always calms and centers me. The most challenging part for me now is the emotional sobriety piece. Which for me is to try to get along better with my fellows; usually my husband, my friends, and my family. My husband's been in and out of recovery, and that has been a big challenge – because he has a God and it's not me.

DB: How have you reconnected with your body since being in sobriety and what do you do daily to increase your health and vitality?

NC: So, I've done so much since I got sober. I never worked out before or did yoga before I got sober. I started doing hot yoga soon after I got sober, and it was a life changer. Then I moved around a bunch and started some different routines. I was doing CrossFit for a while, and different kinds of yoga, and started running for a bit. I also really like to hike; we do that frequently with the dog, as well as now just walking along the beach with friends. Some days I don't do anything except walk Bailey and do my yoga stretches. It's all about balance for me.

DB: How have your relationships changed since being in recovery? Who would you say are the top three to five people you surround yourself with and why are they influential in your recovery?

NC: Before I got sober, I lied all the time, and I mean a lot! When I finally surrendered and got sober was the day that I really stopped lying. I mean, sometimes I'm too truthful; which can get me in trouble. People can trust me now, and they want to be around me more. I got sober in this community with a bunch of other sober women and they became my sober family. In asking about who I look up to – I'd have to say it's the women that I got sober with who are my tribe, my touchstones, my girls. And the sponsors I've had. Since I moved around a lot, I have had a few sponsors who helped me get through so many of my life's ups and downs, and I still talk to most of them today. Most of my friends have been through a lot of loss, sadness, and tragedy in recovery and when I see that they can go through anything, that is what inspires me and makes me want to be a better version of myself.

DB: Why?

NC: Because they show me how to live a better life. Basically, it's me getting out of myself and not listening to my head. I have that negative voice that keeps telling me; "You're not good enough, you're not smart enough, you're not pretty enough, nobody wants you, etc." I still have that voice after almost 15 years in recovery. Sometimes it's louder than others. When I'm in that space I call somebody and share what's going on with me or I journal about it. I just talk to people who I value for their recovery and sobriety.

DB: What's your spirituality lifelike and why do you think spirituality's important for growth and sustainability in recovery?

NC: When I first got sober and I heard you had to find a God, I was like, okay, cool, I can do that. I was raised Catholic, but it was important for me to find a Higher Power that I could do business with. I lived right by the ocean in my early sobriety and using the ocean and nature as my Higher Power worked for me. Going through life, I've had to learn how to enlarge my God throughout my sobriety as life throws us curve balls. It's very important for me to have that connection where I'm feeling like I can trust God. That's been my biggest challenge, especially in the last year or so. I am really trusting the universe and trusting whatever else is out there, as they can manage my life better than I can.

DB: What was the one tell-tale moment in your life that confirmed in your mind that you needed to seek treatment and recovery and why?

NC: It was my second DUI, I was 37-years-old and I was living my life the same way as I was at 19. I was drinking, using cocaine 3-4 days a week, and realized that I can't keep doing this. I was living this life of rinse and repeat. The same crazy cycle of addiction. However, I had no desire to get sober though. I just had to get a court card signed – so I walked into a meeting and as soon as I walked into that meeting, I knew I needed to be there, but I didn't want to face myself into thinking that I had a problem that I needed to take care of. I went out and drank for a week and had my moment of clarity – nothing good has ever happened when I'm drinking and using. I went back to that meeting because I figured I had nothing to lose. That was my mentality going into recovery – let's give this sobriety thing a shot. And here I am.

TARA CONNER

"If you're someone who's in recovery, and you're aggro all the time, you've gotta do something different, because I can promise you, I didn't get sober to be miserable."
– Tara Conner

Bio: Tara Conner is a Television Personality, Actress, and Recovery Advocate. Through her work, she shares her experience, strength, and hope with audiences throughout the United States. Conner was crowned Miss USA in 2006. During December of that year, she entered the Caron Treatment Center and completed 30 days of treatment for alcohol and drug addiction. She has since celebrated 11 years of sobriety. Tara hopes to raise awareness that addiction is a disease and that many people go on to lead a healthy, productive life in recovery. She especially wants educators, families, and professionals to know that sobriety at an early age is achievable and that it greatly enhances life's possibilities.

"It's so important to understand that addiction is a family disease," said Conner. "I experienced this firsthand within my own family. But I've also learned that through treatment and recovery you can break the cycle."

In 2017, Tara joined forces with Greg Hannley of SOBA Recovery. Together, they are beating down the doors of our politicians, and raising awareness for long-term recovery solutions. Once a month, they are joined by actor Daniel Baldwin on their television show

SOBA Living. Each episode highlights current events, potential problems, and solutions to combat the opioid epidemic.

Tara's next journey consists of "Recover Out Loud Townhalls", where she travels to communities in the United States creating a space for debate and conversations in each town. She hopes that by shedding light on the problem, they will come together and show their truth's. Conner said, "We can't change anything until we know what the problem is."

Last year, Tara did her first TEDx Talk, and is currently finishing her first book.

Occupation: Television Personality, Actress, and Recovery Advocate

Drug of choice: Opiates

Length of sobriety: 13 years

DB: What do you do to stay sober on a daily basis, and what's the most challenging part about it?

TC: For me, I have to go to a 12-Step program pretty much on a daily basis, because I am a real one. I'm one of those that my life is on the line, so I know that I have to take action every single day. I do that through being of service, going to a meeting, and working with others, while just trying to stay on top of it. It really doesn't get hard. I feel there's a misconception about recovery that it's a constant struggle. I don't think that it has to be. If you're struggling, that just means you have some work to do. I just try to stay on it and to avoid any type of struggle. If I do start struggling, I have tools that I've learned through recovery to get through it. I just have to use them.

DB: Now, how have you reconnected with your body since being in recovery, and what are some things you do on a daily

basis to increase your health and vitality?

TC: I go through phases where I'm painfully aware of everything about my body, from my digestive system to cholesterol levels and my energy levels. It took me awhile to truly try to incorporate mind, body, and spirit. I definitely am not diligent with it. I do my best, but, sometimes I just don't have the power to go to the gym or don't have the power to eat a healthy meal. I think it's just part of life. If I could diet every single day and if I could keep on a specific "vegan-only this that and the other," than I would. I think that it's something that you have to work at. It's taken me a little while just to say "Okay, more fruits and vegetables" and try to eat leaner meats. I definitely try to watch my diet, but I still can sometimes turn into the girl with "the gas station diet."

I also try to do my best to work out pretty consistently. That way, if I have indulged, it makes up for it because I love sugar. It's just a part of our makeup. Sometimes, I have to try to balance it instead of beating myself up for having Dominos. I will just make the decision, say "Okay, I'm gonna treat myself here," but I'm gonna try to keep it healthy for the next few days and go to the gym and really just go at it. I do things such as the "Thor workout," which is traditional weightlifting. But, I've done things such as Barry's Bootcamp as well. I always try to mix it up a little bit, but it is very important to me. I feel it should be important to everyone.

DB: How have your relationships changed since being in recovery? Who would you say were the top three to five people you surround yourself with and why are they influential in your recovery?

TC: Okay. Before I got sober, I didn't have relationships, I had victims. I used to live my life just in survival mode, and every relationship that I had, I truly needed them to be a certain way for me to feel comfortable. That's just not how life works. Relationships are an "ebb and flow," and it can't just be this selfish entity that says, "What can you do for me?"

It took me a long time, honestly, in recovery to just love myself. I didn't have a relationship with myself, so therefore I relied on other people to make me feel whole on the inside. When I was about eight and a half years sober, I woke up one day and realized, "Wow, nothing's gonna make me feel better today." The pizza is not gonna make it better. Going to a movie is not gonna make it better. Him coming back is not gonna make it better. Nothing could fix it, and that's when I truly realized that I had to work on me, because recovery's an inside job.

Sometimes, in this society, where we're all preoccupied with what's next, and keeping up with the Joneses, I think we forget to just try to get in tune with our own spirit and understand what makes us tick. When I really did a lot of work on myself, I switched from "What can I get out of life?" to "What can I put into it?"

My relationships now are relationships. They're healthy. I have my best friend. I call her my wife, her name is Melinda. We've been in each other's lives the entire time I've been sober. She's watched me go through every "ebb and flow," and every high and low. She's seen me at my best and she's seen me at my worst. She just loves me through it. I feel over the past few years, I've been able to be there emotionally for her as much as she's been there for me.

I have my fiancé. He's a "normie." He has an incredible story, and he hasn't had his lack of hardships, but he's just very positive. He inspires me to work harder and to be better. He's just innately kind. I kind of mirror that. I have sober sisters that are like sisters to me. I have my friend Laura. She and I got to know each other when I was selling cars, when I was broke in sobriety. Here we are, years later, roughly seven or 8 years later,. I would take a bullet for her. My family life has gotten better. It's no more pointing fingers and being, "This is why I feel this way, and you did this, and blah blah blah." It's more of "Okay, we all did the best job we could. Let's all put it in the past and move forward."

I can actually love people for where they are, and not have to take offense to everything. I had to learn a really hard lesson that this world wasn't designed to make me comfortable. Humans are flawed. We're flawed individuals. We're gonna let each other down, because it's part of the human experience. Through really jumping into the work and getting whole within myself, I've been able to be far more empathetic. I can have compassion. I can pretty much find the best in the worst situation with anyone.

I went from being a needy friend to being that friend that people feel as though they can come to with anything in the most nonjudgmental way possible. I really value my relationships today, because at the end of the day, that's what's important to me. My family's important to me, my growing family and my dog. I had to make an amends to my oldest dog, Gracie, because when I was in "sodriety," I mistreated her. I didn't give her the attention that she deserves. Now, every single day, I make sure that that dog gets great food. She gets lots of love. She gets pets. She gets toys. She gets whatever she wants. That's my living amends to her. I have two other animals that I take care of, Roxie and Gypsy, and they're like family also. I just know that it's not about me anymore.

DB: What's your spiritual life like, and what do you do on a daily basis to integrate it into your life, and why do you think spirituality's important for sustainability and growth and recovery?

TC: For me, spirituality is the most important part of my recovery. When people used to say that, I used to say "Yeah, yeah, whatever." I was pretty bitter in my first few years because I had this idea of what God was, and I had this idea that was impressed upon me through different churches that I went to and through family and whatnot. It wasn't my own idea. The God concept that I had before wasn't my concept, so I couldn't have a relationship with this God thing because it wasn't my own.

I've been seeking my entire life. I remember before I ever drank or used or did anything, as far back when I was 3-years-old being in the fetal position, begging this God to please help me. At the end of the day when it gets really bad, it's the best I can do to lay on the floor in the fetal position and say, "God, please help me," and that's great. But now the way that I do it, and this is a "dumbed down version" of finding a relationship with God: I figure out what it is that I'm powerless over. What dominates me? Is it a conversation that I had earlier dominating me, meaning I can't think of anything else, so what do I do? What do I need?

I think about what is it that I need right now. Sometimes I just have say, "God, I need you to be a hug. God, I need you to be my friend. God, I need you to be protection. God, I need you to be my dad. I need you to be my mom. I need you to be Ryan Gosling," whatever it is. I also ask God for the things that I can't have. I think that we all have a side of us that can get envious or jealous or greedy or whatever. When I see those things crop up in my life, I'll ask God, "I need you to be excitement for others. I need you to be acceptance. I need you to be humility."

It's an active way of creating this relationship that I now have, because when I figured out what it was that I needed, when I could give it to God. After I gave it to God, I started realizing that the things that I lacked before, I don't lack anymore. I still have opportunities to grow. I feel I'm always going to be teachable, and I think it's important for all of us to be teachable, because we're not it. As I said, it's not about me anymore. On days that I'm not feeling too spiritually fit, I kind of have this thing that I do. I'll take my body for a meeting or to go help someone, because for me, that's taking my body back to God.

I'll take my mind through step work, and call my sponsor, and have him work with me. That's me taking my mind back to God. Then I try to be of service, whether it's just calling someone else, picking up chairs at a meeting, or just doing something for someone else. It doesn't even have to be in the recovery world. I try to take my spirit into service, and taking my spirit back to

God. I feel I'm taking my mind, body, and spirit in three different ways. I can be feeling shitty the entire time, and also be kicking and screaming the entire way, but at least I know that I've taken the action to align my will to a better alignment.

DB: What was the one moment that confirmed in your mind you must seek treatment and recovery, and why?

TC: Well, I have a weird story. When I went into treatment, it wasn't necessarily a choice. I could have said, no. "Screw you Donald Trump and Miss USA. I don't care. I quit." For me, it was a divine intervention. I'm one of those people that if you come up to me and say, "I think you have an issue with this," I'll blow it off and say, "Well, we all have issues." In that case, back in 2006, I was on the front page of every newspaper. They were trashing my name left and right. They were bringing my family into it. I was the type of famous that I wanted to be, but not for the right reason.

It's one thing if one person tells you, "You've got a problem." But, when you have an entire collective world telling you that you're a hot mess, you kind of have an open mind, and that's what happened. I just got an open mind at that time. That open mind was enough to keep me sober, and to take the direction that I was given through treatment, and the continual work of going through a 12-Step program and staying in touch.

Truly, when I really realized that I was gonna die from a sober state, I was 8 and a half years sober. That's when I had to make the decision, not other people making the decision. But, I had to be the one to say, "Okay, my way's not working. I don't know, you might, so I'm gonna follow your direction." It wasn't until I truly started following direction wholeheartedly from other people that I started getting results.

A lot of people get beaten into a state of reasonableness through drugs and alcohol. I definitely "kind of" did that. I was beaten into a stage of open-mindedness, but 8 and a half years sober being untreated, I beat myself in a state of reasonableness through just being me. I was the problem, and I could really see that. So, I needed something to come between me. I used to just have this microwave God where I'd say, "Okay, I need you to fix this. Cool, thanks." I really had to create a relationship with this infinite power that lives in all of us.

It took me hitting my knees, literally and figuratively, and saying I'll do whatever it takes. Whatever I need to do, I'll do it. When I started doing it, I started growing. I don't know that we have to get sober and be miserable. I wish I would have known that in my first year, but now I try to tell people, we don't get sober to be uncomfortable. We get sober to live a happy, joyous, and free life. We should have freedom and happiness, and know peace. We should be able to attain that.

If you're someone who's in recovery, and you're aggro all the time, you've gotta do something different, because I can promise you, I didn't get sober to be miserable.

MASTIN KIPP

"100% of addiction is caused by unhealed emotional trauma."
– Mastin Kipp

Bio: Mastin Kipp is a number one best-selling author, speaker, and Creator of Functional Life Coaching™ for people who are seeking rapid transformation in their lives. He has been featured on the Emmy Award show, Super Soul Sunday, and recognized as a "thought leader for the next generation" by Oprah Winfrey. Mastin has built a highly successful international personal development company that helps people create rapid change, connect to who they really are, and live their lives with passion and purpose. Through his writing, online courses, in-person seminars, and international retreats, Mastin has worked with over two million people in over 100 countries around the world. Oprah recently also named Mastin "one of 100 awakened leaders who are using their voices and talent to elevate humanity," alongside other teachers such as Tony Robbins, Caroline Myss, Deepak Chopra, Dr. Brené Brown, Marianne Williamson, and Eckhart Tolle to name just a few.

Occupation: Best-Selling Author, Speaker, Creator of Functional Life Coaching™

Drug of choice: Cocaine

Length of sobriety: 15 years

DB: What do you do to stay sober on a daily basis and what do you think is the most challenging part about it?

MK: Well, I think in the context of cocaine, it's not hard for me anymore because I'm not around it, right? Let's see, so 2018 . . . Last time I was around a bag of cocaine unintentionally was probably 2008? And I was just around it, it was in a room where I was. And I felt that same, oh let me come over and join you, and I left. So, I think that the most important thing, when it comes to addiction, especially if it's something very clear like a drug addiction, alcohol, it's different if it's sugar, right? And food? But it's important to not have it in your environment.

So I don't associate with people who do that drug, I don't put myself in environments where that drug exists, and also since, I've done a lot of work on the insides of my body to understand what's going on my body, and there's a lot of reasons why I chose that specific drug and sugar as a coping and really self-medication. That's the real issue. I was trying to self-soothe and self-medicate, basically. And the technical term in the therapeutic, mental health space was, I was trying to self-regulate my emotional state.

And if you look at my brain scans, I have three or four different forms of ADD and ADHD from the Amen Clinics, two traumatic brain injuries, and so at that time it was . . . cocaine was like a focuser, it was helping me get things done, and it was really, in many ways, compensating, illegally and very expensively, both in terms of finances, emotional costs, and health, it was trying to help me make up for this brain damage that I had, basically. So, when I went to the Amen Clinics and got my brain scan, they said well it makes total sense that you would have a drug history of cocaine because of the way that your brain organizes.

What ended up happening, actually, was I ended up getting really clear on the foods I'm supposed to eat and not eat, and then also I actually now take prescription medication for my brain based on the Amen Clinics brain scans, which is the most advanced scan in the world. And I'm happy with it, because it's really great, and it's a different version of a drug I used to take that I stopped taking because it made me feel awful. But it's a new iteration of the drug, they came out with a different type of way to deliver it, and I really feel like myself. I don't really have a desire to use, if you will, because I'm helping my body get its needs met. Now, when it comes to sugar, that's a different story (laughs) . . .

DB: How have you reconnected with your body since getting into recovery, and what are some things you do on a daily basis to increase your health and vitality?

MK: I quit cocaine cold turkey. I dumped it, I flushed it, and I was done. And a week or two later, I felt like shit, man. You know, you're coming down and all the brain is like, where is my fuel, you know? And it was really bad. But I remember having this moment of, I wanna feel as good off the drugs and I did on the drugs. Because there's this thing about drugs where there's this moment, there's a window where you're like, ah, that's how I wanna feel. And then it very quickly passes. And then you don't feel that way. And I have a lot of compassion for anyone who has addiction, 'cause it runs in my family and I have a lot of clients who struggle with it. There's usually a core trauma associated with addiction, either very obvious trauma or sometimes less obvious traumas.

And so the thing about trauma, and addiction, is that when you're coping and you're using, you're actually usually not associated with your body. Now, you might be addicted to working out, but you're addicted to the physical appearance. Maybe you're addicted to controlling or constricting food, but you're not paying attention to your body. When you start to get sober, one of the things I realized, unfortunately at the time, is that I had to get associated with my mental states in my body.

When you first realize that, it's not like, yay, let me fuckin' celebrate that. It's like, fuck, God damn it, now I gotta feel my feelings. A thing I don't wanna do. But you have to descend back into how your emotions are feeling, and how you're feeling in your body. And that journey took me into things like Kundalini yoga, to help really regulate my emotional state. The breath is so powerful an emotional regulator, everything we're learning about the polyvagal theory, and how the vagus nerve is regulated by exhales and inhales, and the diaphragm impact vagal nerve tone, which is basically a fancy way of saying the way that you breathe is based on . . . helps you feel better, and helps you not be depressed and not be anxious, and all that type of stuff. Calms nervous system down.

It took me into functional medicine, learning about dysbiosis and the microbiome, and all my bio markers. I have a Cholestech LDX machine at my house, where I do my lipid profile, my cholesterol three times a week and I measure that, and adjust based on the measurements. I do a lot of IV therapy now, I do a lot of glutathione injections, I do a lot of trauma therapy and my coach/therapist is one of the best in the world, very trauma informed, and has helped me get associated with my body. And then being a professional speaker and coach, I'll do times where I'll do 15 days in a row, 12 hours a day, speaking, coaching on stages, doing interventions, coaching for hundreds of people. I have a whole prep, couple months of prep for that. I'm actually just starting up again today for my next event in December.

So it's definitely made me hyper-aware of my body, hyper-aware of recovery, hyper-aware of my emotional states, and getting a lot of specialized support has been very important, too. So, I mean, it's almost like a full-time job, now, because in many ways I'm an athlete. It's how I view myself, because of the amount of demand I have energetically form my body to put out every day. So, if you look at somebody like Tom Brady, taking care of Tom Brady is a full time job, because he has such a huge demand on his body energetically and performance-wise. And as an entrepreneur and a coach, and someone who's gonna deliver 15 days of 12 hours a day of content to people and being very present and dealing with very deep issues, I've had to adopt that sort of athletic mindset as well. So, it's a huge focus.

DB: How have your relationships changed since being in recovery? Who would you say are the top three to five people you surround yourself with and why are they influential in your recovery?

MK: Yeah. Great question. I think that my relationships are very different. Back in the day when I was using, if you didn't do cocaine I wouldn't talk to you. It's like, next. Oh, you're weird. The funny thing about cocaine is everyone has really great ideas, but they never leave the table. You know what I mean? That's kinda how it is. And I was in the music business, and very much in this sort of misogynistic environment, sort of participating in all that stuff, unfortunately, and I was 19, I didn't know what I was doing. And I was enabling other people and their addictions, I was very rude and curt, and angry and toxic in my own emotional states, and very codependent. Very much making other people's needs more important than my own, and that manifested into angers and resentments, stuff like that.

So very different, very, very different than today. Today, it's a very core inner group of people, and most of them I've known for at least a decade. And they're healthy, and they're amazing. I think the most important person you'll ever pick as far as your peer group is your partner. And I think of all the choices I've ever made in my life, I've fucked up a lot of choices for sure, I've made some good ones, I've made some not good choices, I've made some pretty good choices, but I think the best choice I ever made is my partner, Jenna. And she is like a unicorn. She's amazing, she is someone who I aspire to become better for, and she's someone who I spend a lot of my time with. That's probably one of the best choices I've ever made.

It's actually the best choice I've ever made.

DB: What's your spiritual life like? And how do you integrate

it into your day, and why do you think spirituality is necessary for sustainability and growth and recovery?

MK: Yeah, I think spirituality is so vague. What is spirituality, right? Is it doing a yoga class and saying namaste? Is it praying? Is it reading a Bible or sacred prayer? Is it chanting? Like, what is spirituality, right? So, I think that the way I would think of it is more a sense of purpose. And what I mean by that is, what are you here for? What motivates you? A purpose is something that is making you want to get up out of bed in the morning and it stimulates goals, it stimulates action. And it's a reason why. There are different things that can stimulate purpose, like doing it to prove the nay-sayers wrong, can happen, like fuck you, I'm gonna prove you wrong. How dare you. That's a big motivator in the beginning of sobriety and any journey.

I think at some point, when I take care of other people can motivate people, big time. Taking care of your family. And now, it's for me also about mission. My moon shot is to end emotional trauma in my lifetime. And I have a very personal relationship with my creator, I do believe in some type of creator. And I'm not here to tell anybody else how to have that relationship because it's so personal. It's like a meal plan, like my meal plan is different than your meal plan, and my relationship is different than your relationship. And I'm not judging you and if you judge me, cool, but don't judge me, you know?

And I used to really mess with people's faith. Especially if they were very dogmatic about it. I stopped doing that because someone's faith is like their certainty. So, I think that the goal is to have a personal relationship with something larger than yourself. It could be a mountain, a sun, the ocean, or it could be gods or spirit. You could be a Christian, you could be a Buddhist, you could be an atheist, you could be agnostic, you could be a course in miracles person. Doesn't matter, because an atheist can still go to see a sunrise and feel awe. They can go to a beach and feel a part of the ocean if they swim, you know? They can go to a mountain range and feel connected to something. They can look up into the night sky and go, holy shit, wow.

I don't think there has to be this specific god or spirit that has to be worshiped. I think it's all about relationship and the latest research in the polyvagal theory suggests that the markers for mental health and the cues for mental health and, vis a vis, also sobriety, okay? Sobriety and mental health are kind of the same thing. That's built into relations, embedded into relationship, the cues from mental health. So, we are relational beings, and Jesus said in the Gospels, you know, where two or three are gathered, there I am in their midst. And he's talking about coregulation, is what he's talking about. Where you can't do it in isolation by yourself.

And I think that's one of the biggest problems today, is that people isolate like crazy. Even though we seem more connected online, there's so much isolation happening. And so I have a very personal relationship. One of my favorite things to do is get up at 3:30, 4:00 in the morning and 'til about 11:00, just kind of have my creative time. And cardio, and creative time, and for me, my relationship is less about chanting mantras and prayer, and more about just a knowing that I'm connected to all that is, and all that is connected to me. And everything that's happening in my life is happening for a purpose and a reason to help me grow, especially the hardship, and that the way that I sort of commune spiritually is through the creative process of writing or whatever it might be. When I write or I create something, that's a meditation for me.

And what is meditation? Meditation is just bringing your focus to a single point. That's what it is. So, I don't think you have to sit down, on a pillow, and cross your legs and put your hands in Gyan mudra, close your eyes, and breathe through your nose, to meditate. I think you can meditate in the gym, training. I think you can meditate writing, I think you can meditate walking, there's a walking meditation. There's lots of things that can bring your attention to a single focus.

You know, The Rock talks about how weightlifting is his therapy, and that's a great example. It doesn't have to be on a yoga mat, but it could be. I think it's a very personal thing.

DB: What was the one moment that confirmed in your mind you must seek treatment or recovery, and why?

MK: That initial desire of I want to feel as good off the drugs as I did on the drugs was kind of the first thing I thought of, like hmm, maybe I should do that. And then I think that as I've grown and the business has grown, I've clarified my purpose and my mission, and I have a relationship, I think that each phase when something new comes into my life, I want to get the most out of it. I want to maximize it. And especially when I become aware of any time that my actions could negatively impact somebody I care about, that's when it's really like a call to be like, "hey, what's going on here?"

And then also when you go down the rabbit hole of medicine and you start getting blood work and all that shit, you know I had certain biomarkers come back where you're like, "you know Mastin, that's not the best cholesterol reading, you need to do something about that." So, there've been wake-up calls for sure, but I never had a moment of, alright, time to get into recovery. I mean, we're all recovering from trauma, right? Self-care is recovery. I just have more thought of it as how can I create more health? Or how can I get more done, or my lower back is going out like crazy, I need to speak for two weeks in a row, how can I get that worked out?

So I've always had a very functional and purposeful approach to things, I don't like to do things to do things. I like to have a reason to do it. I've always been motivated by that. And it's always been applied to a relationship or seminar I have to deliver, or something.

I would like to add just one thing. And I think it's important to say it. 100% of addiction is caused by trauma and unhealed trauma. 100%! So, when people say, "Oh trauma doesn't cause addiction," they don't have a contextual or broad enough understanding of what trauma, emotional trauma is. People think that trauma is, I was molested or I was abused, or something very egregious happened. And certainly those things are traumatizing, certainly. But what they don't realize is that, like in my example, okay? Both my parents, amazing human beings, good, well intended souls. They never laid their hands on me. They did everything they could to take care of me. And my father has unprocessed trauma from the war, being a combat medic. My mother had unprocessed trauma from her childhood, and from having a broken back and three or four major operations where she died twice. And the focus was on taking care of her.

So the message for me was very subtle, and it said your needs aren't important here. Now, you could say, Mastin how could you say that? You're a White guy, you're in Kansas, you have privilege. And all those things are true. And I still got this message as a child that the focus has to be on somewhere else. That's called neglect. That's what that's called. Not intentional neglect, not blaming my parents neglect, but the message my nervous system got was your needs will never get met. And that wound is called a relational wound, and you can have well-intended wounds. Doesn't mean there has to be negative intent.

And that is what manifested in my coping and relationship problems later in life, my drug use later in life, so people have to have an understanding that grade school can be traumatizing. A divorce can be traumatizing. And if you didn't have emotional resilience growing up, you could go through something later that's traumatizing and it could hit you harder than somebody else because you didn't have the nervous system strength to navigate it. So, there could be complex trauma, there could be relational trauma, I mean, trauma is passed down epigenetically from the parent to child.

So, it's really important that people start to expand their view of both mental health diagnosis and addiction. Because the root cause of mental health issues, and the root cause of addiction, is the same thing. It's core trauma that has not been identified or addressed. And I want to be quoted as stating 100% of addiction is caused by unhealed emotional trauma.

JANE VELEZ-MITCHELL

"We're all a work in progress and I make a lot of mistakes and I make a lot of compromises. The only thing I don't compromise on: I'm not going to drink today and I'm not going to kill to eat."
– Jane Velez-Mitchell

Bio: Jane Velez-Mitchell is the founder and editor of JaneUnChained.com, a digital news network focusing on animal rights and the vegan/compassionate lifestyle. #JaneUnChained's video news feed airs LIVE reports from around the country on facebook.com/JaneVelezMitchell numerous times a day.

Jane has won four Genesis Awards from the Humane Society of the United States for her reporting on animal issues. VegNews named her Media Maven of the Year in 2010. In 2013, Mercy for Animals awarded her their Compassionate Leadership Award. In 2014, Jane was honored for fighting animal abuse by the Animal Legal Defense Fund. In 2015, she received the Nanci Alexander Award at PETA's 35th anniversary. In 2017, she received Last Chance for Animals' Sam Simon Award and Woodstock Farm Animal Sanctuary's Woodstock Warrior award.

For six years Jane Velez-Mitchell hosted her own show on HLN (*CNN Headline News*) where she ran a weekly segment on animal issues. Previously, Jane reported for the nationally syndicated Warner Brothers/Telepictures show *Celebrity Justice*, where she did numerous stories on animal issues championed by celebrities.

Previously, Velez-Mitchell was a news anchor/reporter at *KCAL-TV* in Los Angeles and *WCBS-TV* in New York. She is the recipient of a *Los Angeles Emmy* and a *New York Emmy* for her reporting. Velez-Mitchell is a graduate of *New York University* and began her career with reporting stints in Ft. Myers, Florida, Minneapolis, and Philadelphia.

Velez-Mitchell is the author of four books. Her 2014 non-fiction *New York Times* bestseller, *Exposed: The Secret Life of Jodi Arias* offers a detailed psychological analysis of a salacious trial that gripped the American public. Her other *New York Times* bestseller is her memoir, *iWant: My Journey from Addiction and Overconsumption to a Simpler, Honest Life*. That work received the 2018 Experience, Strength and Hope award from *Writers in Treatment. Secrets Can Be Murder* delves into the secrecy and deceit embedded in tragic scenarios. *Addict Nation: An Intervention for America* with coauthor Sandra Mohr focuses on our culture's addictive nature and our obsession with overconsumption.

Velez-Mitchell directed and produced the documentary *Anita Velez: Dancing Through Life* which won a *Gracie* award in 2001. She lives with her partner, Donna Dennison, and their four companion animals in Los Angeles.

Occupation: TV Anchor/Animal Rights Activist

Drug of choice: Alcohol

Length of sobriety: 23 years

DB: What do you do on a daily basis to maintain your sobriety, and what is the most challenging part about it?

JV-M: I stay sober by staying involved in the joys of sobriety which means being with other sober people. Working my program of sobriety, I think that's fair to say. When I stop working it, things go south. When I stop being active in my sober community, sober world, sober friends, sober get togethers, that's when things start. My alcoholic personality manifests and it does it pretty fast. I've learned that prevention is . . . inoculate yourself against this disease which is a disease of amnesia that constantly tells you or is sitting there waiting to tell you at a moment of weakness, "It's okay. It doesn't apply to you anymore. You can have just one." Those thoughts are there waiting to erupt at a moment of weakness. So, the best way to inoculate yourself is to do whatever it takes to remind yourself of why you got sober in the first place and that usually involves talking to other sober people and sharing your experience and your story. I share my story. My story did involve incomprehensible demoralization. I was lucky in the sense that I was never arrested. I didn't lose the job or the house but it definitely impacted my reputation. I had a reputation as a lush. I wish I didn't have that. But you know what they say, don't regret the past, try to use your experience to help somebody else.

Twenty-three years later, sure there's still some people who remember my drinking escapades and the stupid things I did and the embarrassing things I did. That's not gonna go away. The vast majority of people I meet now, they don't think of me as an alcoholic, they think of me as a vegan, as an activist, as an animal lover, as a journalist, as an author. None of that would have happened if I hadn't gotten sober. They say there's no mess you can't clean up and sure, there are some messes that you can't clean up. Terrible things. But I feel like I tried to clean up the mess that was my life and do a living amends. That's a big part of my story is to try to . . . when I was drinking all I cared about was partying, going out on the weekends, going dancing, amusing myself, and getting ahead at work. Becoming better known, getting more money, blah, blah, blah. Actually, it really wasn't about the money, it was more about just moving up.

Now, I have other values. I care about being of service. I care about trying to make this world a better place that's why I started a news network for animal rights called JaneUnChained.

com. We're a digital news network that had 16.5 million video views on Facebook last year. I put all my energy into that now. I've taken all the energy that I used to put into partying, and putting it into something that is gonna make the world a better place. Some people say alcoholics have a lot of clichés but they are truisms is what I call them. They say if you wanna have self-esteem, do esteemable things. Take esteemable acts. That's so true. I feel that very strongly that my self-esteem has increased by pulling myself out of gutter of alcoholism and doing as many esteemable things as I can. Do I still have character defects? Hell yeah. I can be hot tempered, I can be overly dramatic, but not compared to the way I was and I'm aware of those issues and do try to work on them. I would guess in my work for animals and the environment and for I am doing a living amends. When you work on veganism you're also working to eliminate human world hunger because if we all went plant-based, we could eliminate human world hunger. It takes at least 12 pounds and up to 25 pounds of grain to produce one pound of beef. All of this work that I try to do with the animals, it's really about trying to make the world a better place. It's the leading cause of climate change, it's the leading cause of habitat destruction, wildlife extinction. By working on those issues . . . not to mention health problems: heart disease, cancer, etc. By working on those issues, I feel like I'm living amends and I've gone from this superficial narcissist who really just wanted to have fun and had a gallows sense of humor and prided myself in not taking anything seriously. Many alcoholics have that sort of reverse pride is what I'd call it. We're proud of the stupidest things. Like, "I could drink you under the table." I was proud that. Now, I'm proud of other things. I'm proud of doing things and taking actions that will hopefully make the world a better place.

DB: How have you reconnected with your body since being in recovery, and what are some things you include in your daily life to increase your health and vitality?

JV-M: Addiction is a complicated thing and when you give up one thing, your addiction will often jump to something else. When I gave up alcohol . . . when I was in my disease, I did not care a whit as to whether or not I ate anything. I would go and have a salad over five or six chardonnays and that would be fine. Then when I got sober, all the sudden, candy. Oh dear. I started to notice candy for the first time. Sweets, is what I mean. That has been something that I think a lot of people deal with is that the addiction jumps. I have to really work at trying to have healthy sweets because it is definitely something that I grapple with. It's hard for me to fall asleep if I don't have something sweet at night. But I'm trying to do healthy stuff, it's got bananas and strawberries and instead of produced sugar, maple syrup. Alcoholics are often served candy, cookies, and coffee to get their mind off alcohol. I'm just a garden variety alcoholic.

One thing I realized when I got sober, I thought I was hot stuff. I'm a bad girl. I'm a partier. When I got sober, I realized, I am such a garden variety alcoholic. A dime a dozen. Basically, I never even got a DUI. I would go and make a fool of myself at parties. This was my specialty. Now, when I see people doing that, I'm so turned off. People at parties who are slurring their words, I'm repulsed by them. And to think about how people must have been repulsed by my behavior. Suffice it to say that sometimes we think we're all that in our disease and then we realize it was pathetic. It's those kind of memories that keep me sober. A couple of things. One, I'm having fun in sobriety. When I got sober I thought, I will never have fun again. I will never go dancing again. I will never karaoke again. I will never go skiing again. I will never go on vacation again. I will never have fun again. And guess what? I'm having more fun than I've ever had in my entire life. There's a certain relaxation that comes with it because, toward the end of my drinking career, I didn't know what the hell was going to happen. It was off to the races and who knew what was going to transpire. I would say, toward the end of my drinking career, it made me increasingly anxiety ridden. You know what they say, first it's fun, then it's fun with problems, then it's just problems. At the end, I wasn't having fun. I was anxiety ridden. I didn't trust myself. I was anxiety ridden at a party because I thought am I going to make a fool of myself again? When I gave up alcohol, I thought I'll never be able to enjoy a social occasion but actually the opposite occurred. Being relaxed was a huge benefit because I knew I really couldn't make much of a fool of myself, certainly nothing in comparison to what I used to do. And if I did make fool of myself, well, at least I would remember it.

As somebody very wise told me. She said, "Jane, nothing you do sober will ever be as embarrassing as what you've already done drunk." There's a lot of freedom in that. There's freedom to say . . . life, you don't have to take it so deadly seriously, we can have a little fun and accept the fact that we're gonna make mistakes and things are gonna get screwed up every so often and just be a little lighter, more carefree. Frankly, I just feel such a relief that I am not that practicing alcoholic any more. I would wake up in the morning and say, "Who was that person?" And then realize, that person was me. I'm just so grateful and I enjoy being sober. I have fun in sobriety. It's very important to have fun in sobriety.

DB: How have your relationships changed since being in recovery? Who would you say are the top three to five people you surround yourself with and why are they influential in your recovery?

JV-M: My girlfriend, my partner. I'm gay. I drank to suppress my sexual orientation, that's an important fact that I need to bring in. Alcoholism is multidetermined. It was genetic. My dad was an alcoholic. High functioning but still an alcoholic. I also am gay and I was very concerned about letting that secret out which luckily I did right after, very soon after I got sober. I had nowhere to run, nowhere to hide and I realized that I just couldn't stuff it down anymore. My girlfriend is sober. We met at a gathering of sober people. I think it's very important to try to have a sober relationship or at least somebody who doesn't have a drinking issue. You can have a relationship with somebody who is not necessarily an alcoholic in recovery but I think it's best if that person does not drink to access and drinking isn't a big part of their life. I don't think I could be with anybody like that. So, my girlfriend, number one. Number two, I surround myself with people who have similar values. I personally believe that being of service doesn't just extend to our fellow humans, I believe it extends to all beings that are capable of feeling pain and suffering so I surround myself with people who have had the lightbulb go on as well and realize that we don't need to kill to survive. All this talk about we've got to kill these animals to live, we've turned our planet into planet slaughterhouse and I surround myself with people who have woken up and understand that we do not have to torture and kill to survive. That's definitely who I surround myself with.

DB: What is your spiritual life like and what do you do on a daily basis to integrate it into your life, and why do you think spirituality is important for growth and sustainability in recovery?

JV-M: Beware of people who run around saying how spiritual they are. There's a phrase, it says, "spiritual materialism." That's people who use their so-called spirituality as a commodity. The ultimate example would be the corrupt preacher who is getting wealthy off of his poor to modest income parishioners. There are plenty of other people running around saying that they're spiritual but are their actions in line with those values? I believe that Thich Nhat Hanh, the famous philosopher said . . . and he said, "Peace is every step in every decision we make throughout the course of the day." That's how I judge whether people are spiritual, not by what they say or whether they self-describe as spiritual. It's the decisions they make on a minute to minute day by day basis. Let's face it, we live in a consumer culture and a lot of the decisions we make throughout the course of the day are what are we gonna buy? What are we gonna eat? What are we gonna wear? I try to ask myself, "Am I making ethical, spiritual decisions in my personal choices?" Yes, we discuss food and I don't believe that killing is spiritual. I don't think you can run around saying you're spiritual while you're killing on a daily basis. Especially when you don't do it yourself, when you're hiring somebody else who doesn't really have a choice of what job they're going to take. They're doing the throat slitting. It's definitely hypocrisy and not spiritual in my opinion. Killing is no kindness, to put it bluntly. Then, also, the choices about whether we're going to make this world cleaner and less self-destructive. Even little choices about should I have a plastic cup? Should I get a straw? Should I recycle? Do I have all of that mastered? No. It's very hard to practice those kinds of principles every day in this culture where it's almost becoming impossible to buy something that's not plastic, you know? We've plasticized the world and we're destroying it. I wouldn't wanna say I'm coming from on high, that I've figured it out. I do a bunch of stuff that when I think about it, I go, "Why did I do that?"

We're all a work in progress and I make a lot of mistakes and I make a lot of compromises. The only thing I don't compromise on: I'm not going to drink today and I'm not going to kill to eat. I wasn't born, let's say vegan or sober, for sure. But we're a work in progress and it's never too late. It's never too late to get sober, it's never too late to stop killing. All these things are things that we... progress not perfection. I just want to say, I'm not coming from any lofty plane. I do get irritated . . . my tone can go south really fast and I can get irritated with people and I'm still working on that. I get frustrated. I notice that people who are really spiritual are often able to stay calm and cool no matter what. I aspire to that but I'm not there yet. I'll tell you that.

DB: What was one situation you found yourself in that confirmed in your mind that you must seek treatment and recovery and why?

JV-M: There were many times where I had made a fool of myself, got drunk at a party. The time I got sober, I finally had a number to call because one of my best friends from college had recently gotten sober and we used to party together. A lot. He was like, "Jane, you need to get sober. You need to do this." I was like,

"Mind your own business. You're not my mother." Then I made a fool of myself at this party. It happened to be an interesting kind of this is your life kind of party. Everybody I knew was there. It was almost like the very people who would show up at an intervention had arrived early. A lot of people. My ex-husband, my agent, my agent's husband, some of my best friends, my then boyfriend, work colleagues, good friends, and I got drunk. Which definitely involved tequila and definitely when tequila entered the picture, all bets were off. I could sometime keep it together or keep it to slurring when it was just chardonnay but when tequila entered the picture, watch out. And that's exactly what happened that night. I was carried out of the party over my boyfriend's shoulder.

The next morning I woke up, he was nowhere to be found. I thought, he's gone. I felt incomprehensible demoralization. Those factors had been there before but the key difference was I had a friend who had told me "You need to get sober" and I had a number to call and I called him. I literally said, "I'm turning myself in. I need help." And funny enough, after I got off the phone, I walked back into the living room and my then boyfriend was sleeping on the couch. Had I seen him sleeping on the couch . . . this is the kind of die-hard alcoholic that I was . . . had I seen him sleeping on the couch, I would not have made the call because I would have known, "Oh well, he didn't quite leave. I can manage this. I can smooth this over." But I thought I had really destroyed relationships, friendships so I am so happy that I had that friend to call. That was it. I would say that . . . what happened was a shift in my psyche. I went from "I will not drink today" which never worked to "I don't have to drink today." That was the shift. I would say that a lot of my cravings just disappeared. I had a psychic shift. I was very, very lucky.

DR. STEVE DANSIGER

"And the other thing is too, is that meditation, the way I was taught it, my teacher used to always say meditation is not a practice of the mind, it's a practice of the body."
– Dr. Stephen Dansiger

Bio: Dr. Steve played CBGB and Max's Kansas City in the late 70s; drank, played in a toy rock band and then got sober in the 80s; became an international educator and rocker again in the 90s; and a sought after clinician and meditation teacher in the 2000s. Dr. Steve has attempted to cure Marc Maron on WTF, become a master EMDR therapist and provider of EMDR Therapy Training with the Institute for Creative Mindfulness, and helped set up the premiere Buddhist addictions rehab center, Refuge Recovery Centers. At the center he developed and incubated the MET(T)A Protocol, a design for addictions agency treatment using Buddhist Mindfulness and EMDR Therapy as the anchor. He gives regular Dharma talks in Los Angeles and internationally, is beginning production of two podcasts, seeing patients, and supervising and guiding young clinicians. At all other times, he is wrangling and entertaining his 9-year-old daughter. Dr. Steve's book *Clinical Dharma: A Path for Healers and Helpers* is available in paperback and Kindle. His collaboration with colleague Dr. Jamie Marich, *EMDR Therapy and Mindfulness for Trauma Focused Care*, was released by Springer Publishing in November 2017. His new book *Mindfulness for Anger Management* is due for release in November 2018 by Althea Press.

Occupation: EMDR/Mindfulness/Meditation Therapist and Coach

Drug of choice: Alcohol

Length of sobriety: 30 years

DB: What do you do on a daily basis to maintain your sobriety and what's the most challenging part about it, would you say?

SD: Well, you know, it's a very different answer today than it used to be. I'll be clean and sober 30 years in March, so the answer to that is very different than what it was when I first got sober. I could just do the quick and dirty is that when I first got sober, I did go to meetings. I got sober in AA in New York at the end of the '80's, which was actually a really great time to be in 12-Step in New York. There were just a lot of young people getting sober.

I have a lot of friends who have the amount of continuous sobriety that I have, that did it that way at that time. I went to a lot of meetings. I didn't have a job and I knew that I wanted to stay sober. I didn't even know what it meant to want to stay sober until I got brought into the 12-Step program by a friend. I had made sort of vague promises to myself at times but in AA, I ran into these people who seemed pretty happy about being sober.

I soon picked up exercise a lot in the beginning; so, getting into my body and looking at the different ways that I could support my recovery and the different ways that I could deal with emergency situations, like dealing with that hardest part, the sort of urges that I would get in the beginning that didn't seem to be even connected to any particular trigger. It would just be so powerful that I'd be like, "Oh, what am I even gonna do here?"

What I would do is I would take that very fundamental advice, I just gotta get through this day. And sometimes it would look very sober, but other times I'd look like a guy white knuckling it. But, the fact is that I got through that day.

So, then as the years went by, months and years went by, it became less about being in a fist fight with a bottle of Jack Daniels and those urges weren't really coming and it was just a matter of addressing life as a person not completely escaping life through substances.

So, each of the challenges along the way has presented itself. I'm not gonna use even though my Mom just passed away. I'm not gonna use even though my kid was born. You know, each of these huge events that bring on strong feelings. In the past, I would medicate those strong feelings and so now I've found a multitude of ways I can do something different. I can do something physical. I can do something mental, emotional. I can do something spiritual. I've got all of these different tools but just basically they're my ways of being in this world. Meditation has played a huge part in all of it. At the basis of everything is my meditation practice, which began when I was brought to a retreat at a Zen monastery and I learned how to meditate.

So, that's the foundation of everything. And then from that I'm able to apply mindfulness to any situation, any recovery tool. Today it's all about my community. Meaning, I've just got the most wonderful friends and family. Plugging into the joy of my work and really being engaged in my work. And knowing that the only reason I'm able to do the work I do is because I'm not intoxicated and that I've spent a lot of time not intoxicated so I have this focus and energy that allows me to be of service to people. I can try and see if I can transform suffering. And it has to do with being able to live within the structure of what life has to offer, which includes a deep, deep sadness at times and deep, deep joy and being able to just be with that. As opposed to trying to amplify the joy and escape the pain.

DB: How have you reconnected with your body since being in recovery? And what are some things you do on a daily basis to increase your health and vitality?

SD: These days I work backwards. These days I'm big on walking and hiking. I was gonna get back into running, but again like I said, I'm 55 and there's been body changes that I'm trying to be mindful of. I know that there's a lot that the body can do, but based on sort of my history of my exercise, I would say my body stuff has gone up and down, in and out, over time.

So right now, a lot of walking. In the past there's been yoga, there's been working out. Like working out with weights. Working out doing cardio. Cardio beyond just the walking. I like cycling. I really like long distance hiking. Backpack style hiking.

Then, I've gone through phases where I revive things from when I was a kid. When I was a kid, up until the age of 12, I was very physical and played baseball, soccer, roller hockey, all kinds of sports; team sports. I haven't really revived that in my life. There have been times where I've gotten involved in softball games and things like that.

That's the majority of it, solo working out. Going for walks, hiking with friends. Sometimes going through phases where I'm more involved with yoga or lifting weights or other forms of cardio. Tennis, I went through a period of tennis coming back and I have a plan. I have my tennis instructor picked out to get back into tennis.

That's where it stands now. And the other thing is too, is that meditation, the way I was taught it, my teacher used to always say meditation is not a practice of the mind, it's a practice of the body. So, yeah, it's not burning calories in the same way nor is it working on the neuro chemistry in the same way, but it is definitely working on the neuro chemistry because I'm allowing myself to just sit and be a body sitting on the ground. And it's a very different experience than being a body sitting on the ground that's trying to think big thoughts and making myself anxious with them.

That's another way I actually look at that as a way I take care of my body, because meditation lowers the heart rate, blood pressure, the breathing rate. All of which is really good for the body. Helps reduce stress much like exercise through the endorphins and dopamine and all the rest of the chemical changes. In addition to the physical changes, it's super healthy.

I don't know if you were going to bring up food, but I've tended to be more vegetarian than not over the last 30 years. Right now, I'm vegan again. I did five years of veganism at one point.

I sort of really became aware of the importance of being mindful of nutrition in terms of taking care of my recovery.

DB: How have your relationships transformed from when you were using to now being in recovery? And who are the top three to five people you surround yourself with and why are they influential in your recovery?

SD: Well, in the end, it's funny the only people that are in my life from my days of using are the people who also got sober and a few people that I hung out with in high school and college who didn't use. You know what I mean?

I remember I have this one friend from my first college where I got basically kicked out after two years from drinking. And I asked my friend when we reunited, reconnected, I said, "Were there more people like you? It didn't seem like anyone was not drinking." And he's like, "Yeah, there were hundreds of us that were not drinking."

Anyway, so I find myself looking back on my relationships when I was using in a less judgmental and severe way than I used to. Like, I used to think that I was using them, and they were using me. But I did have a lot of sweet relationships, but I tended to destroy them. I was the one who set fire to a lot of relationships because I usually was the more severe alcoholic or addict in the equation.

So that's what it was. Very passionate relationships with people and then someone would go nuclear. Usually me going nuclear or encouraging them to put the nuclear device in action.

In recovery I always had, for the most part, sponsors in 12-Step. I've always had therapists along the way. And I've had a couple of friends, like spiritual friends. People who are Zen Buddhist Monks and things like that. People who are part of my crew that is about the care of Steve, the care and feeding of Steve.

I think I was pretty much a people person when I was using. And then towards the end of my using I started to isolate much more. And so once I kind of got a little clear eyed and a little bit less fearful, I really just dove into having relationships. So those relationships are generally very reciprocal. People are not using each other. People are feeding each other and we're lifting each other up.

So I've got, for instance, a couple of friends, a few friends, who moved out here to LA from New York around the time I did and now we're still buddies. We see each other all the time. And now we all have kids and our kids play with each other and stuff and it's just an amazing thing to be able to be sober and clear eyed and just participate in life.

Then I have my best friend. My best friend has been my best friend for almost 30 years. I met him at a meeting. He's said something like, "Hi. I think your glasses are cool." I said, "Okay, that's cool." And then we just started talking. Then he was the one who brought me to the Zen monastery for that retreat. Now, one of his boys is my godson. We're across the country from each other, so we're on the phone every day or two just having this friendship.

So yeah, it's almost hard to put into words. The difference is that I'm present. I'm involved. I am truly part of the relationship and I know it and so does the other person.

And I feel like also recovery, being in recovery, has given me some tools so that when conflict comes up I'm in a much better place to resolve it. Because conflict is part of everything, It's part of relationships and friendships. So, I feel like the reason I have some long-standing friendships is because I also have these conflict resolution tools that I use.

DB: Who are the three to five people who you hang out with now and why are they influential in your recovery?

SD: I've been so busy lately that it's more like I touch into my people. So, I would say the top two are my wife and my daughter. Even though my kid is 9-years-old and so I don't expect her to keep me regulated, but we coregulate. She keeps me on point. She keeps me honest. She keeps me focused on the fact that I'm not the most important person in the room. And I just enjoy being a Dad so much. I mean it has been ridiculous. The last nine years has been my favorite thing.

And then there's my spouse who I've been with for 12 years now. We have one of those marriages where we've had our challenges, we continue to have challenges, and then we go in there and meet them, and then also find the joy, not just in parenting, but in just being together.

Right now, because I'm sort of in transition, right now the person who I wrote my last book with and who I work with on training people in EMDR, it's a long-distance working relationship. She's in Ohio, but she and I have become through the writing of that book together on EMDR therapy and mindfulness, and addressing trauma, with that and addiction, we already were close colleagues, we already had a friendship, but being in constant contact with her has really shifted my recovery to a really good place. I'm in this transition period, and I'm in this next phase of recovery. And her presence has been really instrumental in that. And then, all the colleagues that I have, either in a lateral fashion, at the institute that I train for, and all the colleagues that I work with training them in therapy, and in directing, clinical operations at different places. That is a huge part of my recovery, because it's collegial, but it's also pretty deep, there's a deep friendly aspect to it all. And we're all on this sort of boat together. We're in like the chief lifesaving boat going around to all the other boats with the people in it, trying to provide the care. So, in that boat, we're caring for each other.

And so that's a huge part of my recovery. And I currently still, at the moment, I have a therapist, and that experience of still being in therapy environment for myself allows me to kind of have a place where all these relationships can be monitored and nurtured. And then I can go out and be better in those other relationships. So I think those are the top ones.

DB: What is your spiritual life like, and what do you do on a daily basis to integrate it into your life, and why do you think spirituality is important for growth and sustainability and recovery?

SD: So you know, again, I came through the 12-Step door, and so that was my formal introduction to returning to the idea that spirituality is even a thing. I had a very deep breakup with God, or all things related to spirituality when I was 13 and my cousin was killed in an accident. And he was like an older brother figure, and I was just like, "Alright, I'm done with anything that has to do with whatever that might be." So, when I got to 12-Step and I was, "Oh. Oh, God. Oy." And so, I just started to consider it, and I actually turned into very open minded, and really went on a very, very deep spiritual search. All options were open, so what happened was when my friend brought me to that Monastery, I was about four months sober, something like that. I was like, "Oh, I think this fits." And so it's a longer story.

I've called myself a Buddhist for many years, and in 1998, I lived at the Monastery for a year, and I took a Buddhist name, and I took lay precepts and. But I still have a loose enough definition of what it means to be a Buddhist. It as much as I'm more concerned with living the path, so living the eight-fold path that Buddha laid out, which takes care of everything that the 12-Steps take care of, and pretty much every other spiritual path takes care of. Which is developing more wisdom, living ethically, and in the Buddhist's case, really focuses on developing mindfulness. And so I do that daily, in a formal way where pretty much won't miss a day of meditation, formal sitting meditation.

I also do walking meditation. I will go to a group, a Dharma sitting and participate. I teach Buddhist mindfulness, so I put myself in those environments and have myself meditating. I teach classes that put me in the space where I'm always reading texts that grow my wisdom and my understanding. And the beauty of it is, and this is part of 12-Step and other things too, particularly in the Buddhist philosophy or Buddhist spirituality, being wise in my speech, being wise in my action, and being wise in my livelihood.

So, I'm told, or it's been suggested to me, that three-eighths of the path that I'm on is what I'm doing and saying, and then how I'm operating as a person in the work world. So, I can't help but focus on it. So, everything that I'm doing and everything that I'm saying and everything that I do at work and everything that I'm thinking and feeling has these spiritual aspects, spiritual ramifications or spiritual application. I'd say my mindfulness practice is in my primary spiritual activating tool.

The suggestion I often give friends or clients is something I read from a book, *A Gradual Awakening*, by Stephen Levine, who is a famous Buddhist teacher that passed away a few years ago, and he wrote something to the effect of definitely when you discover that you want to look at spirituality and you want to find a path, go ahead and go to the spiritual smorgasbord for six months. And then at the end of six months, pick one thing, and do it for at least two years to see what it's really like to participate in something.

So, in a sense, it's what I did. And I even went back to the smorgasbord. I went to Interfaith Ministry School. I didn't finish, but I went through more than a couple years of it. So, I've always been open to the many paths, and the many paths lead into one. The path in particular that I found that makes sense for me to walk has been this Buddhist path.

DB: What was one tell-tale moment that confirmed in your mind you must seek treatment and recovery, and why?

SD: Well, there was a tell-tale moment that I didn't listen to about two years before I stopped drinking, where I was in the emergency room with alcoholic gastritis, and my mother was with me because I had been visiting them when I was struck with the attack. And the doctor came in and he gave me that look, you know? That look of, "I know exactly who you are, and I know exactly what your problem is," and I knew he knew. I was like, "Oh, it's all over now." And he said, "How much do you drink?" to me. And I said, "I don't know, a beer now and then." He looked at my mom and he's like, "Does he drink?" And I did a lot of not drinking around her, and she said, "I don't know, probably a beer now and then."

So he's said, "Well, I don't understand, because his liver's enlarged, we ran his tests. I can't really think of another explanation, based on the rest of his testing, like why else that would be true." And I left, and I drank for another two years. So, then it was like a long, slow, decline into what I would call more of a spiritual-emotional bottom, less than that physical bottom. I just got that place where I couldn't drink and I couldn't not drink, and I tried to stop drinking, sort of on my own. And the only way that I could find to do it was to lock myself in the room with my girlfriend at the time, and not leave the house, and then go to bed.

So that wasn't going to be sustainable. The last tell-tale sign was when my last drinks were like three beers, when I had been sitting with my ex-girlfriend on my left, and my girlfriend on my right. Ex-girlfriend said, "Drink. You're boring when you don't drink."

Current girlfriend said, "Don't you dare," because she had been trying to help me not drink. We were trying to do this project of not drinking. And I drank that night. I had maybe not had a drink for a couple weeks at that point, and in three beers I went through my entire usual cycle of what would take me many drinks to do, which was first drink I was loosened up and I felt good, and I was like, "Yay drinking." Second beer I became lampshade guy, entirely too loud, thinking I'm funny, and then third beer I became the morose suicidal drunk.

When I woke up the next day, I was kind of like, "This is over." A friend of my girlfriend had been trying to bring me into an AA meeting for about nine months. It was as they say, attraction, not promotion. She was really just letting me find my way there and I got in touch with her, I said, "Alright, uncle, take me to your people." And so, it took. I got fortunate that way. I got fortunate that way or I just really was done. Between the physical bottom from a couple years earlier, and then just realizing I was done. The other thing too was that I was a musician at the time, and this band that I had been in kind of got fake famous and was kind of maybe going to the next level and broke up all of a sudden. That was part of what drove me to the place where I was just really super miserable and wanting to drink more again, and sort of just pouring alcohol on that problem.

So, I kind of came to the conclusion sort of toward the end too that I had been instrumental in the breakup of that band, and I realized that my being a drunken fool was not serving me or others in any way that was positive. So that was another sort of sign or impetus to get help. And in New York, back then, and still to this day doesn't really have a big rehab culture. Out here in LA, there are rehabs everywhere. And in New York, back then especially, you just went to an AA meeting. Either you went to an AA meeting or you flew to California to a rehab if you had sort of heard about it. So that was the path. That's how I availed myself of some kind of treatment . . . was to go to meetings.

EDEN SASSOON

"And I heard my father's voice, and I heard to me what would be my higher power . . . both talking and I actually had a visualization. And I saw my Dad and I saw what in my mind's eye what looked like Jesus and they were talking. They were basically saying you are more than this."
– Eden Sassoon

Bio: Eden is the outspoken daughter of legendary beauty icon Vidal Sassoon. Influenced by the impact her father left on the industry, she has made her own mark with her full-service salon EDEN by Eden Sassoon, and two luxury Pilates studios in Los Angeles. Her desire to forge her way led to her building the nonprofit organization Beauty Gives Back, which unites the hair industry in fighting the global water crisis.

Occupation: Health and Wellness Advocate

Drug of choice: Alcohol

Length of sobriety: 6 years

DB: What do you do to stay sober on a daily basis and what's the most challenging part about it?

ES: Oh, Dougie. Well obviously that question evolves daily or yearly or . . . I mean six years ago I would have given you completely different answers. So today I wake up in gratitude and I give it to God or a higher power and for me I do call that higher power God. And I realize that I am such a small part of this massive universe that we live in and that kind of puts my ego in check. Not kind of, it does. And that I am one with everybody and that the person next to me could be suffering just as much as I am or was. I think it's a moment to moment thing. The addiction I think, by the grace of God was released and so I don't struggle with alcohol. I don't struggle thinking about it. I don't struggle wanting it. I think I struggle more with other emotions that come up that relate to addiction, maybe it's food. Maybe it's whatever it is on a deeper level that I want then and I need to check myself, why do you want it? What does it mean to you? Where does this take you? And just sort of try to be in every moment as is in a peaceful, happy way and that keeps me centered.

My challenges now are more with (and have always been with) for one, letting someone love me. I turn back to myself. If I'm not capable of loving myself 100% then no one else will ever be capable of that. Sobriety doesn't play a part for me in that. I would say the closest challenge as far as alcohol to me would be food. That is more of a constant daily struggle which plays a part in my self-esteem. I guess part of me wants to go to OA (Overeaters Anonymous) and figure it out. I mean granted, when we're in meetings and using the program you just have to substitute food for alcohol or whatever your addiction may be.

DB: How have you reconnected with your body since being in recovery and what are some things you do daily to increase your health and vitality?

ES: Oh, my body. I don't know that when I was drinking that I realized I had a body or anything for that matter. In six years I've had to really work on reconnecting with self—"self" being mind, body, spirit. My body is part of who I am 100% because physically I am more of a physical person. Others might be more of a mindful person or a spiritual being and I think I'm all three.

But if I'm not using my body then that goes back into the cycle of self and self-hatred and overeating and these other things that I work on. I've come to realize that my body is my vessel to get through this journey and I need to be as healthy and strong and useful to myself as I possibly can be.

DB: How have your relationships changed from being in recovery and then who are the top three to five people you surround yourself with and why are they influential in your recovery?

ES: My relationships have ended in recovery and thank God. But, that's by choice. I think when you come to find yourself you need less people around; when you take something out of your life that you've had in your life for so long, you will have to make new friends or new people will just organically come because I do believe we're all energy and if you're creating this energy or I was creating the energy of not being sober and chaos in my life, then those are the people I surround myself with. And now it's very, very, very different. I don't know if I have very many friends. The people that I surround myself with are the people that I work with.

I'm actually going through a transition right now with really sort of surrounding myself with my children and those that I work with and/or exercise with. I'm single. I choose to really be with myself as much as possible, even when I'm with myself if that makes sense, to understand things about me. When somebody is added to my life if they don't add to my life then I choose to be alone. In any way, friendship, lover, even my children sometimes, I say let's have a time out.

People need to choose wisely and let the right energy in. And energy attracts energy, right? So, what you give off you're going to get back.

DB: Absolutely. Now what's your spiritual life like and what do you do daily for spirituality and why you think it's

important for growth and sustainability in recovery?

ES: I think that's a huge question. For me, spirituality is everything because again, I am this spiritual being in this physical body. The physical body I think traps us and limits us and our potential. So, if you can take that energy and realize within the walls of your mind that you are so much bigger than that, therein lies a lot of freedom and possibility and creation. It's not really day to day. It's again, every moment releasing the pressure of I am my mind and my body in this small 5' 4" package of a little woman and knowing I'm a powerful being.

Because beyond that is, I am capable of anything. And trust me, my mind holds me down too. I think whether it be yoga, meditation, Pilates, physical fitness in any way, the choices we make through our diet, who we allow in our life and spend time with, this is all part of being and being present and being in the moment. To me, the past doesn't exist. The past only shows me limitations of what the future can hold. And that's very good because there are no limitations but the past creates that sense that there are

So since it doesn't exist why do we tend to hold onto it and why do we think about it? And why do we dwell on it? I don't do that. Here I am. And so it is.

DB: What was the one situation you found yourself in that confirmed in your mind you must seek inner treatment and/ or recovery and why?

ES: I wish to God that I only had one situation. But there were many: many of blackouts, many of vomiting in public, many random nights of who is this person? Not me, the man next to me. A lot of things that today I sometimes look back and think "wow". Wow, it's incredible. And thank God that I am here now because I don't think that anyone can do that forever. So again, once you make the choice of living a certain lifestyle or being in your present moment and you're connected to who and what you really are and that energy, then you can't go back.

So everything I did and where I was, which was complete chaos, and then the me in the moment, it might have been considered fun but that's not fun. That's also another question that people ask"what do you do for fun?" And I'm like, what does that even mean? Life is fun. This moment should be fun. It's as if you're saying my life isn't fun and you're asking what I do outside of myself for fun. So the original question, I woke up one day on the edge of my bed and thank God I was dressed and I actually went into my closet to go on my hike and as I'm getting dressed, I'm crying.

And I heard my father's voice, and I heard to me what would be my higher power . . . both talking, and I actually had a visualization. And I saw my dad and I saw what in my mind's eye looked like Jesus and they were talking. They were basically saying you are more than this. You have so much potential. What are you doing? Really kind of coming at me hard in my mind and my father had a way of doing that for all the right reasons. And I just kept crying and crying and crying and then as the morning went on and I got on the mountain I realized that that was it.

This was my day. And then a godshot about an hour later, I ran into a sober friend of mine, Nick. Immediately I called my ex-husband and said, "I'm going to go down to a meeting tonight." And he said, "Well I have a thing. You need to keep the kids." And I'm thinking to myself, "Did he really just say that to me? Maybe he doesn't understand." So I said, "You know what Nick? What can we do?" He says, "Get in the car." Within 10 minutes we were up at the Hills Treatment Center and that was the beginning of my journey: December 5, 2012.

DOUG'S TWO CENTS ON SPIRITUALITY

I consider myself a Christian. I do not judge anyone who is not. I believe in God and believe Jesus died on the cross for my sins. That's my belief. It may not be yours.

Spirituality is a beautiful thing. It helps keep you centered. Many people in who have struggled with addiction feel spirituality is a crucial part of recovery, while others disagree. Christianity, Higher Power, Buddhism, Muslim, Judaism, or meditation are many forms of spirituality that people enjoy practicing. I love meditating. It calms me and helps me to relax. Statistics show that meditation is growing in popularity and is very beneficial for us mentally. Doing acts of service or being in nature are some other ways that people in recovery embrace spirituality. As I keep reiterating, there is no one way. Do what works for you. Spirituality also teaches us to be more forgiving. Maybe you need to forgive a parent, sibling, lover, or someone else. Heck, it could very well be you that needs to be forgiven. Just because you forgive someone doesn't mean you forget, but you are making a decision to no longer let that anger or resentment be a burden in your life.

Here are a few tips to help you add some spirituality in your life:

1. Write down one thing you are grateful for every single day. We tend to get caught up in the things we don't have in our

lives instead of what we do have. We look at what others have instead of what we have. If we spend all of our lives focusing on the things we don't have, we will be unfulfilled. Start with what you have.

2. Have faith. Many believe faith is the opposite of fear. Faith is believing in the unseen, believing that life will be better tomorrow than it is today. That's the essence of faith, that things are going to work out.

3. Look at some of the spirituality practices that are mentioned in this book. See if some of those resonate with you and how you could start to incorporate them into your life.

4. Love others for who they are. Agreeing with them and loving them are two different things.

5. Think of someone you might have harmed. Make that phone call or take a step to amend that relationship or at least apologize.

RICKY BYRD

"I love the gym . . . helps my mind and body.
I think clearer when I'm in that mode."
– Ricky Byrd

Bio: Ricky Byrd is a Recovery Troubadour and Rock and Roll Hall of Fame 2015 Inductee with Joan Jett and The Blackhearts. He is Founder/CEO of Ricky Byrd's Clean Getaway Cleangetaway. nyc and a Certified Recovery Coach/CARC + CASAC T. Byrd has performed, recorded, and/or toured with Joan Jett and The Blackhearts, Roger Daltrey, Ian Hunter, Southside Johnny, Paul McCartney, Ringo Starr, Joe Walsh, Alice Cooper, Mavis Staples, Billy Squier, Darlene Love, Smokey Robinson, The Beach Boys, Brian Wilson, Jimmy Page, Steve Miller, Steven Van Zandt, John Waite, Ronnie Spector, Graham Nash, Don Felder, Bruce Springsteen, Dion, Elvis Costello, Bill Medley, Paul Shaffer, Bonnie Bramlett, Bobby Whitlock, Sam Moore, and Billy Joe Armstrong to name a few. Byrd has recorded three solo CD's: Tough Room This World (Live) – 2001, Lifer – 2013, Clean Getaway – 2017.

Occupation: Musician, Recovery Troubadour

Drug of choice: More

Length of sobriety: 31 years

DB: What do you do on a daily basis to maintain your sobriety,

and what is the most challenging part about it?

RB: I still go to as many Community Support Group meetings as time will allow. I try and call a few people in recovery on a daily basis, as my friend Will G. says, "I'm checking in so I don't check out." I also have a few people that call me on a daily basis. All of that keeps me connected to Recovery. I do a lot of work in the recovery community, including my Recovery Music Groups at treatment facilities around the country. Keeps it all real green for me. Now that I'm certified as a Recovery Coach and Drug and Alcohol Counselor (in training) I come into contact with people struggling and I get to help which in turn helps me by keeping me grateful to be clean and sober. I'd like to say I pray every morning but I am usually rushing somewhere and forget. I do have a better day when I remember to hit my knees. Good news is you can stop any time of the day and say the serenity prayer. If you stay around for the miracle, all of these things become second nature and part of your routine like drinking and drugging once was.

DB: How have you reconnected with your body since being in recovery, and what are some things you include in your daily life to increase your health and vitality?

RB: I love the gym . . . helps my mind and body. I think clearer when I'm in that mode. Unfortunately when I went back to school I fell out of that good habit. I'm about to rejoin as we speak. As far as eating healthy, well I go in and out of that world! Sitting on the couch with a guitar in my lap is my stress reducer most times.

DB: How have your relationships changed (types of people, length/meaning of relationships, etc.) from when you were actively using to being in recovery?

RB: Well when I was using most of the people I hung out with were using. Now most of the people I associate with are either in recovery or never had an issue with it. I'm not the drug and alcohol police so what other people do is none of my business, yet when it starts affecting your work or personality it's no fun to be around. I'm sure I was a piece of work as well.

DB: Who are the top three to five people you surround yourself with and why are they influential in your recovery?

RB: I don't really surround myself with anyone. I need to be a loner sometimes and sometimes I like to be around people. I also do not need to talk recovery 24/7, but a lot of my relationships and people I hang with come from long friends I know from community support group meetings. Being around my 17-year-old daughter reminds me how I would never want her to see that guy from the active addiction days. That alone is a powerful recovery tool for me.

DB: What is your spiritual life like and what do you do on a daily basis to integrate it into your life, and why do you think spirituality is important for growth and sustainability in recovery?

RB: My spiritual life gets stronger or weaker depending on how much recovery work I'm doing on myself. That simple. I have a condition that pushes my buttons, tells me I'm worthless and wants me to be in pain. You can't be spiritual when you live in fear instead of faith. When I'm working recovery it makes me want to help others, move forward in spite of fear, admit when I'm wrong, face life head on. Accept things as they are and not as I would have it. That's spiritual to me.

DB: What was one situation you found yourself in that confirmed in your mind that you must seek treatment and recovery and why?

RB: There were many near misses. I almost died and kept using for four more years. I just hit the final wall and made a call. That was my beginnings. I was looking in the mirror drunk, high, nose bleeding, heart beating out of my chest. And with the gift of desperation at hand I picked up the phone. I was DONE. Then I learned how to stay DONE a day at a time. Over 30 years later I'm still chuggin' along on the Recovery train. Sometimes it's easy, sometimes it's difficult but as long as I don't pick up the first one I have a chance to be happy, joyous, and free.

LEONARD BUSCHEL

"I could literally tell you about any day I've lived through in the last 24 years. Ask me about any New Year's Eve, any birthday, any hospital stay. I could tell you where I was. By looking it up, not by remembering anything."
– Leonard Buschel

Bio: Leonard Buschel is a Philadelphia native, and a very happy Los Angeles transplant. He is California Certified Substance Abuse Counselor with years of experience working with people struggling with addiction. He attended Naropa University in Boulder, CO. Mr. Buschel is the founder of Writers In Treatment whose primary purpose is to promote "treatment" as the best first-step solution for addiction, alcoholism, and other self-destructive behaviors. Leonard is the director of the nine-year-old REEL Recovery Film Festival & Symposium®, and for five years has been the editor/publisher of the weekly *Addiction/ Recovery eBulletin®*. He also produces the annual Experience, Strength and Hope Awards® in Los Angeles. Recipients have been Academy Award winning Lou Gossett, Jr., Astronaut Buzz Aldrin, and Duran Duran founding band member, John Taylor. Celebrity guests appearing on stage have included: actors Robert Downey, Jr. (*Iron Man, Air America*); Ed Bagley, Jr. (*Saint Elsewhere, Arrested Development*); Tony Denison (*The Closer*); Joanna Cassidy (*Body of Proof, Blade Runner, Boston Legal*); Jack McGee (*The Fighter*); Ione Skye (*Say Anything*); Danny Trejo (*Machete*); Joe Walsh (The Eagles); broadcaster Pat O'Brien (*ABC Sports, Access Hollywood*), plus comedians Bobcat Goldthwait and Alonzo Bodden. He just celebrated 23 years clean and sober.

Occupation: Will get later . . .

Drug of choice: Cocaine/marijuana

Length of sobriety: 23 years

DB: What do you do on a daily basis to stay sober and what is the most challenging part about it?

LB: I have gone to at least two AA meetings a week for the past 24 years.

The most challenging part is, every once in a while, I imagine a tumbler of Vodka with a little ice sitting next to me. And I think if I drank it, every cell in my body would sing like members of a celestial choir the words "you're home, where have you been so long?"

DB: How have you reconnected with your body since being in recovery and what are some things you would do to increase your health and vitality?

LB: Well, I don't eat meat because I feel like eating meat symbolizes death, and I want my body to be alive. So, I don't eat meat because I don't want to absorb the fear that the animal had right before it was killed. Before the animal is slaughtered, fear enzymes that have been stored in it's body, pumps the chemicals, into its blood stream and muscle mass. Then I end up eating their fear.

I go to the gym twice a week with a very a spectacular trainer. Since I am too lazy to do it myself, I need someone sort of like a workout sponsor that tells me what to do. You could say that I have a gym sponsor that I work with. Her name is April.

I also walk at least a mile and a half a day and on good days I walk 3 to 4 miles.

I drink a spirulina drink every morning. Live spirulina that goes in a bottle of chilled water. It's my favorite beverage to drink in my morning AA meeting. Or on alternative mornings, I have homemade miso soup, which is made up of live digestive enzymes. The ingredients and ambiance of miso soup are very similar to the seawater from which we all emigrated, many years ago before passports or murderous border guards. So, I start the day up with something alive.

DB: How have your relationships changed since being in recovery? And who would you say are the top three to five people you surround yourself with and why are they influential in your recovery?

LB: Not as many one night stands. (laughs)

Loving less drama. And trying to be less critical and non-judgmental. I don't exclude anyone from my inner circle, whether they are using or not.

I surround myself with my dog and my family. I love hanging out with my friends, and the co-director of the REEL Recovery Film Festival, I think I spend more time with them than anybody. It's your coworkers you need to co-exist with. You spend more time with those people than you do your family. I also try and make friends with the occasional unpleasant characters who visit me in dreams.

By nature, I'm pretty much as an isolator. Oh, and I have a really good friend who is a chemistry professor and seems to be able to answer all my science questions that seem to pop up on a regular basis. For years, I would have him travel with me before the internet. I hate not knowing sometimes. Although, I think it was Voltaire who said, "Doubt is an uncomfortable condition, but certainty is a ridiculous one."

I was always asking him questions about the galaxies, time, molecules or quantum physics. And I love the people in my home group, even though I only meet with them twice a week. It's important to love your home group.

DB: What is your spiritual life like and what do you do on a daily basis to integrate it into your life, and why do you think spirituality is important for growth and sustainability in recovery?

LB: Every morning for the last 20 something years, I sit in front of my altar and light Japanese incense and sit there for 5 to 15 minutes. No matter what, whether I'm in a hotel or staying at a friend's house.

And every night I sit in front of my altar, light Japanese incense and I just smile at a photograph of Jesus that I have at my altar. I bought it in Jerusalem when I was there as a smuggler, and before it was an apartheid state. After that, I bow down to a mantelpiece that has pictures of my mother, my father, my brother, and my sons, just to acknowledge my ancestors and my family for their contribution to my life. Also, on the mantelpiece is a small wooden box with the ashes of a woman I loved who died because she accidentally injected a deadly amount of coke and speed into her vein. Every night before retiring, I write in a journal about anyone I was with that day, where I went and what I did that day. I don't necessarily write down my emotions but I write down every meeting, woman, movie, every play, every person I saw that day. And I've done that for 24 years. I could literally tell you about any day I've lived through in the last 24 years.

Ask me about any New Year's Eve, any birthday, any hospital stay. I could tell you where I was. By looking it up, not by remembering anything.

And I do that because I think if I don't acknowledge in a tangible way that I existed for even a day, I might have forgotten that I did.

Maybe it's my version of those caves paintings that they did back when they were doing cave paintings. Just to remind myself that I actually lived for a day, it's very important to me. And in the morning I hold two gallon bottles of water in front of me, and I bend over and let them pull me down, so they stretch me.

And I sing, "row row row your boat, gently down the stream, merrily merrily merrily merrily, life is but a dream," ten times. It stretches my body and it reminds me of the mortality of life.

I say that alcoholism and drug addiction is people seeking or looking for spirit. They take spirits because they are looking for spirits and I would hate to get to the end of my life and still believe that I am my body. Because then I would really be pissed off about dying. The Buddhists say every time they meditate it's a rehearsal for death. That's one of life's challenges you only get one shot at.

DB: What was the one situation you found yourself in that confirmed in you mind you must seek treatment and recovery?

LB: Not being able to sit through a massage and having to get up and go outside to throw up.

I said to myself, "what's wrong with this picture? This is not why I moved to California." And literally, within a half hour, I was on the phone with the Betty Ford Center. That same morning I woke up in my bed and I felt like I was in a hole. Literally, I felt like I woke up, not in a grave but in a cave. And I thought, "Oh my god, how did I get here?" And there was no way out. This hole I came to was unfathomably moist and cold. The sides of my crypt were dripping limestone and ancient rain water. An hour later I kept throwing up during the massage. It was 3 months later I realized that the 12 steps was my way out. That I could slowly find my way out of this deep hole.

And I realized this is not what I had in mind for myself and one miraculous coincidence after another had me driving to a rehab a couple of weeks later. But, the moment really was throwing up during the massage. I thought, "hmmm, what's wrong with this picture?" My bottom was palpable. I wouldn't call it a moment of clarity. It's a moment of, not just fear but abject terror. And I had to admit that I needed to stop doing drugs for a month.

The first year was an exploration of sobriety. I wanted to see what it was like. I had been using everyday for the previous 26 years, and I thought, "Okay, I'll do this for a year and then I'll decide which way I want to live." And when I had my first year, I thought this no drugging and no boozing was a better more sustainable way to live. And I made a vow to god, that my life would be that of a non-drinker and a non-drug user.

JULIE REISLER

"Because I was really good at hiding it. Because I didn't want anyone to know that I was miserable or upset or hated myself. I wanted no one to know that."
– Julie Reisler

Bio: Julie is a Doctor of Potentiality. Author and Life Designer® Julie Reisler is the founder and CEO of Empowered Living, a life design and personal development company. Julie is a multitime TEDx speaker, host of The You-est You® podcast, and meditation teacher on the popular app, Insight Timer. Julie has a master's degree in health and wellness coaching, with a concentration in nutrition, and more than twelve certifications in leadership, health, and well-being. Julie runs a coaching program, Monetize Your Purpose, for change-makers, entrepreneurs, and coaches. Julie is the author of the *Get a PhD in YOU* series and creator of the documentary and course, *Hungry for More*. Julie is also on the faculty at Georgetown University in their coaching program and is a Lululemon Ambassador. Julie is passionate about helping you to master your inner world so you can crush it at work and beyond. To learn more about Julie, go to juliereisler.com.

Occupation: Life Design Coach

Drug of choice: Food/sugar

Length of sobriety: 15 years

DB: What do you do to stay committed on a daily basis? And what's the most challenging part about it?

JR: Okay. Yeah, it's definitely daily practice for me. I would say the first and foremost important thing for me is getting quiet and going within and meditating. It's not always the same amount of time because I live a life with kids sometimes. So sometimes it's two minutes. Sometimes it's 30. But some form of connecting to my higher self every morning is crucial. I would also say intuitive journaling, where I just write and ask myself higher level questions and try to answer them from an intuitive place. So, for me, it's really connecting to my higher self, to the universe, to infinite intelligence, to something greater than myself. I also have a practice. I look in the mirror, and I just try to connect with my eyes and feeling a sense of love and gratitude for who I am, and just being alive. I would say those are a couple things I do every day, no matter where I am, what's going on.

I think now what is challenging is my life has different time constraints. I wanna say it carefully. When I'm taking my kids to school and we're running late, you know, how many times you do that becomes condensed. So, for me, it's being flexible and not judging myself, and doing the best I can and/or getting my ass up earlier, which I'm not the best at. So just setting that intention. But there are many mornings, especially when I'm driving them an hour to school, and we're getting ready, and my son's coming in while I'm meditating and jumping on my lap, then it doesn't happen the way I would want it to, and understanding that that's perfectly fine. That's valid and that works too. It doesn't have to be perfect, or done the same way. So probably around my kids' schedule is one of the bigger challenges, and when I'm traveling, and that probably can throw it off too. But I always find time. There's always time to meditate, to go within, to journal. I always can find time, and I do find time. It's kind of a non-negotiable.

DB: So how have you reconnected with your body since being in recovery? And what are some the top things you do on a

daily basis to increase your health and vitality?

JR: That's a great question. I, for me, one of the things I don't do is I don't weigh myself anymore. As a recovering food addict, I do not weigh myself on the scale. I haven't known my weight . . . a couple of times, I've had to find out. Just the doctors made a mistake, or was at the gym and went on one of those . . . tells you your muscle weight. But I generally . . . I haven't weighed myself in almost 15 years. That's very loving. I don't.

So, another thing I do is, sounds kind of funny, but I like to, before I go in the shower, just do a quick scan sending love and light to my body, fully there, present in the mirror before I go in the shower to just kind of connect that I'm healthy and well. I'll do a little prayer and gratitude for my body. In terms of movement, for me it's really about what's the most loving way to move my body. And that can look like anything from walking, hiking, swimming, yoga, Pilates, dancing, weights. Sometimes high intensity, but oftentimes it's more fluid movement. It's less about pushing myself, and it's more about being in the flow and being in an inspiring divine finely connected state.

I dance. I love dancing . . . the big one for me, I find that it just helps me to kind of clear out the cobwebs. And then I try to do some sort of stretching or, you know, I taught Pilates. For me, getting connected to what's called your powerhouse. Just that central . . . It's also known as the solar plexus chakra, the place where we have our divine will and confidence. I like to do something almost every morning. I try every morning to do something that activates my core. And more from a spiritual perspective. Like not just, "Okay, I wanna have great abs." It's not just that. I wanna feel confident and secure and sturdy and grounded and expressing from my divine will.

DB: Now, have your relationships transformed since being in recovery? And who are the top three to five people you surround yourself with? And why are they influential in your

recovery?

JR: My relationships, oh wow. Well, I'm not a victim. I mean, I take full responsibility for my life. 100%. And I feel like I have very connected honest, loving, light-filled powerful relationships that are genuine, that are authentic, that are nourished, nourishing, positive, empowering, supportive relationships. I mean, I'm not in a state of people-pleasing anymore. I really look to get my answers from within. And I like to support whoever I'm around, around their recovery or journey. I just feel like the people I surround myself with are also . . . whether they're in recovery, and most are, but some are not, they're living in a mindset or lifestyle around taking responsibility for their life, looking for spiritual connection, looking to be their best self, looking to uplift and empower others. It's a growth abundance mindset. That's the life I live in, and those are the people I surround myself with.

DB: What is your spiritual life like, and what do you do on a daily basis to integrate in your life? And why do you believe it's important for sustainability and growth and recovery?

JR: I feel like I've always been connected to some aspect of, you call it God, or higher power. What I can tell you is over the last probably 10 years, the deeper . . . I've been in recovery for 15, since 2003. And since meditating and really making it a daily habit of journaling and having trusted friends and sponsors that I talk to, to me, honestly, my spiritual connection, my spiritual practice, is the most important. My relationship with me and my higher self, let me say it that way, is the most important thing about my life. Hands down, no question. Before my kids, before my husband, before my career. Because when I am connected to the sacred being that I am, and I believe we all have this, then I am in a state where I am literally receiving guidance. I am acting in a way that's in a positive mindset and integrity. I'm hearing my intuition. Everything for me comes from that place first.

And the times that I've not done that are when I've had breakdowns with food, or around myself, or around relationships. For me, spirituality is about connecting to the God essence within me, the divine essence, my higher self. Not my ego. Not me as a mistake from the past. Me as an eternal being. And that is something that is the important thing to me, and that guides everything I do every day. And that's why I start every morning with meditation. It's the first thing I try to do. Which has been challenging. It means not checking my phone. It means going right to that place of connecting.

Part of what I also do, I'd say is, I'm a big get on my hands and knees, put my head down to the ground, hands up in kind of an open gratitude position and surrender. I try to start my day every morning with a surrender and asking, "God, Creator, Divine, what would you have me do to be of the highest service for me and for the highest good of all?" And that question has really guided me. "So how can I be of service?" And that act of humility. I don't always know the answer. And I really don't. And everything I do tries to come from that place of, "Show me," and then listening. And really is, that for me . . . I mean, my whole life is around spiritual connection. That's probably the most important thing.

DB: What was the one situation you've gotten yourself in that confirmed in your mind you must seek treatment and/or recovery, and why?

JR: It was in May 2003. I'd had many times where I'd eaten in secret or eaten crazy amounts of food and been sick. But it was this one after noon, I was in a job that I thought was okay, that I didn't love. And there was a meeting. And in my office, I had a six-pound bag of tie-dyed M&Ms from Costco. And I thought I would just take these small Dixie cups. I thought I would just have a few. You know, I would just have one. One cup. And, Doug, I have no idea. It could have been 40 cups. I lost track. But I ate a couple pounds of M&Ms. And I got so ill, I was out of work for three days. And it brought me to my knees, to the point . . . I mean, it did bring me to my knees, yeah. But I considered taking my life over it. I felt disconnected, so sick, so out of control, so embarrassed, so ashamed, so lacking in love for myself, so much self-loathing.

That was when I . . . I mean, I literally remember getting in my car, and it was a choice between ending my life or going to an OA (Overeaters Anonymous) meeting. And I did not wanna go to the meeting. I thought there would be a lot of weirdos. And I, thank God, heard a voice that said, "Just go to the meeting, and the rest will unfold." And I did. Thank God I went to a meeting. Because that's what changed my life. I mean, I just really considered ending my life. I was that miserable.

And the funny thing is, you would never have known it. I smile a lot. People had no freaking clue. No clue. Because I was really good at hiding it. Because I didn't want anyone to know that I was miserable or upset or hated myself. I wanted no one to know that. I also wanted no one to know that I was stealing their food when I'd go over to hang out, or in my office, or from CVS. I mean, I stole people's food all the time. I hid it. So, there was a lot, a lot of shame. I think I told this to you earlier. It's not really so sexy to be found with Twinkies in your car. It's not like having a six pack. That looks a lot cooler. Eating Twinkies and M&Ms, not so cool.

DARREN PRINCE

"I hang out with people in recovery because of their positivity and spirituality."
– Darren Prince

Bio: Darren Michael Prince (born February 6, 1970) is a sports and celebrity agent who grew up in Livingston, New Jersey. Prince started a mail order company selling baseball cards at the age of 14 called Baseball Card City and also traveled around the country doing trade shows. At the age of 20 he sold his company for $1.0M and formed Prince of Cards which became an industry leader in private autograph signings for sports and celebrity memorabilia with athletes and celebrities. A-List celebrities like Muhammad Ali, Magic Johnson, Pele, Joe Montana, Smokin' Joe Frazier, Dennis Rodman, Hulk Hogan, Pamela Anderson, Carmen Electra, and Jenny McCarthy all worked with Prince.

In 1995 Prince started a new venture called Prince Marketing Group (PMG) which represented athletes and celebrities for marketing deals consisting of endorsements, licensing, TV, Movie, book deals, autograph signings, and appearances. His first client to sign with the firm was none other than Magic Johnson. Soon after, Smokin' Joe Frazier, Hulk Hogan, Pamela Anderson, Chevy Chase, and Dennis Rodman followed.

In 1998 Prince sold his memorabilia company Prince of Cards for an undisclosed amount.

By 2003 with PMG growing at an enormous pace they then added Hulk Hogan, The Late Evel Knievel, Roy Jones Jr., Scottie Pippen, Motley Crue frontman Vince Neil, and Ric Flair as clients. Since 2009 PMG has added several iconic actors from Oscar Nominees Burt Reynolds and Mickey Rourke to recently Charlie Sheen in 2016. PMG also has negotiated the only licensed trading card deals for the now President Donald Trump, Jennifer Lopez, Britney Spears, and Joe Manganiello.

If you ask Prince his biggest and most important accomplishment, he would say it is being a recovering addict, having celebrated nine years sober, and a public recovery advocate and speaker who has appeared on Dr Oz. He was an invited guest by President Trump's administration to the White House for the Opiate Epidemic Summit on March 1, 2018. Darren has been a board member and has assisted in fundraising for New Jersey's largest and oldest drug and alcohol rehab center, Turning Point in Patterson, NJ. His clients Magic Johnson, Dennis Rodman, Micky Ward, Vince Neil, Chris Herren, and the late Smokin Joe Frazier have all attended Turning Points Annual Gala, helping to raise hundreds of thousands of dollars to help people in need get treatment and save lives. Prince himself was the honoree for Turning Points Hope and Recovery Gala in October of 2017.

In 2018 Darren Prince released his memoir, *Aiming High*. It quickly became an international best-seller in four countries and on October 6, 2018 made it to Amazon's #1 new release list. Soon after, Darren became a representative for Banyan Rehab Treatment Centers. On October 24, 2018 Darren was one of 225 invited guests to the White House for the historic signing by President Trump of the $6 billion bill to help fight the opiate epidemic. Currently Darren is a highly sought-after keynote speaker often speaking to students in high schools about avoiding the pitfalls of addiction and learning to feel comfortable in your own skin and hanging with the right crowd. In his presentations Darren talks about his secret hell of a 23-year plus opiate addiction while representing some of the most iconic figures of our time. "The sports/entertainment industry is a small world and very competitive," says Darren Prince, CEO of Prince Marketing Group. "Prince Marketing Group has prospered over the years by delivering out of the box thinking for clients and building relationships through the practice of good business and effective networking."

Prince Marketing Group is currently a multimillion-dollar business that has negotiated over $200 million in deals and has secured marketing deals, arranged signing/memorabilia appearances, commercial licensing, product endorsement, voice-overs as well as negotiated television and movies deals. Darren is a true entrepreneur as he has been able to continuously reinvent himself and continues to grow his business over the years. He has been featured in outlets such as *Your World With Neil Cavuto,* The *Big Idea with Donny Deutsch,* CNN's *Anderson Cooper 360, Hannity & Colmes,* ESPN, *New York Times, Wall Street Journal, New York Post, USA Today, Forbes' Sports Money, On the Record With Greta Van Susteren*, Howard Stern Radio, CNBC *The Closing Bell*, and a variety of others for his marketing expertise.

Occupation: CEO Prince Marketing Group

Drug of choice: Opiates

Length of sobriety: 10 years

DB: What do you do on a daily basis to maintain your sobriety, and what is the most challenging part about it?

DP: I pray and attend 12-Step meetings. I also work and talk to others in recovery. The most challenging is I travel a lot so with the different time zones around the world and jet lag I make as many road meetings as possible. Just in the past two years I have been in meetings in Sydney, Monaco, Montreal, Fiji, and London because I love being connected to my spiritual brothers and sisters.

DB: How have you reconnected with your body since being in recovery, and what are some things you include in your daily life to increase your health and vitality?

DP: I work out five to six days a week and diet outside of the handful of cheat meals here and here and sugar fixes lol! I need to always try to stay in a relaxed state so between praying and staying away from drama or people who bring drama that is key for me

DB: How have your relationships changed (types of people, length/meaning of relationships, etc.) from when you were actively using to being in recovery?

DP: I am more attentive for sure but still have my ADD moments, ha-ha! But I am a better listener now, and my family, earth friends, and clients actually come to me now for advice because of the way they see me living.

DB: Who are the top three to five people you surround yourself with and why are they influential in your recovery?

DP: I hang out with people in recovery because of their positivity and spirituality. My guys at PMG who are agents here and deal with the daily grind know the way I like things as well as how I like to live and look at life . . . it's a great fit for me. And my fiancé Priscilla is a very positive person who has a very short fuse for BS and drama so we get along great for that reason lol!

DB: What is your spiritual life like and what do you do on a daily basis to integrate it into your life, and why do you think spirituality is important for growth and sustainability in recovery?

DP: I know that I didn't get to almost 10 years sober on my own. It's with the help of others and my own higher power. I have had so many God moments as I like to call them and they happen when I stay in the day and live in the moment and find a positive in every negative. When I learn to "Say what I mean, mean what I say and NOT say it mean," when I decide it's better to "Feel alright then right" this way I hold onto my own serenity and happiness and don't engage in BS and that keeps me centered in spiritual but of course I am not always perfect at it. Spirituality is the key cause it is a way of life that we were never used to while we were using. So, the more we do to stay in the middle of spirituality and on that beam the better our sobriety will get and easier to deal with life on life terms is to deal with and accept.

DB: What was one situation you found yourself in that confirmed in your mind that you must seek treatment and recovery and why?

DP: I just knew my life revolved around pain killers . . . nothing from waking up, walking, talking, eating, working happened without pills in my system and I got to, as they say, that jumping off point. I was a functioning addict and in face many people still didn't think I had an issue but the truth was my ex-wife saw the hell I was in behind closed doors and I eventually hit my own bottom. The day of July 2, 2008 seemed to be the worst day of my life but looking back now it was simply the Greatest Day. I am so blessed to turn my bottom into my beginning and I certainly could not do this alone.

MAIA SZALAVITZ

"The exercise stuff I kind of think of it like the opposite of drugs, which is like it hurts first and then you get high. It is good and it does give you a sense of achievement and a sense that, hey, I can actually get better at something."
– Maia Szalavitz

Bio: Maia Szalavitz is the author of the *New York Times* bestseller, *Unbroken Brain: A Revolutionary New Way of Understanding Addiction*, which is widely recognized as an important advance in thinking about the nature of addiction and how to cope with it, personally and politically. Her book, *Help at Any Cost: How the Troubled Teen Industry Cons Parents and Hurts Kids*, was the first to expose the damage caused by the "tough love" business that dominates adolescent addiction treatment. She has written for numerous publications from *High Times* to the *New York Times*, including *TIME*, the *Washington Post, The Guardian, VICE, Scientific American,* and *The Atlantic*— and she is author or co-author of five other books. With Bruce D. Perry, MD, PhD, she co-wrote the classic work on child trauma, *The Boy Who Was Raised as a Dog* and also *Born for Love: Why Empathy Is Essential— And Endangered*. She has won awards from the National Institute on Drug Abuse, the Drug Policy Alliance, the American Psychological Association, and the American College of Neuropsychopharmacology for her 30 years of groundbreaking writing on addiction, drug policy and neuroscience.

Occupation: Writer/Journalist

Drug of choice: Heroin and cocaine

Length of sobriety: 30 years

DB: What do you do to stay sober on a daily basis and what's the most challenging part about it?

MS: I sort of consider myself in recovery rather than sober. What do I do? These days, it's just been so long, that my routine is pretty well done and I don't think about it all that often. It kind of becomes a funny thing because I was only using drugs between age 17 and 23 and so being 53 now, that's like a very short portion of my life. So, it sometimes feels weird to identify myself only as that portion of my life, if that makes any sense. I certainly do not take any cocaine and heroin. I make sure I avoid doing that. If I were to have to have pain treatment, hopefully I will not use opioids for pain treatment, but if I did I would want to take them very carefully under supervision. I would certainly not, not take them if I needed them because I know that if you think that white-knuckling it in pain is safer than getting safely treated with medication that somebody is watching you with, you're more likely to relapse from agony.

Thankfully, I, aside from once a few years ago when I had to have some dental work, I have not been in that situation and when I had teeth removed or something, I talked to people and I took the medication as prescribed and that was that. In terms of, you know, I think what helps keep me emotionally okay today, certainly I am still on my antidepressants, which is Prozac and Wellbutrin. I am exercising. I work with a personal trainer and have recently begun weight training. Yay, I can now deadlift 200 pounds.

This is something I never thought I would get into. My husband's also really into swing dancing so we do that and take lessons of that as well. I have my husband and my family and my good friends who are my social support. I love music. I, in terms of managing feelings and just generally staying on an even keel as much as possible, music, exercise, that sort of thing, talking to friends, getting massages, just being supported, talking to people online. All of those things really help me be who I am and function reasonably smoothly as opposed to being chaotic.

At this point things are super good for me right now. Again, knock on wood. I got married around four years ago and that's been great. We have a lovely cat. He's sick, which is sad, but he's 18. I do know my book has done really well, my friends are doing well. Sure, I freak out all the time over the horrible political situation, and that stresses me out a lot, but there hasn't really been a situation where I felt close to relapsing.

I should add that for the first five to seven years of my recovery, I was quite involved in 12-Step programs and I did find the social support there useful. I did not find the antimedication attitude there useful, but certainly there were plenty of people who did not have that attitude and I did find that community to be helpful. I moved away from it after the medication started to work and I just started to feel more grounded in general and more annoyed with when I wasn't getting serene. So, I figured also that because my own beliefs about how to deal with addiction are not traditionally 12 Steps that I felt I would feel uncomfortable trying to "12 Step somebody." I wanted to continue to work in the area, but I didn't want to be disingenuous basically.

That was part of my story because that was the only thing that was on offer when I went into rehab in 1988. I could've done perfectly fine with something else, I have no idea. I don't want to say that that wasn't there.

DB: How would you say you've reconnected with your body since being in recovery and what are some things you do on a day to day basis to increase your health and vitality?

MS: Let's see . . . so, I do workout. I am doing the weight training twice a week. I do some random, boring cardio, like the elliptical, probably once a week or something and then I go kayaking with my husband sometimes. We do swing dancing which is definitely exercise. All of that has been really helpful. I used to run for a while. I'm sort of more into the weights at the moment. The exercise stuff I kind of think of it like the opposite of drugs, which is like it hurts first and then you get high. It is good and it does give you a sense of achievement and a sense that, hey, I can actually get better at something. This is kind of cool. That's especially important as you get older because if you sort of close down and don't allow yourself to experience these things, you won't learn as well and it won't exercise your brain appropriately.

DB: How have your relationships changed from actively using to now being in recovery and what are some things you do now to surround yourself with the right people and who would you say are the top three to five people you surround yourself with and why?

MS: One of the things that was difficult for me, I am probably on the autism spectrum and I, as a kid had a real hard time with relationships and that was part of why I loved drugs so much because it made me feel comfortable and feel like also I had something to bring to the party. If you bring cocaine, people kind of always want you to be there. I don't have that severe insecurity or self-hatred anymore. I used to just think people would only tolerate me if I had something they wanted, like if I was famous or high status or had drugs or something.

Now, I realize that is kind of a horrible way to feel and I actually do have good friends and I do believe that they actually like me, instead of constantly worrying about that and the antidepressant medication kind of gave me a way of not being so obsessive about what does this person like me? What do they think of me? Maybe I should leave?

It's more just like I'm able to be present and not be so self-obsessed or something. It's interesting because also as a kid, I was always sort of told I was selfish and bossy and a lot of that was around trying to manage sensory and emotional overload that came from situations that would be normal for other people, but that were too intense for me. The medication reduces that intensity and so then I don't have to work so hard to manage that and then I can be there for people.

Well, two important things I really learned in recovery are to be grateful for what I have and to appreciate it. Also, to be able to be happy for other people. That kind of doubles the amount of happiness you can have in your life. Instead of being jealous or horrible when something good happens to somebody, I am genuinely happy. I can sometimes be a little jealous too, but that's just human.

My husband's great. My best friends are great. My sister, my brother, my cat. I'm a big believer in cats. They keep you sane. Warm, fluffy, purry, although our cat actually does not purr that much. I just love to see them and I find them very soothing. The other thing I have to say also for self-soothing, I really love the beach so I try to get to the beach as much as I can, or just be by the water. I have great people in my life and also my nieces and nephews. It seems like for so long I was so desperate to make my way in my career and to feel useful and to feel connected and all of those things have happened now, so it's just kind of like, wow, this is really weird.

DB: What is your spiritual life like and what do you do on a daily basis to integrate it into your life, and why do you think spirituality is important for growth and sustainability in recovery?

MS: It's interesting because I have always throughout my life been terrified of death and trying to come up with a way to believe that stuff goes on and we're all part of something. I genuinely, truly want to believe that that is the case and that and, you know, kind of like the Buddhist view, like we all were one, we got born, we manifest ourselves into squirrels and then we come back into that at some point. But, I'm also a very sciencey person so it's like, hmm, maybe it's not that. It's interesting. For me, I am always also obsessed with trying to be a good person and trying to be useful and trying to make the world a little bit better, at least reduce harm. A lot of that for me is about being there for people who need me and writing the stuff that I write and speaking out against inequality and inhumane policies and just trying to do what I can in my own small way to make things better. For me, that is spiritual because you are working for the good of humanity, even though that sounds very pompous.

DB: What was the one moment or situation you found yourself in that confirmed in your mind you must seek treatment and/ or recovery and why?

MS: I've written about this, but it was basically I was in my apartment and I was out of heroin and sort of beginning to have withdrawals and this guy and his girlfriend were there and he had this heroin and the stuff I had was not working, it was bad. It was probably like powder of some sort that was not heroin. So, I found myself begging him for some, which might not have been bad and then I just realized, "Oh maybe I could seduce him or something." I was not at all attracted to him. That was like a really horrifying thought and I thought, wow, this is not good. I've never really thought about doing things that I feel would violate my own self in order to get drugs and there's other people who would be fine with that, but I'm not judging them, but I couldn't. I knew that I needed help and so I actually went into treatment the next day.

ROB KOWALSKI

"I guess the most challenging part about staying sober would be, when life starts hitting you, I guess, you don't have that option to numb the pain."
– Rob Kowalski

Bio: Rob Kowalski, is a Speaker/Writer/Advocate, and Entrepreneur as well as a "reformed bad boy." Once the biggest stripper and nightclub promoter in his hometown of Baltimore, MD, he had a life-changing encounter with Jesus and is now passionate about sharing his story with others and creating ways off the dead-end road he once glorified. He is the Founder and CEO of CityFam, a non-profit organization that advocates for the power of community to transform an individual, a city, and even the whole world. He is also author of the book *Why Waiting Works, How Fast Sex Prevents Us From Finding Love and Long-Term Happiness*, the self-proclaimed most practical book ever written on sex.

Occupation: Author, CEO/founder of Cityfam

Drug of choice: Alcohol

Length of sobriety: 6.5 years

DB: What do you do stay sober on a daily basis, and what's the most challenging part about it?

RK: So I have a pretty good routine that I follow. For me it's I wake up early. I usually visualize. I read a little bit in the mornings. I read. I spend some quiet time with God. Usually look at my Bible app, read a couple of verses out of there. And sometimes I do affirmations. It's basically a lot of the principles that I found in the *Miracle Morning*. But I was doing several of them anyway, sometimes sitting quiet with God, talking to Him, and just listening, reflecting. So those are the things that I do in the morning to kind of set the tone for my day. I like to work out in the mornings at least a few times a week. You know, it's hard. It keeps me sane, like always that feeling of accomplishment afterward. And then I have to work regularly, regardless of how I feel. You know what I mean? Because sometimes you can be on that verge of depression. Like you're right on the brink; you could go either way. And if you succumb to it, it just gets worse. So I tend to . . . I have to work.

I go to church on Sundays. I volunteer regularly. I life coach a little bit just to stay focused on my goals. And then I socialize with the right people, because that's part of it, too, especially for me. It really fills my cup to be around people. Because of the community, I cultivate it through CityFam, I'm able to still do fun things that, to me, it really prevents me from backsliding. Because if I get bored or lonely, that's not good, because then I'll get depressed. And if I get depressed, then I won't stick with it. You know what I mean? So those are the things I do regularly to stay sober.

I guess the most challenging part about staying sober would be, when life starts hitting you, I guess, you don't have that option to numb the pain. So you kind of just have to learn to take it. And for me, I wasn't used to taking it. Until six years ago, I pretty much gave myself all kinds of vices to comfort myself. Of course, they produced negative benefits down the road, but it's in the moment. And I'd have to say that's the hardest part. And then the other probably hard part is, you have to avoid a lot of places that you used to once go, a lot of things that you used to once do, because they could be potentially dangerous. You really have to get creative with finding fun, finding activities that are still fun to do so you don't burn out, so you don't relapse and use again. And then the people to do them with, really, which can be challenging, too, not only the things to do but the people to do them with. I guess that's what I would say.

DB: Have you reconnected with your body since being in recovery, and what are some things you do on a daily basis to increase your health and vitality?

RK: I definitely work out a lot harder now that I'm sober. I mean, I've always worked out. I was never getting up and going to the gym at 5:00 in the morning, 5:45 in the morning before.

DB: And what are some things you do daily to increase your health and vitality?

RK: I think all those things that I mentioned have increased my health and vitality. Everything from, obviously, the workouts, I'm definitely in the best shape that I've been in. I might not be the leanest that I've ever been in, just because food has kind of turned in my life a little bit. My body fat is probably in the teens, and I've been lower. But I'm healthy because I'm definitely doing more cardio and more well-rounded things instead of just lifting. But even volunteering, it's good for your health. Being around people and genuinely having real genuine friendships and laughing, like that's healthy. I haven't read the papers, but I know that there's health benefits to laughing. So, I would say a lot of the activities that I do to stay sober are probably really good for my health, too. Yeah, I don't know if that's kind of a cop-out, but that's what I'll answer.

DB: How have your relationships changed since being in recovery, and who are the top three to five people you surround yourself with and why are they influential in your recovery?

RK: Man, my relationships have changed drastically. Before I got sober, my friendships would suffer because I would live recklessly. So, I think it was my 38th birthday party. I remember . . . I was not yet sober but wanting to get sober, but I hadn't gotten sober. And I had a birthday party, and it was hardly five or six people who showed up, or whatever it was, and they were just like people that I went out with and drank with. I remember less than two years later, when I turned 40, how many people I had at my birthday party. This was a year and a half after getting sober. I had all of these great friendships, better relationships with my family, better relationships with everyone. I mean, I was a better son, a better friend, a better citizen, just a better person all the way around.

I liked myself more, because I wasn't just living for myself. Like most addicts, I was just trying to get to the next high. Mostly it was just alcohol, but sometimes it was drugs, sometimes it was girls, was my high. But, yeah, I started trying to make a contribution in other people's lives, and my relationships improved like night and day. So, I would say, for the people that I hang out, you said three?

DB: Thoughts on top people?

RK: Okay. I would say Chris Lockemy, the pastor of Epic, he's a great friend and a mentor to me, and he's just one of the best human beings I've ever met. So, when I first was trying to get sober, I just really stuck to him like glue, knowing that he would rub off on me if I spent time with him. The other person was Lori Lockemy, his wife, and she's my life coach. She really helped me get clear about what my goals were, and that really motivated me. It pushed me through the pain of the change, because I knew where I wanted to go. Where up until then, I really hadn't. It was very easy just to not get sober, because I didn't have a clear vision for my life. She would be number two. And both of them I trust highly, so they can speak into my life if they see anything, and it's not like I would feel attacked in any kind of way by them. So them.

Billy Loften, the guy I started CityFam with, a really great person, friend, loves Jesus. He's normal, meaning like sometimes you get people that are overly religious and you can't relate to them. But he's not like that at all. And me and him, he was my wing-man for the past six years. And then Ginny, I would say I spend a lot of time with her, mostly just in the office. But she's the director of operations for CityFam, been a friend of mine for 20 plus years. We're birds of a feather. We came from a similar place. We're in a similar place now in our lives, and she's probably my number one wing-woman, girl, just to hang out with.

DB: What's your spirituality life like? And what do you do on a daily basis spiritually, and why do you think it's important for sustainability and growth in recovery?

RK: So I definitely spend some time with God every day. I typically read a little bit. I talk to Him in the mornings. I talk to Him sometimes throughout the day. But God speaks to people differently. And I don't know how He speaks to everyone, but I know how He speaks to me. And a lot of it is through feelings, like how I feel. Like I really feel like I'm in tune with Him in my gut and my spirit, so He leads me in a lot of ways like that. Things will feel right. They won't feel right. And that's how He kind of leads me. But He's instrumental in my life in everything. Like He makes all the decisions for me. I'm not trying to do anything by myself. So how is He instrumental in my sobriety? I mean, if it wasn't for Him, I wouldn't have got sober.

Because even as much of a mess as I was making, and even with all the problems . . . even the way I felt about myself and I was creating problems for myself, I don't think I would have gotten sober without Him, because I liked the lifestyle too much. So, for me it was I didn't want to let Him down, because He loved me and He forgave me and He called me and told me He had a purpose for my life. And I knew what it was. So, like I said, completely instrumental in my sobriety, because I just don't know that I would have done it without Him. And now He gives me the power to stay sober even through hard times. I would say yeah, completely instrumental.

DB: What was the one situation you found yourself in that confirmed in your mind you must seek treatment in recovery and why?

RK: Man, I've got more than one. I've gotten a few. I mean, I knew I needed recovery. I'd gotten arrested in Ocean City one time. I walked into a stranger's house. I was black out, and I walked into somebody's house not knowing. I was just that drunk. And I woke up, I'm in jail, and really couldn't even remember why I got locked up. And that was pretty bad. I got my second DUI, which I ended up getting off of by the grace of God, but that was really a wake-up call for me. I remember being in jail and just thinking that the madness had to end. And it didn't end right away after that, but it was not long after that. And those were probably the two big things that really stood out for me, I guess.

DAMON WEST

"When I came back in that court room and the judge said, you know, 'Damon West, you are hereby sentenced to 65 years in the Texas Department of Criminal Justice,' it took my breath away, Doug."
– Damon West

Bio: Sentenced to 65 years in a Texas prison, Damon West once had it all. He came from a great family, in a home full of God, love, support, and opportunities to reach any dream. A natural born leader, with good looks and charm, and a three-year starting quarterback, he appeared to be the all-American kid living out his dreams.

Underneath this facade, however, was an addict in the early stages of his disease. After suffering childhood sexual abuse by a babysitter at the age of nine, he began putting chemicals into his body to alter the way he felt, starting with drinking and smoking. By the age of 12, he would escalate to marijuana use. In his mind, he was not hurting anyone by smoking pot; in reality, he was feeding the monster that is addiction.

After receiving a scholarship to play football for the University of North Texas, Damon left for college on a wave of euphoria at his prospects of playing Division I football in Texas. College presented Damon with many new opportunities in life. He began college as a student-athlete and got involved in campus life, joining the Lambda Chi Alpha fraternity. When his football career came to a premature end, due to an injury in 1996, against Texas A&M, Damon lost all direction.

Football had become so much of his identity that he no longer knew who he was; his purpose and reason for existence were lost to him. Feeling the pressure of the existential vacuum, Damon chose a dark path on the road of addiction, abusing harder drugs like cocaine, ecstasy, and prescription pills to go along with the alcohol and marijuana.

After graduating in 1999, Damon's life would take him to the United States Congress, political fundraising for a presidential candidate and then into the world of Wall Street, with a position to train as a stockbroker for one of the biggest banks in the world, U.B.S. It was at this last stop that Damon was introduced to methamphetamine for the first time; he was instantly hooked. The lives of so many innocent people would forever be changed by the choices he made in order to feed his insatiable meth habit.

After three years of committing property crimes (burglaries of homes, buildings, vehicles, as well as auto theft) and other drug-related crimes, with a dozen other meth addicts, a Dallas SWAT team finally caught up with Damon and arrested him on July 30, 2008. Or, as Damon refers to when speaking, he was not "arrested" so much as he was "rescued."

After reconnecting with his family and his faith in Dallas County Jail, he began the long process of paying for his crimes. The consequences of his behavior earned him a life-sentence of 65 years for engaging in organized criminal activity. With a promise to his parents to come home as "someone they will recognize," Damon left for prison.

Prison life began with a violent baptism-by-fire. Armed with the knowledge that "you don't have to win all your fights, but you do have to fight all your fights," he battled for his right to exist independent of a gang. Clinging close to God, his family's unwavering support, a 12-Step recovery program and all the tools available to him, Damon emerged from prison a better man spiritually, emotionally and physically. On November 16, 2015 he walked out of prison on 58 years of parole.

Today, Damon works for the Provost Umphrey Law Firm in Beaumont, TX. When not out speaking to students and athletes about the dangers of drugs and the consequences of bad decisions, he spends his free time volunteering, doing service work, attending 12-Step recovery groups, exercising, and enjoying his new life with his family and faith community at St. Elizabeth's Church. His message is both a cautionary tale and one of hope and perseverance in the face of the most extreme odds.

Occupation: Motivational Speaker

Drug of choice: Meth

Length of sobriety: 10 years

DB: What do you do on a daily basis to stay sober and what's the most challenging part about it?

DW: On a daily basis to stay sober, it's like you get up in the morning. In The Big Book they have a 30-second prayer: "God, offer myself to thee. Develop me and do with me as" . . . that prayer. I have my own variation of it that I got when I was in prison, a two-part prayer, and I say it every day when I get up just to remind myself my role to play. It's, "God, put in front of me what you need me to do today for you and let me recognize it when I see it." I don't want to miss those things, you know. That kind of gets me back on track. I've got people around me. One of the questions you said you wanted to ask was the five people that we know that are in my recovery circle. Those five people, we'll get into that, but those five people, man, part of their job is to make sure my feet stay on the ground and my head stays out of the clouds, keep me humble, make sure I'm humble. If you see Damon West not being humble, speak up because you and I are addicts, Doug. If we lose humility, we're in trouble. Not only are we in trouble, but we may have victims that are in trouble too that we don't know about yet.

I stay tapped into my higher power and the cool thing about it, Doug, is we get to pick our own higher power. My idea of my higher power doesn't have to be like anybody else's. You know, I'm Catholic, Doug, but it doesn't necessarily mean that my idea of God is the same idea as the Catholic Church. My idea of God is my idea of God. I do, I have a concept of God, a supreme being, a higher power, but it's mine, man, and I have a personal relationship with that God. There's a guy that I know that wrote a book. His name is Bob Bodine, and I can get you in touch with Bob probably. Bob wrote a book called *Two Chairs*, and *Two Chairs* is basically the concept that you get up in the morning and you set two chairs out and you sit in one of them and you put your higher power, God, you ask him to sit in the other chair and you have a conversation in the morning to start your day. Now, I don't do this every day. I should. But, in the morning you have a conversation with your higher power and you kind of get your instructions for what's going to go on that day. You know, you sit there and listen.

It's meditating, Doug. You meditate. You listen. The rule is the 80/20 rule. You listen 80% of the time and talk 20% of the time because the thing about it is, your higher power knows what you're thinking, what's going on in your life. I mean, why would you be the one talking 80% of the time? I think that's what's been wrong in my life at different points when I was living in my addiction is I wasn't listening. I was always talking. I was always the voice that was too much noise. So, in the mornings I try to shut up and listen. I try to shut up and listen. I try to absorb some stuff before my day gets started, before it gets crazy. But, you know, I stop myself all the time throughout the day and I'll say The Serenity Prayer. Some days, Doug, you know this as a recovering addict, it's not one day at a time. Some days it's 20 minutes at a time, 1 hour at a time.

Some days are easier than others, but you've got tools in recovery. You've got tools. You can call somebody. I call my sponsor all the time and I'll run decisions by him. That's another thing to try to stay spiritually fit in my program of recovery is if I've got a thought that I'm not real sure about I'll call my sponsor and say, "Hey, man, here's what I'm thinking. What do you think about this?" He'll tell me. He'll say, "Hey, man, that's the dumbest thing I've ever heard or go for it. That's a great idea." You know, spiritually, mentally, and physically, Doug, I've found that those are three areas I have to try to work on every single day or I don't feel right. I don't feel well when I don't work out spiritually, mentally and physically every day. You know, we are what we eat. When you're talking about what you eat, not just food, you know, because that's going to be the physical part, but spiritually and mentally, man, what are you feeding yourself? That's what I ask people all the time in these presentations. What are you feeding yourself spiritually? What kind of books do you read? Mentally, what are you feeding yourself? What kind of videos do you watch? What kind of websites do you go to? What are you feeding yourself today? Because that's what you're going to look like on the outside too, you know.

One of the things Jon Gordon put on his social media one day that I just loved is that leaders are readers. That's true. You've got to get out there and read. You've got to absorb other people's ideas, other people's thoughts and be open to all of that. I try to read. I try to read stuff every day. I mean, I read stuff at work all the time, but one of the things I think I can improve on, Doug, is backing off of social media some and using that time for other things that are important. I've found here lately, you know, my girlfriend and I, we've got a house together, so it's been a lot of work. I've found that I don't prioritize my time well, and I have extra time in the day when I think, man, I just don't have time to do something. Yeah, I do. I mean, I spend about an hour or two a day surfing on social media and keeping up my brand, who I am.

You do the same thing. You have a social media. You have a brand you're building. Those are just some of the things I do every day. I try to stay tapped into it. I go to meetings, you know. Two to three days a week I'm in meetings and I guess the most important thing that I try to find is ways to help other people, Doug, because that's the most important thing.

The most important thing is to give back and help others. Servant leadership is the term I use for it, to go out and do service work. That's that second part of that prayer, man. You know, put in front of me what you need me to do today for you God, but let me recognize it when I see it. When I see an opportunity to help someone else, I've got to jump on it and take it, man. That's not something I can pass up because people have jumped out to help me.

DB: How would you say you've reconnected with your body since being in recovery and what are some things you do on a daily basis to increase your health and vitality?

DW: You know, on a daily basis, boy, we're talking a lot time because like I said, I haven't prioritized getting my workouts in. That's one of the areas where I've slacked off and I hate that, but you know, when I got into recovery in prison, that was one of the things. I'm talking about getting fit spiritually, mentally, and physically and so I started working on myself in prison. I'd do a lot of pushups and pull-ups and jogging and running, man. That's where it's at for me, Doug. I love to run. I love to release the endorphins. I like the quiet. I like the peace. Running, for me, is very meditative. When I don't run for a while, which I haven't got to run much in the last two or three weeks. I don't feel right. I'm not as centered. I'm not as grounded, man. That's one of the things I'm getting up in the morning to go do is jog because I've been neglecting it man. But, I love to get out there and run and just listen, you know. Sometimes I'll have my headphones on, Doug, and nothing's even playing in them, you know.

DB: How have your relationships changed since being in recovery? Who would you say are the top three to five people you surround yourself with and why are they influential in your recovery?

DW: I have the ability now to have mature adult relationships whether it be a personal relationship, relationship with a friend, relationship with my mother and father and brothers, or a romantic relationship like I have with my girlfriend. I have the ability to be a mature adult, and part of that is to be responsible and here's the biggest part about recovery. I have learned that whenever I am wrong, I have to admit it and move on, but the trick about this is, is that the person you've wronged doesn't have to accept it, and you have to be okay with that. I have to keep my side of the street clean. If I'm keeping my side of the street clean, then I can have a normal relationship. Communication, Doug. I can communicate now in relationships better than ever before because, hey, man, I want that exchange. I want you to know that I'm curious.

If something's on my mind, Doug, that's another thing about recovery that's helped me out in relationships is we're different. We're wired different, Doug. We're addicts. Our thing like this happens. It's a cycle that happens. We have a thought and a thought gets in our head. Let's say you're an addict, and it's a thought to go drink, you know. The thought gets in your head and if you don't do something with that thought in your head it's going to sit there and it's going to become an obsession and you will obsess over it and obsess over it and obsess over it, and eventually one day it will become physical, man. You'll put in. I know now that when I have a thought I've got to get it out, you know. Let's say it's with my girlfriend and something she said that I didn't understand or maybe not agree with, I'm going to tap her on the shoulder and say, "Hey, Kendall, listen, here's what just went down in the conversation. Here's what you said. Here's how it made me feel. Am I on the right track?" Because I have learned, Doug, that as an addict, man, I have the uncanny capability of going down a rabbit hole into a parallel universe and all kinds of scenarios happen out in my mind that have never even happened.

You've got to step back and go look in the mirror and say, man, you're a crazy person. I have become, in my mind, the scenarios and stuff that played out in my head, but none of these events are real and it's fear that drives that, man. Fear does that to us. So, I have had to learn in relationships and recovery that hey, fear is a natural thing, but what are we going to do with it when it comes in? You know, if you have a fear of something, talk about it. If I have a concern about something, I talk about it. If I've done something wrong, I admit it, you know. I admit it. The thing about this is, too, that I tell people that I have any kind of relationship with is here's the deal. If I'm wrong, I'm going to admit it, and there's no such thing as an I'm sorry, but . . . the minute you put a comma at the end of the word sorry, it's not an apology anymore. "I'm sorry, but, you know, that's not an apology." Here's the deal that I want. All I want from you is what I'm giving you. I don't want anything more, anything less. If I'm putting that in I expect you to put that in too. Let's have a normal relationship.

I've had the ability now, the opportunity now, to have mature adult relationships for the first time in my life and that's because of recovery, nothing else. The other question you asked is the three to five people. The first person, the one that lives with me is my sponsor. My sponsor and I are tight. I met my sponsor when I was in prison. He was the guy that brought the meeting into the Stiles unit, to the maximum-security prison where I was doing my time. He was the guy who brought the meetings in every Wednesday morning, the AA and NA meetings. He's a volunteer. You know, he lives in the area where I live because Stiles unit is in Beaumont, and I live, right now, right outside of Beaumont, the next town over. So, I told him, and I would always tell him, when I get out of prison one day, I'm going to come find your home group and that's going to be my home group too.

You know, Doug, it was funny. He would kind of laugh at me. He's bringing a recovery meeting to a maximum-security prison, man. This dude gets lied to more than the police. So, he would kind of laugh it off. But, man, November 16, 2015, the day I walked out of prison, it was a Monday, I showed up that night at that meeting because I had my mom look it up online. I asked her to look it up online and she did, and they had a Monday night meeting that night from 7:00 to 8:00. I showed up there, man. He saw me and there were tears in his eyes. He's like, man, "You made it, Damon." I said, "I made it, man, and I need a sponsor big time." So, he became my sponsor, and we're close. We're really close. We talk all the time. I would say to him . . . I would say my parents . . . I mean, I paroled out of prison and had to live with my parents. Up until now I've lived with them the whole time I've been out of prison. So, we've gotten closer.

My brothers. Let's just put my parents and my two brothers, Brandon and Grayson, in this same little spot for one person because you're like a little unit, your family.

Another person that I'm really close to is my girlfriend, Kendall. Kendall, she is neat. She's a nurse practitioner. My mother is a registered nurse. One of the qualities I've found in people in medicine, particularly nurses, is this quality that you don't see in all people, and it's empathy. You know, empathy's not guaranteed. Empathy is a choice, Doug. I have found somebody that is good with empathy because that's what she does in her career. She's a nurse practitioner, so she takes care of people that are in need. Nurses, for the most part, that I've ever encountered, they see somebody that's hurting and they want to fix them. It doesn't matter what they've done. It doesn't matter their background, what their financial situation is. They just see a human being in need and they want to help. When Kendall and I started dating, she knows that I'm an addict and I'm in recovery and as someone in medicine she understands that addiction is a disease. She understands the disease concept part of it really well and she encourages me to make my meeting. She knows that my life, my freedom, our happiness, if we're going to have a happiness together, depends on me making my meetings and me staying in my program of recovery. She would be the next person I'd go to.

The last person I would say is my boss, a guy named Chris Kirchmer, the guy that gave me the job at Provost Umphrey Law Firm right out of prison. You know, he and I have become really close personal friends. Of course, he's still my boss, so I work for him, but I mean, this is the guy, Doug, when I got out of prison and I would go to for things like, "Hey, man, you know, I haven't seen a doctor in a long time to have a full physical, a prostate check and everything. Who's your urologist, Chris? Who could I go to? What kind of doctor could I go to?" So, he would help me out finding the right doctor to go to for something like that. Or, you know, "Hey, Chris, somebody just gave me . . ." because I had all hand-me-down stuff. Hell, I still wear hand-me-down clothes, you know, but it didn't all fit, so I came to Chris, kind of embarrassed and I was like, "Chris, man, I've got all these second-hand clothes that I really like, but I need a tailor to go to." He found me this little Vietnamese lady in Port Arthur that he goes to as a tailor. He says, "You go there and tell her my name."

The point is, is that Chris is someone that I've turned to over and over throughout this new life and this second chance and he's always been there. He's always been there and he's been there with great advice. He'll come to me for stuff too, for advice, and I like that. I like that exchange. He's just is a close personal friend. These are the people I go to all the time, Doug. These are the people that are in the program of recovery. They also know that I have to be in my program of recovery or I'll give it all away, Doug. That's the thing about us addicts, we give it all away, man. My program of recovery has to come first, Doug, and I'm sure yours does too.

DB: What's your spiritual life like and what do you do on a daily basis to integrate it into your life, and why do you think spirituality is important for sustainability and growth and recovery?

DW: Spirituality, the importance of it, I mean, so look, here's the deal. In my mind, spirituality is your conscious contact with your higher power with God. Religion is a man-made deal. Spirituality is something different, entirely than religion. I think definitions are important, so let me get that out. Spirituality is this, man. If I don't stay grounded to my higher power, you know, it's like that saying in The Big Book. I think it's page 85, I don't know. It says, we have a daily reprieve contingent on the maintenance of our spiritual condition, right.

So, I have to daily maintain that spiritual condition, but that's also a warning, man. That's also a warning that if you don't maintain that relationship and know which end of it you're on, you're in trouble. A constant reminder to me is, like I said, to start my morning out and ask God, man, what do you need from me, man? You know, what do you need from me and let me recognize it when I see it. The main thing is, I don't ask for anything from my higher power. I don't, Doug. I don't ask for health, wealth, happiness, fame, fortune, you know, none of that stuff because I don't control any of that stuff. I don't control any of that. Who am I to ask for it? It's not like God gets up every morning, my God gets up every morning and waits for me to wake up so we can run the universe together, you know. It's not like my higher power is up there wringing his hands, going, boy, I sure wish Damon would get up so we can start the universe up, you know? I've got to be reminded of that, Doug, because I have an ego.

I have an ego, man, that if you feed it, it grows. Whatever you feed grows, Doug. I have to feed that humility. I have to feed that vulnerability. I have to feed those things that keep me locked in a program of recovery, that giving spirit, that servant heart. I have to feed those things. The only way to feed those things is with opportunities to give back, opportunities to help other people. Kindness, Doug. I mean, kindness and empathy and all the things I've talked about that I like in a relationship, you know, I have to be able to go out and give those things freely, freely give it away and not ever ask what's in it for me, you know? There's four things that I control in this life, and I constantly have to remind myself every day. Talk about standing in your spiritual program, man. I remind myself all the time.

When I get frustrated over certain things that, "Damon, unless this is something you think, say, feel or do, then you have no control over this stuff." That's like asking for stuff from God, right? You know, if it's not something I think, say, feel, and do, then I can't control it, man. I've got to let things happen around me. That's the hardest thing in the world for me, Doug. The hardest thing in the world for me is to let things happen, man and not get in there and be the wizard behind the curtain pulling levers, pushing buttons, manipulating everybody to do what I want them to do, because that's what Damon did his whole life. Damon wanted it. Damon did it. Man, no. I've got to sit back and chill out and say, "Hey, look, you know what, God, if it's your will, if it's supposed to be done then it will get done." That doesn't mean I just sit around. You're a hustler, Doug. You get out every day and you work and you have goals. I think that we're expected to do that. Your higher power is not going to do it for you. But, there are areas that you can't control. You can't control if someone wants to talk to you to have an interview. All you can do is get up and keep making those calls.

Another thing that I remind myself that I'm sure you do all the time too, Doug, is I'm going to ask the questions. I'm going to ask. If there's something that I'm trying to do and it's part of my goals or whatever, I'm not going to not ask somebody, you know. All you can do is tell me "no," but if I don't ask you the questions, then I know what the answer is automatically. I have to get up and ask those questions. I have to get up because that to me is living in recovery, man, having the courage to get up and say, "You know what? I'm going to fail this someday, but that's okay because today I'm not going to be drunk. Today I'm not going to be in my addiction. Today I'm free, and that's the thing about it." Like we were talking about a while ago, more people are locked up by their thoughts than by steel bars.

DB: What was the one situation you found yourself in that confirmed in your mind you must seek treatment and recovery and why?

DW: I'll give you the date that it happened. May 18, 2009. It was the sixth day of my trial. Six days is a long criminal trial in Texas for some trial that's a bunch of property crime and no one was hurt physically or anything like that. Six days a jury sat there and listened to victim after victim and police officer after police officer and witness after witness and co-conspirators come up. There were over 50 witnesses at my trial, Doug. After six days of testimony the jury deliberated for ten minutes on my sentence. Ten minutes, Doug. Ten, man. I don't know how much Law and Order you watch, but if a jury's gone for ten minutes and you're at the defense table, they smoked you, man. When I came back in that court room and the judge said, you know, "Damon West, you are hereby sentenced to 65 years in the Texas Department of Criminal Justice," it took my breath away, Doug. That is when I tell everybody all the time was rock bottom for me. Before that, five minutes before that wasn't rock bottom because in my mind I was going to get probation and I was going to get out again and get screwed up. I was going to go get a job like a normal guy and just smoke meth on the weekends, man. I couldn't wait to get out. I could taste the dope, Doug, in that courtroom.

When I got hit with a life sentence—65 is life—when I got hit with that life sentence, it took my breath away, Doug, and when they took me back to my holding cell, I thought, man, this is me. I've got to change. No one else has to change. I've got to change. That was my rock bottom moment. That's when I realized that I had to make a change. I had to do something different, something I had never done before. When I got to prison, eventually I got into recovery and that's when I changed my mindset in prison. Recovery gave me that, Doug. I got into prison and I quit looking at prison as a punishment. I started looking at prison as an opportunity, man, an opportunity to work on myself 24 hours a day, 7 days a week to be the best version of Damon West that the universe could handle. As long as I kept that relationship up and kept proportion up, I mean.

Lack of proportion in my mind is a big problem. I've always thought I was way more important to the world than what I am, you know. I know, Doug, just like you know, that I have something to offer. You know you have something to offer society too, and you found it. You found that thing, that passion, that drive because you have no idea, Doug, who you're going to reach with your book or with one of these interviews you do. If you reach one person, if you help one person get to those rooms of recovery, then you've done what your higher power wanted you to do, just one person, Doug, and I think you've done that.

DANIELLA PARK

"When I got sober it was because I had blown a hole through my stomach lining and almost died before having an emergency surgery."
– Daniella Park

Bio: Daniella Park is a wife, sales expert, business owner, marketer, speaker, blogger, recovery advocate, top achiever at Coast to Coast Computer Products Inc., and the creator of Recovery 12 Step Store and clothing brand "Doing It Sober." Growing up in Hollywood, Daniella worked as a stunt woman, stand-in, producer, manager, and former Vice President of "legendary star maker" Jay Bernstein Productions. For more information or speaking inquiries: info@doingitsober.com www.doingitsober.com

Occupation: Sales and DoingItSober.com

Drug of choice: Alcohol, methamphetamines, cocaine, LDS, hallucinogens, and anything under the sun

Length of sobriety: 12 years God willing

DB: What do you do on a daily basis to maintain your sobriety, and what is the most challenging part about it (if anything)?

DP: Maintaining my sobriety is the easy part or at least picking up a drink or a drug is no longer the hard part. The challenge for me is dealing with the mental defects that are present in my life and my relationships. I'm stark raving sober and I still have a problem getting along with people, my normal temperament is uneasy, and I never feel like I'm good enough, but my ego is through the roof. I have nothing to take the edge away and with my default always being vodka or a bunch of methamphetamines I really needed something new! I had to completely change everything if I'm going to try and stay sober and make it sober throughout my day. I am bodily different than some of my friends and I can never drink safely so I HAVE to find a solution to cope with my issues. My solution is continuously maintaining a DAILY routine of healthy esteemable acts. My checklist is simple but takes action. SMP = spiritually, mentally, and physically. How can I connect with my higher power whom I chose to call God? I find my spiritual connection through praying and being aware of the signs around me that are personal to me and my God. If I am helping another person or being of service in some way my heart is filled. My chances become lower of not taking a drink if I am telling another alcoholic my story or driving another alcoholic to a 12-Step meeting or even just going to coffee or calling someone to see how they are doing. Those simple things work for me period. I struggle with my physical fitness. In the past 12 years in recovery, I have been very fit and other times I have struggled with illness. The great thing about my life now is I don't beat myself up over everything either. This is not something that came right away but something that took practice. When it comes to working out, there has been the most resistance and it's like a snowball effect of crapiness from there. When I don't work out, I eat worse, load up on sugar, and beat the heck out of myself afterwards. Then I gain weight, and EVERYTHING becomes harder. I stop praying and then start isolating. I must take action! If I wallow in self-pity I will stay there until I get into enough pain to either workout or take that drink that could kill me. If I can't do anything or go to the gym, I at least try and take the dogs for a walk. It's amazing how much better I feel when I just get my body moving and how this propels my thoughts towards a healthy direction. It's always progress with this one and a lot of starting over and over.

DB: How have you reconnected with your body since being in recovery, and what are some things you include in your daily life to increase your health and vitality?

DP: When I got sober it was because I had blown a hole through my stomach lining and almost died before having an emergency surgery. The alcohol and drugs after 20 years ate away my lining of my stomach and the bacteria started to drip into my organs basically burning and sizzling them to destruction. I was literally struck sober after this surgery and have had some serious medical issues throughout my years being sober. My bones and joints are arthritic, and I have many bulged disks in my neck. My dopamine levels have decreased so much I became depressed. I was always very dehydrated just in general. I discovered if I drank half my body weight in water, my headaches would go away, and I would be struggling less during my workouts. I started doing physical therapy for the damage that was done to my neck and back over the years and that started helping me gain strength slowly. Everything in recovery has happened slowly for me which has given the gift of patience over the years. Dealing with pain in recovery is much different because narcotics and opiates that help with pain are addictive-these trigger my addictions and the tentacles come out to grab ahold of my mind without me having any control of it. Trust me on that one, you are not unique and cannot control mind altering substances. I am not a doctor and do agree with taking them if desperately needed with the help of a doctor and someone to administer them as needed. I take an antidepressant, ibuprofen 600 mg for the pain, and a non-narcotic muscle relaxer when I can't stand the muscle spasms anymore. I find if I work out a few times a week, take short walks around the neighborhood, eat healthy but don't deprive myself of cheats and take vitamins, I remain fairly healthy and don't get sick or ache as much. I take iron, Vitamin B, Vitamin E, iron, glucosamine, and magnesium every day.

DB: How have your relationships changed (types of people, length/meaning of relationships, etc.) from when you were

actively using to being in recovery?

DP: When I was using and drinking, I had no idea I was suffering from a disease. I had two DUI's by my 20's, spent time in the twin towers jail but still maintained my seven night a week habit of going to Los Angeles clubs. I admit I lived a very glamourous life and rode the high horse of Hollywood for many years, hanging out with the best of them but in the end, I was always alone. My friendships were based on what kind of drug you had and if you had a cool pad to party at the end of the night. Eventually, a woman who came from a high-class Malibu family who never had alcohol in the house, became a lost soul opening my life up to doing whatever it took to have the freedom of living on my own as a functioning addict and alcoholic.

My life today is full of God and full of life. My relationships are strong and meaningful and have lasted for years and years unconditionally. People respect me in the community and I am a business leader and recovery advocate. Every day of my life I have someone I can call for help that will answer my call and be there in a heartbeat for me as I will for them. I have been married for five years and found out I have a sister who has been looking for me for 30 years . . . these miracles would have never happened to me without my sobriety. Thank God!

DB: Who are the top three to five people you surround yourself with and why are they influential in your recovery?

DP: I fill my life with people that want to be healthy, that want to help themselves. I have a sober sponsor who helps me make better decisions and who has helped guide me to live sober. Afterall, I had never lived sober in my adult life and had no clue how to live. My sponsor is a woman who has more time in recovery than me and has things going on in her life that I like or admire or would like to achieve myself. One thing I heard, and it makes total sense to me is, self can't reveal self to self. I am also a sponsor, I help any woman who is willing to get sober and is serious about bettering their life. I am always with my husband, Darren, as he has become my best friend, business partner, and lover. We have created the most amazing life traveling all over the world meeting others who are sober and learning new things from different countries. I try to stay open minded about who I let in my life because you never know what might happen. But I finally have boundaries! If someone is over-stepping, I will be the first to let them know I am not here for more pain. I find myself attracted to people who are in recovery or who live a life based on spiritual principals. I'm addicted to listening to personal growth. My daily habits also include positive affirmations specific for the day.

DB: What is your spiritual life like and what do you do on a daily basis to integrate it into your life, and why do you think spirituality is important for growth and sustainability in recovery?

DP: The spiritual life is not a theory, I must live it. I am very simple with my prayers and attending AA meetings is my "church." I find God has so many things to say through the mouths of other people. If I go to the meetings, I can help others and I can also see exactly what I don't want for myself and get reminded how awful it really was being new in recovery. My prayers consist of, "God help keep me sober today and keep my mind open to becoming more like you" I pray for those in my life and those still suffering. At night, "Thank you for keeping me sober today." Things change daily but those are the main prays that start each prayer. I was always told to make a gratitude list of five things I am grateful for each day or when I become resentful or angry. One of my most favorite teachings was from the Big Book in Alcoholics Anonymous. Step 3: "Made a decision to turn our will and our lives over to the care of God as we understood Him." This to me was the most profound part of my spiritual experience so far. It tells me if I accept things the way they are and believe that God has the taken the wheel, and everything is exactly the way it's supposed to be, I can live in peace. It has given me HOPE. If I have something too big to deal with, I put it in God's hands and let go. A fun thing I remember doing in early sobriety is writing down my issue and flushing it down the toilet and forgetting about it because it always seemed to work its way out if I trusted God. Same concept, sort of! This helps me focus on the more important issues in my life and not get hung up on fear and drama.

DB: What was one situation you found yourself in that confirmed in your mind that you must seek treatment and recovery and why?

DP: After I got out of the hospital from almost dying, I still then didn't think, "Wow, maybe I have a problem?!" I went to the pharmacist and told him that I have staples in my stomach—can't smoke, can't have caffeine, can't drink, and can't take pills and asked if they had a patch that might help me get through my days. Total insanity! He told me to go to a 12 Step meeting next door, I walked in saw the old lady crying and walked out. For some reason, this was my moment. I called someone I knew that was sober and she asked me to meet her at another 12 Step meeting that night. The most pivotal moment where I finally surrendered and gave up total control of my addictions was when I walked into that AA meeting and I was able to relate with other women and felt these women genuinely cared about me and wanted to help. No one had done that sincerely for me in many years and I was spiritually bankrupt! I felt like I belonged for the first time in a long time and it attracted me back over and over. It has helped me stay sober all these years with gratitude, grace, and willingness to help the new girl that was just like me and in turn, I get to stay sober.

BOB FORREST

"I'm constantly involved with new people and people that are struggling and using and I try to give support and encouragement and not be judgmental."
– Bob Forrest

Bio: "Rehab Bob" Forrest is perhaps best known as the straight talking, straight shooting counselor on VH1's *Celebrity Rehab with Dr Drew*. Bob had a long journey in his struggle with addiction, visiting rehab facilities 24 times before finding sobriety in 1996. He has spent the last 17 years being of service, becoming one of the foremost chemical dependency counselors working in the southern California region. For five years Bob was the clinical director and on the board for Musicians Assistance Program/ MusiCares, and he spent eight years counseling at Las Encinas Hospital in Pasadena. Bob's treatment philosophy and counseling services are brought to a client base that extends throughout the U.S. as well as internationally. Bob can also be seen regularly on the CNN and HLN networks offering commentary as an addiction specialist.

Prior to his life in recovery, Bob Forrest was best known as a musician, fronting the critically acclaimed Los Angeles bands: Thelonious Monster and The Bicycle Thief. Bob was heavily acclaimed for his gifts as a songwriter and frontman.

Thelonious Monster was a key player in the hip Los Angeles

music scene of the '80s, playing innumerable shows alongside The Red Hot Chili Peppers, Jane's Addiction, Fishbone, and Guns 'N Roses, among many others. Despite it's ever-evolving lineup, the band released five lauded albums and notoriously performed at Holland's Pink Pop Festival in 1993.

Bob's second band, The Bicycle Thief, came together after Bob met a teenaged Josh Klinghoffer, a guitar prodigy who went on to become the guitarist in The Red Hot Chili Peppers. He also fronts his own band, Dot Hacker, and was voted into the Rock n' Roll Hall of fame as it's youngest member. The Bicycle Thief recorded one album, and released it twice, in different configurations. The Bicycle Thief played many shows at the notorious Viper Room, had a slot at the inaugural Coachella Festival and toured the U.S. playing with The Red Hot Chili Peppers, The Foo Fighters, Stone Temple Pilots, and They Might Be Giants. Bob and Josh have both hinted that another album may come in the future.

In 2011 a documentary about Bob, *Bob and the Monster*, premiered at SXSW and has since seen wide and home video release. In 2013 Bob's memoir, *Running With Monsters*, was published by Crown Books. In 2015 Bob released his first studio album in 10 years, *Survival Songs*.

In the fall of 2016, Bob returned to the stage at McCabe's Guitar Shop in Santa Monica after a 15-year absence, for a sold-out show with musicians including Zander Schloss (Thelonious Monster, The Circle Jerks, Joe Strummer), Mike Martt (Thelonious Monster, Tex and the Horseheads), Josh Klinghoffer (The Bicycle Thief, Dot Hacker, Red Hot Chili Peppers), and Josh Blum (The Bicycle Thief, Sugartooth). A limited-edition vinyl LP, *Bob Forrest + Friends Live 2016*, was produced from the evening's performance and released in April 2017 by Greenway Records.

2017 also saw the launch of Bob's addiction-centered podcast *Don't Die* with fellow counselor Chuk Davis and Mike Martt.

Occupation: Drug Counselor

Drug of choice: Heroin, cocaine, and alcohol

Length of sobriety: 23 years (in March 2019)

DB: What do you do to stay sober on a daily basis and what's the most challenging part about it?

BF: I'm constantly involved with new people and people that are struggling and using and I try to give support and encouragement and not be judgmental, I would say. So, I try to. It keeps you focused on . . . because addicts are so fragile and defensive and emotionally violent. They're challenging to talk with every day. Right? And so it keeps you centered on coming from a compassionate point of view, right? Because you can say, "Oh dude, you should get help." And they go, "Fuck you man. You're rich I'm fuckin' homeless you can't me to get help . . ." You know what I mean? And you say "Well, but I wasn't like that when I was in your situation, like I was homeless too. I had no front teeth and, I know that you're angry and frustrated" . . . rather than just hanging up the phone, like I don't need to talk to a stranger who talks to me like that. You understand? You're always in the emotional mix of compassion. That's what working with others does. I mean there's a lot of misinterpretations of service work and helping others. Like it helps you. Helps me by keeping me centered and humble and compassionate. It doesn't help me, like make me this big shot who helps a lot of people. That's what most people think and I think that's what motivates a lot of 12 Steppers to do it. They feel like they're big shots. I don't feel that way. I feel like it keeps you . . . so, if I'm talking to a kid who calls me, they got my phone off the internet, and I just keep encouraging and trying to give suggestions or if he asked advice, give them best advice I can. When I do that to somebody who's angry and frustrated I say, "Well I gotta go right now" . . . am sorry and they get angry and say you helped some movie star . . . that's how addicts are.

They're defensive and they're reactionary and highly emotional and when I am centered and compassionate towards them and calm, it gives me the ability to be like that with my children, to be like that with my wife. To be like that with people who work for me. Whereas when you use being of service to blow yourself up and be a big egotist about it, then you tend to be that way with your children, be that way in a relationship. Be that way with your coworkers and employees. I see it. I see who does 12 step work to be braggadocio and grandiose. I see how they treat people. They treat them as subordinates. They treat them as people that build up their own sense of self, rather than, work among workers, a parent, a husband. And so, being of service centers me emotionally spiritually, psychiatrically like that.

DB: What's the most challenging part about it? Is there anything still challenging for you?

BF: Well, it's challenging and this has come up repeatedly. Because I'm trying to help people. You know, you can be really simple, just be sober and life will evolve and unfold. Right? Well, the people you're dealing with nowadays don't have what I call the main fundamentals of life. So, like I always say when I got sober, a world of opportunities opened up to me. When a 20-year-old kid from Ohio who's never had a job and dropped out of high school, gets off the opiates, their doctors put them on, and they have no place to live and they have no resume and they have no job skills, no education, and no language skills. There's not a wealth of possibilities opening up for them. And so, I can see why they go back to drugs or do replacement therapy or do all these things because, and the people that got sober in the 80s like me, need to acknowledge that addiction has changed. Addict population has evolved and mutated. It's not the same. I graduated from college. I was raised in the 1960s and 70s. I have the fundamentals of life. We have a generation of young people who have addiction who don't have the fundamentals of life. So, sobriety is going to be a treacherous, agonizing, growing learning experience. And we live in a narcissistic culture that tells you, "You don't have to grow or learn or all of that." So, it's very difficult. And so, I think what's hard for me is sober doesn't mean what it meant when I was younger, when I was getting sober. And in the first 15 years of my sobriety, I have friends who smoke pot, they consider themselves sober. I have friends who take benzos who consider themselves sober. I have friends who periodically go on binges and consider themselves sober. As long as they don't go back to heroin.

That was unheard of. It was understood what sobriety was. And now it's very vague, so that's difficult. I'll give you an example. I just had oral surgery last Tuesday and had two teeth extracted and two posts put in, I had taken no drugs, none. I had the surgery last Tuesday for four and a half hours. I was conscious the whole time because I didn't want valium and I didn't want drugs like that in my system. I didn't take any pain drugs. I took anti-inflammatory Advil.

You won't find many people in 21st century America like me. Because I am so against having my mind altered. So, it's lonely and it's weird and . . . people don't even understand why I did that. And when I got sober, and all the time I was trying to get sober, everyone I met knew why you would do that. So, it's very lonely. It's a lonely sobriety at this point, except for the gift of people struggling and wanting to be enlightened and wanting to get on the other side and wanting to grow and wanting to learn. That's the only thing that matters to me really in this whole space. I don't care if you're dealing with childhood trauma, that's up to you. I care that you become a functioning member of society.

DB: Have you reconnected with your body since being in recovery and what are some things you do to increase your health and vitality on a daily basis?

BF: Well, I do go to the ocean as often as I can. The ocean is a cleansing thing. I have like, hippy dippy spirituality, like body is mostly water and salt, water and salt and somehow being in the ocean . . . I don't surf or anything organized, I just like being in the ocean. I'm going to be in the ocean later today. There's something about the ocean is a purifying and spiritual and it's obviously good for you, swim around, and then like I said, I have two small kids and we go on the trampoline and go to the park and I carry them around. I could never be a guy sitting watching CNN running on a piece of metal machinery. I could never. So, you fill your life with abundance and you are going to be pretty active.

DB: How have your relationships changed from being in recovery?

BF: Well, see, a lot of people in recovery say they are better; some have gotten worse, some become nonexistent and some have gotten way, way better and new relationships are always healthier because I'm entering into them in health. There's not a lot of baggage of past behaviors or past layers of insecurity. So, relationships with my family have healed with some people.

So, in relation to my family, I like to tell people, some relationships may be or are just untenable. They're really unresolvable. I mean I had a very strange relationship with my mother for decades and we actually, I think, got along better when I was using then we did when I was sober and we used together, we drank together, we were drinking buddies and she continued and I didn't. So, I tried to love her and be there for her and be a part of her life. But at a certain point you have to protect yourself. I think a lot of times these recovery books and these recovery people, I think they tend to paint it with rose colored glasses rather than the reality of what it is. I've been married three times, right? My marriage now based on sobriety, based on being 20 years sober when we got married, it's just completely different than my marriage when I was 19 and doing meth and drinking with my wife who was doing meth and drinking. You can't even compare it.

So relationships evolve as you grow, and they become healthier and sometimes, it doesn't look like a Hallmark card. Healthier for me is I keep a safe distance from people who emotionally abuse me and who are sick. You know what I mean? I wish they weren't and I'm not angry about it. I'm not resentful about it. I just chat about it sometimes, but people make their own beds and they lay in them. So, we all have our ups and downs of life and so I think that often recovery is portrayed a little too mandy-pandy, recovery is real. Recovery gets real.

DB: Who are the top three to five people you surround yourself with? And why are they influential in your recovery?

BF: Somebody asked me that other day and it's funny, like only one of them are sober, right? One of them rarely drinks and one of them has never had a drink in their life. And then one of them is pretty much a pothead. So, it's a mixed bag and through the years as you get older you kinda choose more wisely who you ask advice because I mean basically there's 100 people I could ask advice from, and I know the advice I'm going to get from 90 of them. I already know that. I've already gone over that in my head. There is a handful. I would say a count of five. There are five people, four guys, one girl. I don't know what they'd say, but I know it'll make me think about the situation that I'm in a dilemma over. They're very calm. They're very measured.

There are people who like to think, right? And they'll ask more questions than give answers. I seek people like that out. So, if I say, "Hey, I don't know what these guys want me to do, this thing, and I don't know if I should do it or not I've gone around and around and I got to give them an answer. What do you think?" The 90 people will say black or white, do it or don't do it without any more information. The smart people. The people I'd listened to, the people I seek their guidance and mentorship, will ask a bunch of questions about the situation so they can better understand what it is.

I think a lot of people in our society just make black, white, good, bad, right, wrong kind of decisions and so if you ask them the price, they're going to give you a right, wrong, good, bad black, white answer and I want nothing to do with that. I want sophisticated understanding of life and of decisions. And so, I seek people who like one of them, Austin, gives me advice I don't want to even think about. Right? But those are the people that I listen to.

DB: What is your spiritual life like and what do you do on a daily basis to integrate it into your life, and why do you think spirituality is important for growth and sustainability in recovery?

BF: Well, I'm more commonsensical . . . there's some things that I do that you would consider in that spiritual realm. Spirituality, and psychology, and the arts used to be all in the same category. It's modern times where we've subdivided them and consider one, just the spirituality. To me, art and the appreciation of it . . . listening to music, is a very spiritual experience.

Sitting quietly with family or . . . I sat with my kids yesterday outside watching the sun go down. It's as spiritual an experience as any experience I've ever had in a church or at a yoga studio. I try to focus on the everyday, the spirituality in the everyday. I got this music . . . we have a great conductor here in Los Angeles named Dudamel. I love him.

To go see him conduct some of the most beautiful music ever made, ever written is a spiritual experience. Walt Disney Hall, here in Los Angeles, is a temple of spirituality to me. Art and the divine and all of that is just one, it's not separate. I sit quietly in the morning and I look out the windows of my office at a bunch of trees and just appreciate being alive.

When I listen to Father John Misty or Bob Dylan I just feel blessed to be able to hear it. I think what people are trying to find in this spiritual quest nowadays is very selfish and pious. I've just always had this commonsensical thing.

I saw the Pope movie that Wim Wenders made, everybody should see that movie. Pope Francis is talking about what is most important to have in life and he said a smile and a good sense of humor. He didn't say devotion to a deity, he said a smile and a sense of humor.

All around you can formulate your own spirituality, especially nowadays. But, that takes personal responsibility and a lot of people don't like personal responsibility, they like other people to tell them what to do, and then do it. And then, either get the feeling that they want from it or disillusion. Then, they can blame the people who told them to do it.

I'm more like you've got to figure it out to yourself with you as the center of trying to find peace, because spirituality to me represents peace. Peace of mind, peace of spirit, peace of central nervous system. It sounds kind of complicated, it's not.

Spirituality, to me is watching the sun go down with my children, it's listening to Dudamel conduct Beethoven's Ninth, it's laughter with a friend. It's not some other complicated thing. You know what I mean?

It works for me and it works for most of my friends that have that kind of belief. A more commonsensical spiritual belief. As far as right, wrong, good, bad, good, evil, or how most people see the world? I don't see it as that. I see there's explanations for evil, there's explanations for good, and life is a constant choice of what you . . . if you're driven by fear, you're gonna do selfish, and hurtful, and often categorized evil things.

If you're gravitating towards love and acceptance, then you're going to have more of an easy going, "I'm okay, I want to reassure you in an honest way . . ." It sounds really complicated, because it's not black and white good/bad, right/wrong. There's always an explanation for something.

If somebody betrays me or fucks me over, they thought that was the best thing for them to do. Then, that way . . . then, how it relates to recovery is I'm not constantly mistrusting of people or angrily lashing out at people who did something wrong to me or a perceived slight. I'm constantly just like, "Well, that makes sense. That happens in the world."

People fall out of love with you, people screw you in business deal, people usually act in what they think their best interest is. If leaving a relationship with you they think it's in their best interest to do, they will leave. If they think it's best interest to screw you out of a business deal, they will screw you out of a business deal, but that's based on their fears and they have to live with that. I just have to live with whether I screw people out of business, whether I leave relationships because of my own fears or inadequacies.

This all fits together as a puzzle. Spirituality is psychology, spirituality is art, spirituality is how you treat people. It's not a separate thing, religion is a separate thing. Spirituality is a whole thing, all the time. I'm on the freeway right now. You could either drive aggressively, and tailgate people, and honk your horn, and cut people off or you can just go with the flow of traffic.

Honestly, sometimes I drive very aggressively, because I have to get somewhere and I feel bad when I cut someone off or whenever I speed up to try to get away from them. That's just another reminder that I'm not well, I'm not living in that zone that I strive to live in. It's very self-aware, self-related spirituality.

I took my son to see this concert and he's seven-years-old and he was kind of bored and fidgety and I was hugging him and had my arm around him and he fell asleep. I thought, "That's beautiful. That's perfect." I'm here with my son, the orchestra has made him fall asleep. I didn't have that anxiety that other parents might feel like, "Oh my God. The child's asleep." All the judgment, all this horrible, hideousness of our society just doesn't affect me. I'm just so like, "Oh my God. How cool is that?"

Loud music, beautiful music that I can enjoy and my son who I brought who I was hoping would like it, or appreciate it, or be able to understand it couldn't. I reassured him that it's okay not to like it or it's okay to be bored and he fell asleep. That's a spiritual way of life.

People have spirituality all wrong in this country. It's not how long you can meditate, it's not how much you can quote the bible, it's not how much you can quote the AA big book it's how you treat people and how you live in your daily life.

DB: What was one situation you found yourself in that confirmed in your mind that you must seek treatment and recovery and why?

BF: Well, it was interesting. I'm of those things that's quoted in the big book of the educational variety. When my drinking and drugs were affecting relationships I just thought, "Well, this is the wrong relationship for me. I'm a drug addict, you gotta get used to that. You were fine with that early on and now that bothers you." It took a lot of time where romantic relationships ended because of my drinking and drugs, and then it started to affect my work.

I was a musician, I was in a band with people who drank and took drugs. Even they were saying you drink and take drugs in such a destructive way, we don't want to work with you. Then, that kind of woke me up. "Okay. Now." For about three or four years I went through girlfriends breaking up with me and not wanting to be with me because of my drinking and drugs.

Now my work is falling apart, because of drinking and drugs. Still, I didn't want to stop drinking and taking drugs. I would say I did, but I really didn't want those consequences or those uncomfortable things in my life, those uncomfortable relationships in my life to kind of go away. But, I didn't want to stop drinking and taking drugs.

I went to rehab several times for girlfriends and would return back to drinking and drugs within a few months after getting out of rehab. Then, I went to rehab a few times for my band mates and would return back to drugs and drinking after a few months. And then, the courts got involved and I started getting in legal trouble where I got a DUI or I got possession of drugs.

Then, the society themselves were saying, "You know what? You're not a safe person to have out on the streets." That kind of woke me up, and then it starts to add together. Like, "Oh my God. No one wants to have a relationship with me, no one wants to work with me, and now the society doesn't even want me walking around in it. Maybe I should stop taking drugs?"

It kind of added up, but it wasn't one thing. It wasn't a girl not wanting to be in a relationship with me anymore, it wasn't a band not wanting me to be the singer anymore, wasn't the society not wanting me to be out free anymore it was all of it kind of crystallized and came together and made perfect set to me. Because, it ultimately doesn't matter what other people think about alcoholic or drug addict, it matters what the alcoholic or drug addict thinks of them.

Really, I was masterful at manipulating myself into some sort of rational that made sense. I explained similarly, girls would get into relationships with me knowing that I drank and took drugs. They would continue a relationship with me and at a certain point, whether it was at the year point or three-year point or something they would then say, "I can't do this anymore. I can't be around this, you're gonna die." Or whatever they would say.

I would say, "I can't believe that you're saying this, you know who I am. You knew who I was coming into this." That rational made sense to me. Instead of honoring their love and how hard that must have been for them to say that to me or how upsetting my drinking and drugs was to their life . . . how can you have a family with a guy who's on heroin all the time? How can you move forward in life with anything because your boyfriend might die any day? You know what I mean?

I couldn't see their side of it. That inability to be empathetic to other people. I could only just see my side of things and my side of things was always rationalized as, "This is wrong what you're saying and dismissive." I could dismiss their relationships, and then I could dismiss the work stuff. I could just work with other people, but then there's my freedom being taken from me.

I was in jail several times for . . . not that long. A few months here and there. But just the idea of, "Now I'm a criminal. Now I'm in jail." It all just made sense and I really went about . . . after that last event. I just can't drink and take drugs anymore. I really didn't know what that was gonna mean, I didn't know where that was gonna lead. I was just so convinced that . . . I had all these warning signs and I ignored them. Now, all of a sudden I could see them all very clearly.

With most people's sobriety, they call it a moment of clarity. I just had a perfect vision of my life, and what I'd done to other people, and what I'd done to myself and to my possibilities with my life. I just didn't want to live like that anymore. And then, that then pivots immediately to, "How do you stay sober?"

I think I'm a slow learner. A lot of people get sober because their spouses are gonna leave them, a lot people get sober because they get fired from their job, a lot of people get sober because they get a DUI. But, I had to get all of those things and more in order to go, "Oh my God. I should stop drinking and taking drugs. Seriously. I should stop."

CONCLUSION

I hope that you found this book useful, inspirational, and most importantly, relatable.

As you can see with recovery, it's real, it's hard, and it takes a village, but it's worth it.

In short, I think the biggest take-aways are these:

1. Don't compare your journey to others. Instead, use others as a means of inspiration and not as a reason to feel inadequate.

2. Health is everything. Buddha once said, "To keep the body in good health is a duty . . . otherwise we shall not be able to keep our mind strong and clear." So, find a workout regime that you will stick to.

3. Surround yourself with people that bring out the best in you. Keep your inner circle strong. Hang out with people that will push you further in life.

4. There are many paths to spirituality should you choose to pursue one. Again, find one that works for you.

5. Allow your past to motivate and encourage you to become a better version of yourself. Don't let it drain and deter you from becoming the person you were meant to be.

There are many other tips in this book, but these are a few of the common themes I recognized. Feel free to write down your top three to five take-aways and use them to help enhance your recovery or maybe even into recovery.

Please contact me directly through my website if I can help you in anyway. Remember to take it slow and always focus on how far you have come and not how far you have to go.

Best Wishes,

Doug

www.dougbopst.com

Made in the USA
Lexington, KY
30 March 2019